saying
something

INGRID MONSON

saying something

jazz improvisation and interaction

THE UNIVERSITY OF CHICAGO PRESS } CHICAGO & LONDON

Ingrid Monson is assistant professor of music
at Washington University, St. Louis.

The University of Chicago Press, Chicago 60637
The University of Chicago Press, Ltd., London
© 1996 by The University of Chicago
All rights reserved. Published 1996
Printed in the United States of America
05 04 03 02 01 00 99 98 97 96   5 4 3 2 1

ISBN (cloth): 0-226-53477-4
ISBN (paper): 0-226-53478-2

Library of Congress Cataloging-in-Publication Data

Monson, Ingrid T. (Ingrid Tolia)
    Saying something : jazz improvisation and interaction /
Ingrid Monson.
        p.   cm.—(Chicago studies in ethnomusicology)
    Includes bibliographical references and index.
    ISBN 0-226-53477-4 (alk. paper).—ISBN 0-226-53478-2
(pbk.)
    1. Jazz—Criticism and interpretation.   2. Improvisation
(Music)
I. Title.   II. Series.
ML3506.M64   1996
781.65′136—dc20   96-23224
                                                              CIP
                                                              MN

For my mother,
Sonja D. Williams

CONTENTS

ILLUSTRATIONS

Figures

Musical Examples

Notation key

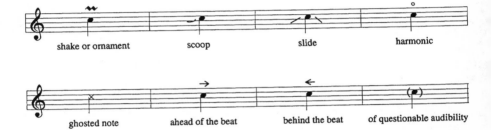

Drum notation

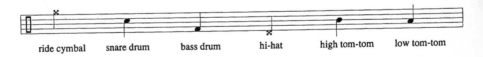

ACKNOWLEDGMENTS

This book is as socially constructed as anything discussed within it. Condensed here are webs of personal, social, cultural, and institutional interactions that have left a deep imprint upon me as well as upon the final text. I am especially grateful for the circumstances that allowed me to talk one-to-one with the musicians who participated in this study: Phil Bowler, Joanne Brackeen, Jaki Byard, Don Byron, Michael Carvin, Richard Davis, Sir Roland Hanna, Jerome Harris, Roy Haynes, Billy Higgins, Cecil McBee, Ralph Peterson Jr., Kenny Washington, and Michael Weiss. Each one taught me something different about the music, life, and how to listen. Without their participation there would have been nothing to write about, nothing to ground the extended embellishments and revisions that invariably go into producing a narrative recognizable as a book. That each one took the time to talk to me was a gift.

New York City has a way of making such things possible, for it is simultaneously the most personal and the most impersonal of cities—full of interlocking networks of people who may know someone who knows someone who with unexpected generosity will help. The jazz community in particular seems full of such people, some of whom are musicians and others who are radio producers, booking agents, managers, critics, bartenders, waitpersons, and researchers. Of particular help have been Becca Pulliam of WBGO radio; Joanne Jiminez of the Bridge Agency; Nancy Hanrahan, formerly with the Public Theater; and Patti Sunderland, whose research on the role of women within the jazz world was conducted at the same time as my project. I thank them for their generous support and friendship over the years.

The ideas presented here have been in progress for many years, aging, maturing, and developing with the aid of many overlapping conversations both inside and outside academia. Those whose comments have materially shaped the content of this book include many teachers and colleagues I encountered while at New York University and the University of Chicago. The members of my dissertation committee— Kay Shelemay, Bambi Schieffelin, and David Burrows—saw me through the initial phases of my research and writing and guided me well. For their comments during the long process of rethinking and rewriting, I am particularly grateful to Paul Berliner, Jean Comaroff, and Michael Silverstein. Myriad conversations over the years have also shaped the final work. Many thanks to Arjun Appadurai, Andrew Apter, Mellonee Burnim, Nahum Chandler, Portia Maultsby, Ron Radano, and Chris Waterman for trading ideas and insights.

For assistance with revising musical transcriptions, special thanks go to Mike Kocour and his extraordinary ear for piano voicings. Additional proofreading of the musical examples was provided by Becca Pulliam, Greg Burrows, and David Stearns. My special thanks to Bob Fried for beautifully rendering my musical examples in Finale.

I have also benefited from the support of several granting bodies over the years, including the American Association of University Women (A.A.U.W.) and the Chicago Humanities Institute. I would also like to thank the staff of the Institute for Jazz Studies—Dan Morgenstern, Don Luck, Vincent Pelote, and Ed Berger—for their assistance in locating material of relevance to my project.

These collective interactions, both sustaining and challenging, have immeasurably enriched my life. To my family—Okolo Ewunike, Sonja Williams, Solveig Daffinrud, and Ellen Monson—my thanks for your love, patience, and support.

A portion of chapter 4 was originally published in "'Doubleness' and Jazz Improvisation: Irony, Parody, and Ethnomusicology," *Critical Inquiry* 20(2): 283–313. © 1994 by the University of Chicago. All rights reserved.

Introduction

Saying Something grew from my musical interest in the contribution of the rhythm section to jazz improvisation. The interplay among drums, bass, and piano in the rhythm section has generally been taken for granted in historical descriptions and analyses of jazz improvisation despite its importance in establishing the feeling and character of a performance. Soloists in the front line rely upon rhythm section players to improvise appropriate rhythmic feels or grooves against which they can weave their improvised melodies. An imaginative rhythm section can inspire a soloist to project his or her most vibrant voice, while disinterested accompaniment can thwart even the strongest artist. Since the late 1920s, when the extended improvised solo became one of the most prominent characteristics of the music, those fascinated by the beauty, power, and complexity of the jazz tradition have focused primarily upon the activities and achievements of individual soloists without considering the enabling function of the accompanists. Although the personal quality of the improviser—his or her magical projection of soul and individuality by musical means—has been rightfully at the core of what writers have wished to emphasize, the time has come to take a broader view of jazz improvisation and its emotional and cultural power.

When a musician successfully reaches a discerning audience, moves its members to applaud or shout praises, raises the energy to dramatic proportions, and leaves a sonorous memory that lingers long after, he or she has moved beyond technical competence, beyond the chord changes, and into the realm of "saying something." Since saying something—or "sayin' something," as it's usually pronounced—requires soloists who can play, accompanists who can respond, and audiences who can hear within the context of the richly textured aural legacy of jazz and African American music, this verbal aesthetic image underscores the collaborative and communicative quality of improvisation. A moment of community, whether temporary or enduring, can be established in such moments through the simultaneous interaction of musical sounds, people, and their musical and cultural histories.

How musicians go about saying something in music and about music—as well as in music and about identity, politics, and race—involves interaction at several analytical levels: (1) the creation of music through the improvisational interaction of sounds; (2) the interactive shaping of social networks and communities that accompany musical participation; and (3) the development of culturally variable meanings and ideologies that inform the interpretation of jazz in American society. This book develops an ethnomusicological perspective of jazz improvisation centered on interaction in this multiple sense. Stressed here are the reciprocal and multi-layered relationships among sound, social settings, and cultural politics that affect the meaning of jazz improvisation in twentieth-century American cultural life.

This emphasis on interaction also highlights the interdisciplinary web in which the discussion of African American music currently takes place. New books by cultural historians, musicologists, and ethnomusicologists have marked the entry of jazz and African American music into an interdisciplinary dialogue of far-reaching significance. The works of Kenney (1993) on Chicago jazz, Peretti (1992) on New Orleans, Stowe (1994) on the swing era, and Tucker (1989, 1993) on Duke Ellington have expanded the historical, social, and intellectual contexts in which we understand the recorded legacy and cultural significance of early jazz and swing. Ronald Radano's (1993) portrait of Anthony Braxton as a postmodern black experimentalist has offered a new direction for jazz studies by posing the interpretive questions of postmodernism. By emphasizing Braxton's complex relationship to jazz tradition and avant-garde experimentalism, Radano challenges the generic, ethnic, and historical categories that have been tacitly presumed in jazz scholarship. Paul Gilroy's work (1991, 1993) has been centrally concerned with the politics of ethnic identity and the music of the African diaspora, particularly in Great Britain. With its emphasis on the relationship between ethnic identity and music, the new interdisciplinary literature portends a reexamination of the way in which jazz history of the twentieth century has been understood.

Such newer works on jazz that focus on politics, social history, and interpretive issues, however, have often excluded close readings of musical compositions and performances. Indeed, discussions of musical structures and cultural issues in musical scholarship have generally proceeded along parallel—decidedly nonintersecting—lines. At a time when musicologists and ethnomusicologists have been invigorated by interdisciplinary debates in the broader social sciences and humanities, the question of what to do about the music itself is as timely as it was when Joseph Kerman (1985) questioned the relevance of musical analysis to the history of music and ethnomusicologists demonstrated the cultural limitations of Western music analysis. On the one hand, poststructuralist cultural theory in the humanities has had difficulty addressing nonlinguistic discourses and practices (such as music, dance, and visual images) that in some respects operate analogously to language and text but in others do not. Music theory, on the other hand, has had trouble relating structural description to aesthetics, meaning, and history. That close readings of musical works can proceed from the constant intersection of sound, structure, and social meaning, and that interactive jazz improvisation has something to teach us about these relationships, are central preoccupations of this book.

In striving for a more cultural music theory and a more musical cultural theory, I do not mean to diminish the significance of work that has preceded mine. Jazz and African American music have not always been welcome subjects in the academy, and this fact has shaped the jazz literature enormously. Most of the historical, biographical, and autobiographical works about jazz, jazz musicians, and their recordings have been compiled by journalists, critics, and researchers without academic affiliation.[1] Works on jazz undertaken in departments of music, by contrast, have generally followed the prevailing conventions of music theory and musicology and paid limited attention to cultural interpretation.[2] In recent years, however, musicologists have questioned their own conventions and relationship to issues of cultural and historical interpretation. There has been a flowering of works on issues previously considered to lie within the province of ethnomusicologists: gender, race, class, sexual orientation, and cultural identity.[3] Musicologists are now less likely to presume an absolute concept of music—one that views analytical frameworks as neutral and objective and structural values as timeless and universal.

The relationship of jazz studies to these trends is somewhat paradoxical. Historically, the concept of absolute music offered a way for jazz enthusiasts to prove to the unbelieving musical academy that jazz improvisation and composition warranted serious attention. By preparing transcribed scores from recordings and identifying musical characteristics highly valued in Western classical music—including sophisticated harmony, complex voice leading, thematic integration (Schuller 1968, 1986, 1989), and large-scale planning (Porter 1985a)—analysts could circumvent the prevailing hierarchical view that improvisation was less worthy of musical analysis than composition.[4] Even when evaluated by the aesthetic standards of Western composition, jazz looked quite impressive. The same standards, however, were also used to disparage aspects of the jazz tradition and allowed scholars to overlook those aspects of improvisation for which there are no analogs in the Western classical music tradition. Musical interaction within the rhythm section and between the rhythm section and the soloist is one such distinctive musical process in jazz improvisation.

The idea that improvisation should be analyzed and evaluated on its own terms and that the musicians themselves are the most authoritative source of knowledge about the music joins the concerns of both ethnomusicologists and members of the jazz community. In the 1970s and 1980s, one of the most important goals of ethnomusicologists was to establish descriptions and interpretations of musical traditions from the perspective of the cultural insiders. The idea that cultural groups have their own theories of musical process and cultural value—often called *ethnotheories*—came as a response to structuralist methods of interpretation in ethnomusicology and to hierarchical rankings of musical systems according to the relative complexity of musical structures and explicitness of musical theory.[5]

Paul Berliner's monumental *Thinking in Jazz* (1994), an ethnographic study of jazz improvisation, provides the most comprehensive and detailed account of jazz improvisation currently in existence, as well as the most detailed exposition of ethnotheory in ethnomusicology. Berliner discusses the ways in which musicians go about acquiring and developing the myriad musical skills necessary to perform at a professional level—from individual musical vocabularies to collective musical interplay—through participating in a community of jazz musicians. He painstakingly synthesizes the viewpoints of sixty professional musicians into a comprehensive account of improvisation that has no peer. No musical parameter is left unexamined, and the complex interplay between composition and improvisation is nowhere presented with greater nuance and detail. The musical examples alone provide a grand tour through the jazz ensemble—its roles, responsibilities, and artistry—that set a new musical, ethical, and epistemological standard for jazz studies. Berliner's commitment to documenting insider perspectives also redresses a long-standing grievance in the jazz community: previous writers had not taken the perspectives and interpretations of jazz musicians seriously enough in their works.

Saying Something has a complex relationship to *Thinking in Jazz,* as Berliner and I have been in frequent dialogue about our work since we became acquainted in 1991. Berliner's comprehensive coverage of improvisational issues, indeed, allowed me to take a different interpretive trajectory with the ethnographic materials about the rhythm section presented here. *Saying Something* concentrates on what implications musicians' observations about musical processes may have for the rethinking of musical analysis and cultural interpretation from an interactive point of view, with particular attention to the problems of race and culture. Stressed here is what the perspectives of musicians can contribute to the reshaping of social analysis.

Like Berliner, I began with the presumption that the best point of departure for an ethnographic study of improvisational interaction would be musicians themselves, rhythm section players in particular. Ethnomusicology as it had been traditionally practiced, however, did not fully fit an urban, heterogeneous jazz scene crosscut by media, multiple ethnicities, and the recording industry. The theories and methodologies of ethnomusicology and anthropology were formed from an ethnographic practice centered in relatively homogeneous, non-urban cultural situations, in which a general presumption of cultural coherence and the transparency of representation went unquestioned. My familiarity with the professional musical world (which I gained as a trumpet player in the early through mid-1980s) convinced me that these assumptions could not go unexamined in the context of jazz. The multiplicity of perspectives within the jazz world, the deservedly low reputation of academics among musicians, the racial politics of the jazz literature, and the sophisticated understanding of the music industry among musicians required a perspective that could take paradoxes and differences in points of view as a given, not as something to be explained away.

The critique of the politics of ethnography and its modes of representation in the anthropology of the mid-1980s, which drew attention to the constructedness of anthropological works and unmasked the arrogance of claiming to "represent" or "speak for" persons other than oneself, was extremely useful to me in thinking about the jazz literature and the implications of an ethnographic project about jazz. The exoticizing, appropriating gaze of the ethnographic observer, so rightly criticized in Clifford and Marcus's *Writing Culture* (1986), can certainly be seen throughout the long history of writing on jazz. In every generation there have been non–African American students of jazz who have attempted to explain the power of African American music with extremely mixed results. For every contribution of musical detail and understanding, one can find a glib and superficial cultural explanation that reproduces and reinforces the most recurrent and virulent racial stereotypes of African American communities. Many musicians resent the presumption of authority on the part of critics who may have no real musical knowledge themselves. Others resent the voyeuristic quality of the outside gaze that emphasizes the social transgressions of musicians (especially sexual and drug-related ones) at the expense of their broader and frequently more mundane humanity. Still others resent the appropriation of their ideas for projects that seem to financially benefit the writers at the expense of the musicians themselves. However well intentioned a writer may be, he or she cannot escape the asymmetrical American social and economic structure in which the music is embedded. No patronizing gesture of downward mobility or ideological position can ever erase the institutional and social configurations of status and prestige in which anyone with the hubris to write books participates.

Nevertheless, I maintain that the only ethical point of departure for work in jazz studies and ethnomusicology remains the documentation and interpretation of vernacular perspectives, contemporary or historical, no matter how much we must rethink the claims we make for them in light of poststructural discussions of representation and the politics of knowing and being. My commitment to the value of vernacular or insider knowledge places me at odds with a considerable body of work in cultural studies, and my serious engagement with poststructuralist thinking places me similarly at odds with established ethnotheoretical thinking in ethnomusicology. Consequently, a secondary theme of this book is the reconciliation of ethnomusicology's traditional preoccupations with poststructuralism.

Chapter 1 is devoted to the research methodologies and presumptions that structured the way I approached interviewing and interacting with musicians active in the New York jazz scene and produced the materials upon which I base my larger argument. My weaknesses and strengths to engage in such research will doubtless be apparent. Of particular importance to the larger argument of the book is the role of language in mediating both the research interaction and the process of writing about it. I do not claim to have transcended any of the ethical dilemmas in which academic scholarship is fraught (for this is impossible), but I have attempted to construct a work in the midst of these social and institutional contradictions that, on balance, gives more than it takes and is aware of the contradictions in which it is embedded.

In chapter 2 I present what musicians have told me about the rhythm section and improvisation. The discussion is organized by instrumental roles: bass, piano, drums, and soloist. Talk about music has been juxtaposed to musical examples, and a social framework for thinking about the musical options and responsibilities of the players is developed. A central point of the chapter is that interacting musical roles are simultaneously interacting human personalities, whose particular characters have considerable importance in determining the spontaneity and success of the musical event. I quote musicians at length in the hope that longer excerpts provide glimpses of their individual personalities, although I have taken these sections from longer conversations whose topics proceeded in a different order. The larger purpose of the chapter is to explain the musical and social frameworks in which interactive improvisation takes place. For those already familiar with jazz improvisation, some of the musical points may seem very basic, for I asked musicians to talk about what generally gets taken for granted in the musical and social structuring of jazz performance. The overlapping layers of participation and interaction, the negotiating and trading of performance roles, and the relationship of musical roles to the production of an aesthetically desirable groove I hope will be of interest to even the most experienced student of jazz.

In chapter 3 I begin the process of interweaving what musicians told me with issues under debate in the academic fields of music, literature, and anthropology. I explore *how* musicians chose to talk to me about improvisational processes—the metaphorical images and figurative tropes that provide an entrée into the cultural aesthetics of interaction and improvisation. Like Berliner, I found that the metaphor of conversation occurred frequently in musicians' discussions of the subject. By examining sociolinguistic literature on conversational interaction as well as literary perspectives on language—particularly those of Mikhail Bakhtin and Henry Louis Gates Jr.—I explore the structural similarities between conversation and musical performance and the relationships among the aesthetics of social interaction, musical interaction, and cultural sensibility.

Chapter 4 places the metaphor of conversation in its historical, or "across time," dimension. Here musicians' comments and Bakhtin's notion of internal dialogism are read against Gates's notion of signifying and W. E. B. Du Bois's notion of doubleness to provide a context for discussing irony and parody in jazz improvisation. With the help of several musical examples, including John Coltrane's "My Favorite Things," I explore musical references and allusions—including, but not limited to, quotations—for their use of transformative resources in African American musical practices to invert, challenge, and often triumph over the ordinary hegemony of mainstream white aesthetic values. Several concepts are developed in this chapter: (1) the idea of intermusicality, or the allusive, intertextual capacity of music as a communicative discourse; (2) a heterogeneous view of African American culture; (3) the influence of African American musical aesthetics on non–African Americans; and (4) the idea that ethnic identities, skin colors, class stratification, and musical identities do not map neatly onto one another, as an essentialized notion of cultural identity or race might presume, but are heavily mediated by cultural activities and social experience. The interactive creation of music and of cultural heterogeneity and identity are viewed as interrelated.

Chapter 5 explores the issue of musical interaction and musical analysis through a close reading of an extended performance: Jaki Byard and George Tucker's "Bass-ment Blues" (1965). With the help of

Byard's comments about the performance, I present an interactive perspective on the large-scale musical intensification that takes place over thirteen choruses of blues. I question whether standard decontextualized harmonic, linear, and rhythmic analysis of musical transcriptions provides a sufficient account of the music in improvisational performance. By looking at the process of getting lost, cooperatively getting back on, and then reaching a musical climax that partakes of humor, quick interactive responses, and intermusicality, I demonstrate that the interactive construction of the musical text and the development of emotional bonds among the musicians through musical risk, vulnerability, and trust during the course of performance occur simultaneously. The chapter closes by employing Michael Silverstein's (1993) theory of metapragmatics to summarize the interrelationships among musical structures, the indexical (or allusive) capacities of music, and the contribution of sound to music's function as a culturally engaged and emotional discourse. Silverstein's ideas, I argue, offer a glimpse of what a more relational approach to sound itself may need to address.

Chapter 6 situates the prior discussion within the field of ethnomusicology, the larger global traffic in heterogeneous—yet asymmetrical—cultural exchange, and the debates of poststructuralism. Viewing the groove or rhythmic feel as a layered interactive concept provides a useful framework for improving our discussions of international musical borrowing and the dialectic between cultural distinctiveness and cultural overlap. Jerome Harris's discussion of hybrid musical styles in African American music, and of how a bass player can inflect the feel of a piece across genre boundaries, illustrates the subtlety with which musical feels and the musicians articulating them project aesthetic feeling. Central concerns of this chapter are the relationship of jazz to the international African diaspora and the place of human agency, lived experience, and vernacular knowledge in the interpretive acts of academia. I am particularly critical of false dichotomies drawn between music and context and between historical and cultural analysis and individual agency.

The importance that musicians who participated in this project placed on both the music itself and the voices of the musical community continually challenged me to consider the implications of musical thinking for issues that extend well beyond the performance setting. In the end, *Saying Something* suggests that a musical image—that of a multi-layered, improvising, interactive, grooving band—may be just as useful to social analysis as the ever-present linguistic images that frame contemporary cultural interpretation. If I begin by suggesting that thinking about language has something to offer thinking about music, I come full circle by suggesting that music has a great deal to offer thinking about discourse. In the coda, I let the musicians remind us that all this talk about music can only go so far.

chapter one
talking to musicians

In 1989, when I was living in Brooklyn, New York, I began the process of presenting myself to musicians, radio producers, friends, booking managers, and others in the role of ethnomusicologist and academic. I began by drawing upon the acquaintances, friendships, connections, and knowledge of the music business I had acquired in the role of musician through several years of professional activity as a trumpet player (primarily) in Boston, Massachusetts. I was, at first, extremely uncomfortable about presenting myself as an academic since hardly any musician I had encountered in my many years as a performer had very much respect for what had been written about jazz improvisation, including me. I did not expect that anyone would presume that my "new," more ethnographic approach would produce much improvement.

Consequently, I began with people who remembered me as someone who played the trumpet: clarinetist Don Byron Jr., bassist Richard Davis, and pianist Jaki Byard. Don Byron I knew best since we had played together in the Klezmer Conservatory Band for six years and had both attended Boston's New England Conservatory in the early 1980s. My reasons for including him in my study were my utmost confidence in his extraordinary musicianship and my knowledge that he would give me honest critical feedback about the project as a whole. At the time, he was just beginning to emerge as a visible leader in the New York musical scene, and he has since become one of the most prominent younger musicians, nationally and internationally, in both jazz and klezmer music. In the fall of 1977, I had taken a jazz history course and an improvisation ensemble at the University of Wisconsin from bassist Richard Davis. I had not seen him since I left Madison, Wisconsin, in the summer of 1979 and was not sure he would even remember me. But when I learned he would be performing for a week at Sweet Basil's in New York in the summer of 1989, I wrote him a letter explaining my project and asking him if he would consider participating in it. I had also taken a jazz orchestration class with pianist Jaki Byard at the New England Conservatory during the winter of 1980 in which I was one of two female students. I didn't think he would remember me either. As it turned out, both he and Richard Davis did.

The remaining participants I met and became acquainted with during the course of the project: pianists Joanne Brackeen, Sir Roland Hanna, and Michael Weiss; bassists Phil Bowler and Cecil McBee; drummers Michael Carvin, Roy Haynes, Billy Higgins, Ralph Peterson Jr., and Kenny Washington; and guitarist/bassist Jerome Harris.[1] I had wanted to include players representing all the rhythm section roles as well as soloists (which they all were), and I was particularly interested in talking to people who had played and recorded with one another. I had also wanted to include players from different generations—older, well-established musicians and younger, up-and-coming players—for I did not presume that the viewpoints of each generation were the same.

Not surprisingly many of the musicians included here know each other and have played and recorded with one another at various points in their careers. Since few performing organizations keep musicians on an ongoing salaried basis, the constellation of musicians with whom any particular performer plays can be extensive. Musicians may be hired for an evening, a week, or an international tour of several months' duration. Bandleaders obtain bookings and then hire band members for specific engagements or recordings. Musicians consequently play with many different ensembles over the course of their careers. Many express a preference for playing in a wide variety of musical contexts (Higgins 1990; McBee 1990), and when called upon to hire or recommend other musicians for an engagement, they draw upon their existing network of contacts. When I talk about communities of musicians being constituted (established) through the face-to-face musical activities they engage in, part of what I am talking about is exactly these networks of musicians who work with one another,

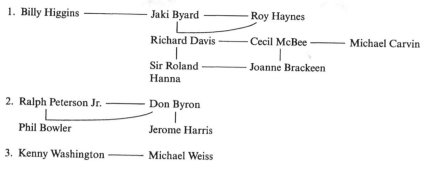

Figure 1   Playing networks among musicians participating in the study

travel with one another, talk about one another, and are viewed by the public in the role of professional musician.

To illustrate the relationships among the musicians included here, I have made a diagram (figure 1) of those who have played and recorded with one another. The diagram is based primarily on discographies of the musicians but includes information from live performances I observed as well. The first constellation includes most of the oldest players in the group; the second and third constellations are comprised of the younger musicians. It is not surprising that the older, more experienced musicians have more extensive networks, and it should be kept in mind that there may be even more extensive interrelationships in this group than that documented here: I may have excluded unrecorded performances, and since the time this was written, some of the musicians may have encountered one another on the bandstand. The networks of playing relationships within the musical world are highly fluid and constantly changing. In many cases I approached musicians who I knew played regularly with one another. Nevertheless, I was not aware of the full extent of the playing networks that existed between participants until after the ethnographic research was completed.

By stressing the activity of music making as something that creates community, I am purposefully moving away from an idea of community that is defined exclusively by a particular geographic location or a particular social category, such as race, class, or gender. Rather, I am interested in the ways in which the latter social categories (and their representations) intersect *within* the activity of jazz performance and recording. My thinking about the community is informed, in part, by the social theory of Anthony Giddens, who suggests that social groups are constituted and reproduced by the recurrent actions of individual agents, whose activities have both intended and unintended consequences. Viewed as a dynamic system through time, Giddens argues, the day-to-day activities of group members express the norms, values, and expectations of a collectivity that extend beyond any one individual. The focus of cultural and social inquiry becomes the question of how the actions of social agents constitute, reproduce, and transform the social entity in question (Giddens 1984, 281–88).

Clearly musical performance is not the only activity that goes into constituting the jazz community, even though it is the most prestigious one. Jazz occurs within the context of an international music industry, and the image we have of musicians is constructed through the activities of many types of agents: musicians, concert promoters, booking agents, record company executives, recording engineers, jazz club owners and employees, radio producers, critics, audience members, and academics. The larger discourse of race within American history and culture forms an inescapable backdrop to the larger music industry, with non–African Americans disproportionately represented in managerial and nonperformance technical capacities and African Americans disproportionately providing the musical leadership and aesthetic direction within the art form. Nevertheless, the jazz world has always been a place where greater black and white interaction has taken place than in the rest of society, and many individual exceptions to this general case could be cited. The legacy of presumptions about jazz musicians and race—as well as the economics of the music industry—is nevertheless present (whether implicitly or explicitly) in any interaction, musical or social, described in these pages. Since, as Cornel West and Andrew Hacker have recently argued (West 1993; Hacker 1992), the United States remains a long way from achieving a color-blind society, the way in which color has mediated the perception and reception of the art form is a crucial aspect of its history, whether it ought to be or not. With this in mind, it seems germane to mention that twelve of the participants here are from African American backgrounds, while two are non–African American; one participant is a woman, and I am a white female.

The observations included here converge around concert and club venues of performance in which these activities, social contexts, and agents meet. The picture becomes even more complicated, of course, when it is acknowledged that any individual might simultaneously or consecutively occupy several positions within the larger jazz world: performers are also audience members, as are booking agents and producers. Some managers and producers might simultaneously be the wives or relatives of musicians. Musicians might negotiate business deals, compile publicity materials, and critique other musicians one night and be the subject of such critiques and negotiations the next. A musician may be a sideman in one band, complaining about the business and musical practices of a leader, and at the same time subject to similar criticisms from the members of her or his own band. Nor does every musician included here play only what falls under the musical category of jazz; the genre itself is subject to conflicting definitions. While I mean to stress the fluidity with which individuals negotiate their positions within the music industry, I would also like to emphasize that the range of options open to any particular individual is structured by whatever is "business as usual" in the music industry at any given moment in time.

Ethnographic Process

Into this larger context I entered as an ethnomusicologist, requesting that busy professional musicians take time out of their schedules to sit in front of a tape recorder and talk to me about rhythm sections and improvisation. I usually introduced myself to musicians at their performances in one of several New York jazz venues active in 1989 and 1990: Sweet Basil's, the Village Vanguard, Bradley's, the Knitting Factory, Birdland, Condon's, Fat Tuesday's, Garvin's, and the Blue Note. I met Ralph Peterson Jr., for example, at a performance at the Knitting Factory in March 1989; Sir Roland Hanna at his performance with Richard Davis and Friends at Sweet Basil's on 5 July 1989; Joanne Brackeen at her duo performance at Bradley's in December 1989; and Billy Higgins at a performance with the Cedar Walton Trio on 22 February 1990 at Sweet Basil's. I explained that I was trying to gather the perspectives of musicians on the issue of the rhythm section and improvisation, that I was interested in their particular thoughts, and that the information would be used in a Ph.D. dissertation in progress at New York University. Although not everyone I approached subsequently participated in my study, I was generally given a phone number where I could contact the musician and from there began what was in many cases a long process of explaining the project further, having my knowledge of and attitude toward the music evaluated, and finding a time and place in which to conduct an interview. In some cases it took several months between the time I introduced myself and the time a formal, tape-recorded interview took place. In some cases, it took several trips to performances to make arrangements, as musicians checked me out. In general, those musicians with the highest public visibility were the most protective of their time and their privacy.

In the meantime, I attended many performances, observed the multiplicity of business and social activities taking place inside New York's jazz venues, and became something of a regular at several clubs. I imagine my presence may have drawn the notice of some: a normally unaccompanied woman, usually seated at the bar (where no minimum was charged), who talked to musicians during the intermissions. I generally went early in the jazz musician's workweek—Tuesday or Wednesday—when the clubs weren't as crowded and it was easier to approach musicians without feeling like one was excessively intruding. As the hour got later, it was not unusual to see other musicians arrive to hear the final sets of their friends. After several months of sitting at the bar and taking regular field notes, I noticed that other people were there for business purposes as well. One evening in April 1990, I sat at the bar at Sweet Basil's and explained my project to jazz critic Howard Mandel; at an after-concert reception at Carnegie Hall, I was introduced to critic Stanley Crouch by Becca Pulliam, a long-time friend and WBGO radio producer.[2] At another after-concert reception sponsored by Philip Morris (to which I had been invited by Joanne Jiminez of the Bridge Agency), I noticed a virtual who's who of musicians, critics, sponsors, and producers. Individuals with record deals, interviews, talent scouting, and other music industry functions on their minds were simply ubiquitous at jazz performances.

In addition to observing and conducting interviews, I began taking drum lessons from Michael Carvin in the spring of 1990 and continued taking them until I moved to Chicago in 1991. Carvin, I had established through the grapevine, was among the most respected drum teachers in New York, having taught many of the best up-and-coming jazz musicians, including Ralph Peterson Jr. Carvin ordinarily did not take beginning drum students, but I explained on the phone that I had considerable professional experience as a trumpet player and, while new to the drums, was not at all new to jazz. After several months of lessons, Carvin told me that the only reason he had agreed to take me on as a beginner was that I had come to him highly recommended by Becca Pulliam. The knowledge I gained of drumming from Michael Carvin was absolutely critical to my musical understanding of the rhythm section.

The experience of preparing this study also forced me to consider the ways in which I was perceived by the musicians. In his sociology of everyday life, Erving Goffman suggested the notion of the frame as a way of thinking about the various "schemata of interpretation" that individuals bring to bear upon their daily experiences. Basing his arguments upon the phenomenology of Alfred Schutz, Goffman suggested that each primary framework "allows its user to locate, perceive, identify and label a seemingly infinite number of concrete occurrences defined in its terms" (Goffman 1986, 21). He also drew attention to the multiple perspectives (or frames) that are brought to bear upon the same situation by various participants in a social interaction (84). Although I presented myself as an ethnomusicologist,[3] I found that the most frequent frame musicians drew upon to contextualize me was that of journalist. Since I wanted to interview them on tape and write about their views about music, I appeared to have more in common with journalists than with any other expected social role within the jazz community. Unlike many journalists, however, I did not have a recognizable byline, could not guarantee that their name and photograph would appear within a reasonable amount of time in *Down Beat, The New York Times, Jazz Times,* or any other jazz publication, and consequently was rather low in the hierarchy of importance as an interviewer. While I tried to communicate that I was working on a dissertation and was interested in more substantial musical discussion than is ordinary in a journalistic interview, the journalist frame seemed to provide the easiest means for musicians to integrate me into a role congruent with their everyday experience in the musical world.

Interviewing

The frame of journalist also involved assumptions about what the interview process would be like: it would take fifteen or twenty minutes and, if necessary, could be done on the phone. The more famous the musician (and hence the more experienced with journalistic interviews), the more likely these assumptions were made. During my research period, I consulted both a radio producer and a magazine writer to ask whether their interviews fit these parameters. Becca Pulliam told me that her interviews were indeed often fifteen or twenty minutes in length; Howard Mandel told me that he preferred to interview in person but sometimes in the interest of a deadline interviewed over the phone.

Not only were musicians familiar with the interview as a concept, they were experienced in a particular interview method about which they had certain expectations. In several cases musicians asked me if I had my questions prepared; in a few cases the musicians adjusted my microphone placement, expressing the concern that I would not be able to hear my own questions on the tape (which did not turn out to be a problem); and in one case a musician who had gone off on a lengthy tangent redirected me to the main topic of the interview.

Nevertheless, I wanted to conduct an *ethnographic* interview, not a journalistic one (although I am no longer convinced that such a distinction is so easy to make[4]), and I hoped to create a kind of interaction that had more in common with everyday conversational situations in the jazz community than did a traditional interview. To this end I prepared tapes of musical examples generally drawn from the recorded work of the musician being interviewed. My goal was twofold: I thought it would be easier for musicians to make musical points with reference to specific examples, and I also believed this process would create an environment more like listening to recordings with fellow musicians than a typical journalistic interview.

Before interviewing a musician, I prepared by reviewing his or her discography and gathering published interviews that had appeared in the jazz periodical literature. I made regular use of the periodical collection at the Institute for Jazz Studies in Newark, New Jersey, for this purpose. From this material I frequently gained knowledge of the musician's background, a sense of his or her network of playing relationships, and some notion of the musician's musical and social opinions. I also spent time listening to his or her recordings and making tapes of the musical examples I thought would be interesting to discuss. I wanted to make sure I knew what a musician had said previously in order not to duplicate information readily available or to waste the musician's time with redundancy.

The success of this interview format varied greatly from musician to musician. Some were quite enthusiastic about responding to music, while others found the suggestion of my playing a musical example perplexing. Jaki Byard liked the excerpt from "Bass-ment Blues" so much that he asked me to play it twice, making different commentaries on each hearing. Cecil McBee, however, seemed to find this process even mildly insulting, reminding me that he *knew* the tune. Kenny Washington selected some of his favorite examples of rhythm section hookup from his extensive record collection for me to hear.[5] As an ethnomusicologist, having specific stretches of music to associate with verbal commentaries was invaluable. Most of the musical transcriptions included in this book are drawn from the examples I played during the course of these interviews. And while I had a general plan in mind when I arrived in the interview situation, I played each one by ear: if a musician didn't seem to enjoy hearing an example, or seemed to find some of my questions uninteresting, I tried to listen for topics that were of interest, encourage expansion upon them, and stay out of the way. On some days, not surprisingly, I was better at this than on others.

The settings in which the interviews were conducted varied widely, and in every case I took the musician's suggestion for a preferred location, refusing only to conduct telephone interviews. I interviewed Phil Bowler, Billy Higgins, and Joanne Brackeen in the public area of Bradley's; Jaki Byard in the basement dressing room at Birdland; Don Byron in his home in the Bronx; Jerome Harris and Kenny Washington in their homes in Brooklyn; Roy Haynes in the public area of Condon's; Sir Roland Hanna in the auditorium of the Minskoff Theater between shows of the Broadway production *Black and Blue;* Richard Davis in the seminar room of the New York University Department of Music; Michael Carvin on a Central Park bench near where he conducted his drum lessons at 5th Avenue and 104th Street; and Cecil McBee in the cafeteria of the Bank Street School.

The most unusual interview setting, however, was Gibralter Transmission at 317 East 111th Street in El Barrio, where I ended up one afternoon with Ralph Peterson Jr. and his family. I had arrived at Peterson's home on the Upper West Side of New York in November 1989, at the time we had agreed upon, only to find Peterson on his way out with his wife, bassist Melissa Slocum, and their infant daughter Sonora T. He apologized for forgetting the appointment and explained that they needed to go pick up his car at the garage and that he would then be available for an interview. I offered to wait, but they suggested that I ride along with them, so we all hopped into a taxi and headed uptown. Peterson and Slocum's vintage Checker Cab, which had been in the shop for transmission work, however, would not start.[6] Its battery needed recharging, and while we all sat in a small (fortunately well-insulated) waiting booth, Peterson said, "Let's start the interview." So we did. Peterson seemed to enjoy the irony (and originality) of the setting, and so did I.

A long tradition of interviews with musicians in jazz periodicals has established the interview as something of a secondary performance genre for musicians. Taped interviews, I would argue, bias for positive reporting. A desire to come across as a thoughtful artist and an inspiring human being with something original to say—as well as an awareness of the role of media in creating public visibility—seems to shape a musician's responses during such an interview. Rarely in my experience did a musician focus on negative experiences when commenting on musical issues; rather, there was a tendency to comment on the ideal aesthetic and communal experiences. But since cohesion in a community frequently derives from conflict as well as sociability, from dissonance as well as harmony, informal conversations were an important complement to the taped interviews. I generally heard negative commentary when the tape recorder was turned off, and consequently I have left many of the negative observations unattributed.

Language and Representation

In *Learning How to Ask: A Sociolinguistic Appraisal of the Role of the Interview in Social Science Research,* Charles Briggs (1986) drew attention to the metacommunicative norms of conversational participants, which in cross-cultural research often conflict with the assumptions of the social science interview format. By "metacommunicative" he means "statements that report, describe, interpret, and evaluate communicative acts and processes" (2). While communicative acts may include verbal and nonverbal signs and cues, metacommunicative acts comment on the process of communicating itself. Linguistic anthropologists have established that there can be substantial cultural, social, and occupational differences in what people presume to be taking place in various communicative events, depending upon their metacommunicative norms and linguistic ideologies.[7] These differences in cultural metacommunicative expectations, Briggs argues, have considerable effect on ethnographic research methodology and the interpretation of communicative data such as interviews or musical transcriptions (39).

While there has been much discussion of the complexities of musical transcription in ethnomusicology (Jairazbhoy 1977; Beaudry 1978; Charron 1978; Seeger 1977, 168–81; List 1974), there has been little consideration of the mediating role of language in the production of ethnographic research data.[8] Transcribing speech, as conversation analysts have documented, is just as fraught with representational dilemmas as transcribing music. In general, transcribed speech looks nothing like written prose.[9] Grammatical irregularities, incomplete sentences and words, repetitive interjections ("you know," "um-huh"), turn-taking overlaps, and unexplained referents pervade the aural speech of even the most highly educated (Schegloff 1986; Levinson 1983, 284–370). Since the conventional representations of interviews in periodicals edit out these ambiguities, many people expect their speech to look like edited text, and individuals reading their transcribed speech are often very disturbed by the experience. What we should instead realize is that the "verbatim transcript" suitable for publication is actually a construction—a highly edited document.

John Gumperz speaks of conversational organization as one part of a larger set of contextualization cues that include

> code, dialect and style switching processes . . . lexical and
> syntactic options, formulaic expressions, conversational
> openings, closing and sequencing strategies. . . . Although
> such cues carry information, meanings are conveyed as a
> part of the interactive process. Unlike words that can be
> discussed out of context, the meanings of contextualiza-
> tion cues are implicit. (Gumperz 1982, 131)

In the last fifteen years, sociolinguists and linguistic anthropologists have stressed the interactive production of meaning in conversation and have demonstrated that metacommunicative norms and contextualization cues vary from culture to culture and can be the source of misinterpretation of ethnographic data. The interactive production of meaning—both musical and conversational—is of course a theme that underlies this entire book, especially chapters 2 and 4.

Here I would like to briefly explore the implications of language representation and cultural miscommunication in the interracial context of American society. Gumperz discusses, in general, the potential of culturally implicit linguistic cues for miscommunication in conversation:

> When all participants understand and notice the relevant cues, interpretive processes are then taken for granted and tend to go unnoticed. However, when a listener does not react to a cue or is unaware of its function, interpretations may differ and misunderstanding may occur. It is important to note that when this happens and when a difference in interpretation is brought to a participant's attention, it tends to be seen in attitudinal terms. A speaker is said to be unfriendly, impertinent, rude, uncooperative, or fail to understand. Interactants do not ordinarily notice that the listener may have failed to perceive a shift in rhythm or a change in pronunciation. Miscommunication of this type . . . is regarded as a social faux pas and leads to misjudgments of the speaker's intent; it is not likely to be identified as a mere linguistic error.[10] (Gumperz 1982, 132)

Consider, for instance, the problem of representing the sonic inflections of African American English. Nonstandard spellings such as *playin', sayin', I'mo, dis,* and *dat* have been used by both African American and non–African American writers to represent perceived pronunciation markers of black speech.[11] The *dis*-and-*dat* style of representation found pervasively in nineteenth-century minstrel shows, on the one hand, carries highly pejorative connotations. On the other hand, the *-in'* ending (which is often found in white speech as well) frequently appears in the written titles to jazz albums and songs to convey a positive, "down home" flavor. Art Blakey's *Moanin'* (1958) and Hank Mobley's *Dippin'* (1965) provide two examples among many. Johnny Griffin's *Call It Whachawana* (1983) furnishes another type of nonstandard spelling used in an album title. The use of nonstandard orthography in these contexts conveys informality, relaxation, and sociability as well as marking "African Americanness" through representation of the sound of African American speech.

What complicates the representation of African American English is the fact that orthographical representations of its pronunciations contain many idiomatic grammatical features—including tense marking and formation of plurals—that are considered "incorrect" in the context of standard written English (Labov 1969; Dillard 1972). A study of "eye dialect" done by Dennis Preston indicates that white middle-class college students overwhelmingly associate nonstandard spellings with lower social class educational achievement (1985). The identification and representation of what Henry Louis Gates Jr. would call "the black difference" in African American language consequently results in a double bind: spellings that convey cultural identity to African Americans and sympathetic non–African Americans imply social and educational inferiority to others (Gates 1988, xxii–xxiii). Gates has written about the effect of this double bind on African American literature (1987).

In view of this paradoxical situation, I have chosen to use nonstandard spellings very sparingly. As one musician who discussed the issue with me said, "I read in standard English."[12] I include such spellings when they seem to be used purposefully to signal ethnicity and when failure to include them would detract from intelligibility. Since African Americans frequently switch from African American idioms to standard English and back in the same conversation—a practice linguists call *code-switching* (Blom and Gumperz 1986)—orthographic changes can represent linguistic changes that carry much cultural nuance. For the most part I have preserved lexicon, grammar, and emphasis in the transcription of aural speech. In one case, a musician asked me to "correct" his grammar, a request that reflects the musician's awareness that his vernacular speaking style is evaluated as "incorrect" by a broader English-speaking audience. In deference to his request, I have made a few tense changes. While it may sound as if I have altered the transcriptions considerably, this is not the case. I am simply making explicit interpretive decisions about language that generally go unreported in ethnomusicological studies. This attention to presumptions about "good" and "bad" speech in American culture is essential in a fieldwork context in which the researcher and the participants ostensibly speak the same language but the former's speech tends to be considered "more correct" than the latter's by the academic community and the dominant culture. The conditions under which these interviews took place and were transcribed, then, were inevitably shaped by existing North American linguistic and social hierarchies.

My musical transcriptions make use of standard Western notational practices as codified by Gardner Read (1979), with the exception of drum notation.[13] Drum parts are notated according to the conventions developed by Jim Zimmerman for the percussion parts appearing in the *New Real Book* (Sher and Bauer 1988, 413). Because Western notation, with some modifications, is used in some capacity by nearly all jazz musicians, it is an insider notation, and there is no overarching problem for the ethnomusicologist in using it, at least not beyond the field's usual debates about the utility of transcription. For this project, which focuses upon improvisational process, transcriptions were extremely useful, and I include them without apology.

Ethnographic Authority

The 1980s witnessed a growing critique within anthropology and ethnomusicology of the politics and ethics of ethnography, and perhaps the most well known essay on the topic is James Clifford's "On Ethnographic Authority" (1988, 21–54; see also Clifford and Marcus 1986). Central to his discussion is a critique of the classic anthropological method of participant observation for its tendency to produce accounts in which the ethnographer justifies her or his authority with appeals to having "been there." These appeals to experience as justification for the author's right to speak, Clifford rightly emphasizes, often mask a bid for authority. Against the experiential "I was there" mode of ethnographic legitimization, Clifford calls for recognition that there is a process of entextualization that occurs as the ethnographer moves from interactive human encounter to mechanical recording of the experience to transcription of speech into language (and music into notation) to the writing of articles and books interpreting the experience.

My attention to language and to interaction, then, is meant to highlight at all levels the constructed character of the endeavor that this book represents. Yes, I was there, but so were lots of other people, who were going about their everyday lives in the context of the professional music world. The absurdity of claiming that I had a more important vantage point than anyone else who may have been there is perhaps more obvious in ethnographic work done in New York City than in that done in the more distant locations associated with ethnomusicology (and the musicians I spoke with would waste no time in calling me on it). What is different about my position is that I have entextualized the events by recording certain types of speech events (interviews), taking notes on what I observed, transcribing recorded interviews and sound recordings, and writing about the implications of the materials in relationship to the debates about music, race, and identity taking place within the academy, the jazz industry, and American society more generally.

I have been constantly aware that this study represents a limited kind of dialogue, one that some of the participants may even have forgotten but that I believe is very important for bringing practical musical knowledges and reflections into productive dialogue with the rarefied world of the academy, as well as with the social, political, and ethical debates taking place within an increasingly transnational context. Not everyone has the time to research and write. That I have been accorded the institutional support to do so is a privilege embedded in the full range of American social hierarchies, no matter how hard I have had to work for it or how ethical I have attempted to be. Despite asymmetrical social conditions, I remain convinced that the academy and the American public have much to learn from interactive jazz improvisation and that the best point of departure—postmodern debates notwithstanding—remains the serious consideration of what musicians have had to say about it.

chapter
two grooving and feeling

A small jazz band provides a framework for musical interaction among players who take as their goal the achievement of a groove or feeling—something that unites the improvisational roles of the piano, bass, drums, and soloist into a satisfying musical whole. The shape, timbral color, and intensity of the journey is at every point shaped by the interacting musical personalities of band members, who take into consideration the roles expected of their musical instruments within the group. I began my study of improvisational interaction by asking the musicians how they viewed these roles—their philosophy, as it were, of their primary musical responsibilities, their observations about what they might do to vary their musical functions or how they might collaborate to ensure that the relevant musical business was being taken care of at any given moment.

Keeping time, comping, and soloing are three of the most basic musical functions traded around the improvising band, and each rhythm section instrument has particular ways of fulfilling them. Each individual musician, in addition, has his or her own idiosyncrasies, peculiarities, and style. In an improvisational situation, it is important to remember that there are always musical personalities interacting, not merely instruments or pitches or rhythms. It is not uncommon for players to express this musical process of interaction in interpersonal rather than musical terms, which makes sense in a form in which performance and the creation of musical ideas are not separated. The often cited soul, warmth, and emotional expressivity of jazz improvisation have much to do with the ineffable and unpredictable musical chemistry among players, who take great delight in recounting their most quirky and magical moments in performance. The unpredictable may be euphoric or anxiety-producing (such as fear of getting lost), but the mixture of expectation and willful departure traded around the bandstand is something the music absolutely thrives upon.

A player's instrumental role is in turn viewed as having a long-term effect on his or her personality. The instrument may be cited in explanation of the player's attitudes, modes of thinking, and musical perceptions: "He's a drummer; that's why he thinks like that." Certain musical limitations may also be accounted for by the instrument, as when a bass player objected to a horn player's musical directions by commenting that "horn players just can't hear low notes." A player's instrument certainly defines his or her musical vantage point, but that vantage point itself is often defined in relationship to those of other instruments. The instrumental roles of piano, bass, drums, and soloist, then, are interdependent and flexible rather than mutually exclusive.

Within each instrumental role there is a range of musical options, from the relatively stable time-keeping function to the relatively free position of soloist accompanied by the rest of the ensemble. As we work our way through the instruments at the bottom of the band, the basic musical choices available to the player at either end of this spectrum—as well as a number of options in between—will become apparent. The background issue to keep in mind is that at any given moment in a performance, the improvising artist is always making musical choices in relationship to what everyone else is doing. These cooperative choices, moreover, have a great deal to do with achieving (or failing to achieve) a satisfying musical journey—the feeling of wholeness and exhilaration, the pleasure that accompanies a performance well done.[1]

The aesthetics of rhythm and the idea of good time underlie every instrumental role in the ensemble. Hence arises the emphasis in this chapter on the idea of grooving and feeling, for they are central to the successful combination of instrumental roles. Bassist Cecil McBee explained the role of rhythm with the image of a wave:

> Given the cultural nature of the music—this being jazz music—you understand that particular pulse which usually is a swing-type pulse, where emphasis is placed on two and

four. . . . The moment you pick up the instrument and put
it into motion you're suppose to *feel* that, and then the
other things kind of ride the wave. (McBee 1990)

McBee suggests that the rhythmic flow is what frames and integrates
the remaining musical elements, the "other things" being harmony,
melody, and timbre. At the heart of this aesthetic is a notion that these
elements must be deployed effectively in time or they won't make
good music.[2]

The swing "pulse" described by McBee, which places emphasis on
beats 2 and 4 as strong beats (in 4/4 or C meter), is a basic element
underlying most African American musics. This emphasis on the offbeats has a noted ability to inspire people to rhythmic participation.
An entire room of people clapping on 2 and 4 in a gospel service, for
example, has the power to motivate all but the most resistant to clap
along. While the character of bass and chordal parts—that is, the style
of the groove—may vary significantly among soul, rhythm and blues,
gospel, and a cappella singing, all of these musics tend to emphasize
the offbeats. How these offbeats are articulated is another important
consideration. A jazz musician is said to have good time if his or her
underlying pulse is steady, strong, and infectious, with emphasis on the
latter. Good time should make you want to "pat your feet," as Count
Basie remarked, or make you want to "march along with it," as drummer Michael Carvin (1990) explained. The idea that good time should
inspire movement remains fundamental.

While time may at first appear to be synonymous with pulse, good
time additionally implies a sense of rhythmic phrasing—an ability, as
Ralph Peterson remarked, "to absorb a large amount of rhythmic variants without being thrown" (Peterson 1989a), and an ability to play
out of time or temporarily suspend the feeling of pulse. In pulsed sections, solid time is the relatively stable element against which a soloist
phrases even more offbeat melodic and harmonic ideas. The stronger
the time feel, the easier it is for a soloist to take risks with solo phrasing. As Michael Carvin put it, "Gravy is nice, but you have to have
something to put it on." At a drum lesson during which I was paying
more attention to interjecting soloistic ideas than to keeping time, Carvin stopped me and remarked that he heard the gravy, "but where's the
dinner?" (Carvin 1990).

Whether prioritization of rhythmic flow is conceived of as a wave or a full-course meal, McBee's and Carvin's emphasis on time and rhythm was shared by other musicians as well. Drummer Ralph Peterson (who also plays trumpet) explained the order of importance as follows:

> I was just having a conversation last night about how important it is—when you're playing a solo—*rhythmically* what the notes say. [It's] almost as important, if not *as* important, as the notes themselves, because if you miss a note and the *rhythm* is logical, then the idea comes across . . . whether you hit the note dead center or not. But if you miss the time—because music is organized sound in time . . . if you blow the time you're more likely to do irreparable damage to that particular section of the music. (Peterson 1989b)

Statements like these do not diminish the importance of harmony, melody, and sound quality in jazz improvisation. Rather, when musicians speak of the central importance of time, they take for granted the harmonic and melodic competence of the player. The point to note is that musicians' discussions of the higher levels of improvisational achievement frequently emphasize time and ensemble responsiveness as the relevant framework rather than, for example, large-scale tonal organization.[3]

The Bassist

Of the bassist's role, Phil Bowler said, "We're the foundation on which everything is built" (Bowler 1989). Bassists spoke most often about the rhythmic and harmonic responsibilities of their instrumental role. Timbral and melodic considerations were often featured in their commentary as well, but these issues were generally discussed in terms of their ability to enhance the rhythmic and harmonic dimensions of the bass position. During a performance, a bassist can make three general types of interactive choices: playing time (walking), interacting melodically (or rhythmically) with the soloist, or playing pedal points underneath the ensemble texture. Cecil McBee described the position of the bass player as follows:

> It's important that the player understands that his musical position is to ascertain the pulse, the harmony and rhythm

all in one. He's the heartbeat. . . . What I mean is *all* are listening to him . . . all are listening to that pulse, that sound
for guidance. The harmonic path, the rhythmic-harmonic
pulsative path that the bass takes serves as a guide toward
whatever improvisation . . . is to occur at the time. (McBee
1990)

The "rhythmic-harmonic pulsative path" Cecil McBee talked about
is created most typically in swing time by what musicians call a *walking
bass line.* The bass line played by Richard Davis underneath Freddie
Hubbard's trumpet solo in musical example 1 illustrates the basic musical features of walking: prevalent quarter-note motion, four beats to
the bar, with some chromatic melodic motion that outlines the harmonic progression clearly. Beats 2 and 4 tend to be played more force-
fully than beats 1 and 3, and rhythmic embellishment of the four quarter notes tends not to disturb the basic quarter-note pulse for very
long.[4] Measures 1 through 4 of this example illustrate a walking bass
line leading from F7 to B♭7.

When asked to lay down the time clearly, a bassist will typically play
a line of this type. As Phil Bowler put it, emphasizing the stabilizing
role of the bass, "It's like the earth—you walk on the earth. The bass
is like the earth" (Bowler 1989). Bowler's image emphasizes harmonic
as well as rhythmic aspects of walking, for the bass usually provides
the lowest note in a harmonic sonority and consequently, as Jerome
Harris commented (1989), is "defining the chordal movement." In this
respect, players' observations about the harmonic role of the bass are
in agreement with standard Western tonal music theory (Aldwell and
Schacker 1989, 69). In jazz, however, the harmonic progression is frequently embellished and extended in performance. Even within the
most mainstream setting, musicians make use of chord substitutions,
alterations, and chromatic voice leading so frequently that the published chord changes to a tune can be said to serve only as a general
framework from which improvisation proceeds. The bassist and pianist, in particular, are expected to have harmonic sensitivity to each
other.

Michael Weiss, a pianist, talked about the way in which a bass player
can motivate his harmonic choices:

The bassist can also have an influence on the harmonic
progression a pianist plays. . . . The bottom note of the

Musical example 1. Richard Davis playing a walking bass line.
Chorus 3. "Blues for Duane." Freddie Hubbard.
(*The Hub of Hubbard*. BASF MPS-20726.
Recorded: Villingen, West Germany, 9 December 1969.)

chord, which is usually the bass player, can significantly
affect the resonance, the sonority that a piano player
plays. (Weiss 1990)

Weiss explained that if the bass note doesn't fit with the chord he's
playing, the chord "won't ring true." Consequently, when playing with
a strong bass player who is not following him harmonically, he must

accommodate the bassist by playing chords that fit with the bass player's improvised line. Pianists also have expectations about how bass
players should respond harmonically to them, as we shall see.

In addition to walking and defining the harmony, a bass player can
interact melodically and rhythmically with the soloist or any of the
rhythm section instruments. This melodically oriented musical interaction is, of course, not restricted to the bass. In musical example 2, for
instance, Richard Davis responds to soloist Freddie Hubbard's triplets
with triplets in the bass (mm. 7–8). Here the bass moves from a walking
line of accompaniment into an imitative melodic figure that fills the
space between Hubbard's melodic phrases. At the end of this passage,
Davis returns to a walking line for two bars (mm. 9–10) and then plays
what musicians call a *turnaround figure* (mm. 11–12). In this case, Davis's line implies a chord progression that leads into the top of the next
chorus: B-flat (IV), E-flat (VII), A-flat (♭III), C7 (V7).

Davis used the image of a conversation to characterize the interactive process in musical example 2:

> That happens a lot in jazz, that it's like a conversation and
> one guy will . . . create a melodic motif or a rhythmic mo-
> tif and the band picks it up. It's like sayin' that you all are
> talking about the same thing. (Davis 1989)

In such moments, the bass player temporarily breaks from the more
routine task of laying down the time and harmonic progression and
responds to something linear coming from elsewhere in the ensemble—the soloist or another member of the rhythm section. A responding figure need not be imitative. In some cases the lines are secondary melodies or riffs, or they are in a relationship of call and
response. Richard Davis likened these interjections to a communicative process, which indeed they are. The bass player, along with the rest
of the musicians, is constantly deciding when to make such interjections. If a bassist makes them too frequently, the rest of the band might
turn and stare or otherwise communicate the equivalent of Michael
Carvin's metaphorical "Where's the dinner?"

Another choice open to the bass player (and the pianist as well) is
to initiate *pedal points,* which function in a somewhat opposite manner
to the walking bass line. The bass player temporarily suspends outlin-
ing the local harmonic progression in favor of sustaining a single pitch
(most usually the dominant or tonic of the key), over which the pianist

Musical example 2. Melodic interaction between R. Davis and F. Hubbard.
Chorus 1. "Blues for Duane." Freddie Hubbard.
(*The Hub of Hubbard*. BASF MPS-20726.
Recorded: Villingen, West Germany, 9 December 1969.)

and the rest of the ensemble can continue playing harmonic progres-
sions. The pedal point is often combined with a rhythmic ostinato,
which contrasts with the straight four quarters of the walking bass line
as well. The basic harmonic function of the pedal point is fundamentally the same as that articulated by theorists of Western classical music: prolongation of a principal chord, often for purposes of emphasiz-

ing an impending cadence or new section of a work (Schenker 1973, 318–19; Aldwell and Schachter 1989, 348–49; Schoenberg 1978, 209). In jazz improvisation, however, pedal points also have interactional and rhythmic implications that contrast greatly with those of their classical counterparts. When a bass player initiates a pedal point, he or she signals a range of musical possibilities to the rest of the ensemble. The pianist and soloist can deviate more freely from the written harmonic progression while playing over a pedal. The drummer is temporarily freed from coordinating with the walking bass and may choose to play in a more active, soloistic manner. This is what Cecil McBee was talking about when he likened a pedal point to an anchor:

> When you choose to go into a pedal tone . . . the drummer
> is really liberated, because, you know, he's got it. You drop
> the anchor so he can build and create around that. . . .
> The anchor is into the water and [the drummer's] the ship.
> (McBee 1990)

The anchor is on the stable end of the continuum of choices an improvising jazz musician can make. The relaxation of the pace of chordal rhythm and the suspension of the walking bass line in some ways necessitate increased activity from the remaining band members. When placed at the right moment and combined with intensified piano and drum activity, a pedal point can provide tremendous support for a soloist's climactic moments.

An example of such an appropriately placed pedal point is found in musical example 3. In the fourth and fifth choruses of his solo on "Blues for Duane," Freddie Hubbard played a repeating riff figure, first in the midrange of the trumpet (chorus 4), then a fragment of the riff raised an octave (chorus 5). This shift in register (mm. 54–55) and the break from the riff figure in the following measure signaled an impending shift in the character of his solo in the following chorus. Richard Davis anticipates this change and responds by initiating a tonic pedal point (on F) in the first measure of the sixth chorus (m. 61). Hubbard plays a more rhythmically dense riff figure, Roland Hanna adds an additional riff to the texture in measure 63, and Richard Davis joins it in measure 64. Hanna and Davis proceed to a rhythmic cadence at the end of measure 64 that marks the beginning of the second four-measure phrase of this blues tune and a climax for the rhythm section.

Musical example 3. "Blues for Duane." Freddie Hubbard.
(*The Hub of Hubbard*. BASF MPS-20726.
Recorded: Villingen, West Germany, 9 December 1969.)

Hubbard continues by playing a concluding phrase and then subsiding. Davis commented:

> Climactic and then they reside. If you're constantly at one level it gets very boring, I would think. So it's almost like a preacher when he starts a sermon—he doesn't start with the climax; he starts with a little foreplay leading you to the subject. (Davis 1989)

It is important to note that the pedal point is effective only if the remaining players in the ensemble react to it and the bass player chooses to go into it at a moment appropriate for the soloist. The subject in this case was emphasizing a climax in Hubbard's solo, but the pedal point can also support the rhythm section in a much wider variety of musical situations. Pedal points can be used to differentiate the

Musical example 3. *Continued*

B section in an AABA form, for example. They may be played in rhythmic ostinatos that set up temporary metric modulations, such as those achieved by the legendary Miles Davis rhythm section, which included Ron Carter, Tony Williams, and Herbie Hancock (Davis 1964). They may help cue the top of a chorus to musicians who have lost their place in the time cycle. Pedal points have also been an important resource for jazz composers interested in extending structural frameworks for

Musical example 3. *Continued*

improvisation beyond the traditional chorus-structured forms. Charles Mingus's "extended forms," for example, often made use of pedal points (Priestly 1982, 35; Mingus 1978, 18–20). Chapter 5 explores the use of pedal points in a more extended musical environment.

There are other musical resources available to the bass player that have interactional implications, even if they are not quite as obvious as the pedal point. Richard Davis identified some of these factors:

Musical example 3. *Continued*

> Then there's certain ingredients that make you reach a cer-
> tain level [of intensity]: repetition, change of octave, some-
> times change of coloration of the notes, a repetitive phrase
> that catches on to something. You know, a musician
> doesn't *talk* about this too much, but it happens—because
> that's where it's at. (Davis 1989)

Cecil McBee elaborated on what Richard Davis called a "change of
coloration" that he called "tone."

Musical example 3. *Continued*

There's certain directions that the bass player can take the
tonality that will *command* various dynamics from the
rhythm section. If you choose to go up into a lighter tone
or over to a smoother tone, you might lose some of the
gravity. If you go down to a stronger tone, by playing
closer to the bridge (where you get a stronger tone as opposed to playing further up on the fingerboard, where you

Musical example 3. *Continued*

get a softer tone), you're going to lose certain dynamics
and you have to learn to manipulate that given certain
tunes, certain passages, certain choruses, certain bridges,
certain feelings . . . you direct the energy. (McBee 1990)

Jerome Harris commented further on the way in which changing oc-
taves can be a resource for the bassist:

Musical example 3. *Continued*

What octave you choose to play things in can change
things around, you know. You can decide if there's some
point of a tune that you want some real oomph in, so you
drop down to the lowest octave. . . . Maybe in the bridge[5]
you might decide to play up in a little higher range
than you had been in and then coming back into the A section, you know, BOOM, you drop down low and it gives

Musical example 3. *Continued*

this new fullness that hadn't been there for a section or so.
(Harris 1989)

In addition to fulfilling the basic functions of providing harmonic
direction and a steady pulse, therefore, a bassist draws on a wide array
of musical options, all of which may have interactional implications.
Harmony, rhythm, pedal points, melodic ideas, timbre, and register
can all be employed in a manner that provokes responses from other
band members and enhances or detracts from the overall musical de-

Musical example 3. *Continued*

velopment of the ensemble. The bass player balances the recurrent demand of keeping good time and harmony with the inventiveness of responding to particular musical occurrences in the band in a manner that creates (or fails to create) musical climaxes. As Jerome Harris summed up the position,

> It's quite a subtle, subtly powerful role. People talk about bass players not really . . . drawing much attention to themselves. . . . But *everyone* in the band is affected if the bass player isn't on the case. And the audience is very deeply affected. They may not *know* what's wrong, but they will know that *something* is wrong. . . . There's a lot of character that a bass player brings to a group. (Harris 1989)

The ability to respond to changing musical events is a theme that recurred in the discussion of pianists and drummers as well. The ongoing process of decision making that takes place in the ensemble perhaps explains why musicians often say that the most important thing is to listen. They mean it in a very active sense: they must listen closely because they are continually called upon to respond to and participate in an ongoing flow of musical action that can change or surprise them at any moment.[6]

The Pianist

The word most often associated with the pianist in the accompanying role is *comping.* Sir Roland Hanna explained that *comp* derives from the term *accompaniment,* while other musicians said that it comes from the word *complement.* In any case, comping refers to the rhythmic presentation of harmonies in relationship to the soloist or the written theme of an arrangement, and the piano and its substitutes (generally the guitar and the vibes) are called comping instruments. Hanna explained:

> It isn't *just* to a soloist that a pianist has to do a comp.
> Let's say an arrangement has been written and the *line* in
> the arrangement is a tutti or unison of several instruments
> playing the same line. The pianist has to be able to fill the
> gaps in that line with a comp that fits perfectly—so that
> you don't feel like you've got *holes* in that line. You've got
> to feel like that little space was there just for the piano to
> play that certain line. He has to comp in such a way that
> the comp fits the gap without getting in the way of the
> line, you know. (Hanna 1989)

In his performance of "Well You Needn't" (New York Jazz Quartet 1975), Hanna's comping is placed primarily, though not exclusively, in the spaces between the melody. Nevertheless, the comping part would make rhythmic sense even if the melody were not being played. In essence, the pianist is expected to improvise an appropriate rhythmic and harmonic counterpoint to the melody or solo. The comp adds a rhythmic layer to the texture provided by the walking bass and the drums. A pianist's comping style is a characteristic feature of his or her jazz piano style.

Many players cited big band accompaniments—particularly riffs and shout choruses—as important influences on their comping style.[7] A shout chorus is typically played at a climactic point in a solo or arrangement and is characterized by fully voiced rhythmic figures with space between repetitions that allows the soloist, rhythm section, or contrasting horn section to engage in call and response. Effective shout choruses raise the intensity level of the musical flow. A riff is a short, repeated rhythmic figure used as a melody or as accompanimental background. Jaki Byard explained how he thinks of his accompaniment style:

> I'm thinking of a big band. . . . Those things that I played
> during that are things I've heard bands do. Those swinging
> clichés, if I could put it that way. (Byard 1990)

The "clichés" to which Byard refers are primarily rhythmic, as he freely departs from diatonic harmony in his own employment of these fig-

Musical example 4. Jaki Byard playing riff style comping.
"Parkeriana." (*Charles Mingus Live in Paris Vol. 2.*
ESOLDUN-INA FCD110. Recorded in Paris, 18 April 1964.)

Alto Sax (Eric Dolphy)

Piano (Jaki Byard)

Bass (Charles Mingus)

ures. Musical example 4, which is taken from an A section of Eric Dolphy's solo on Charles Mingus's "Parkeriana" (Mingus 1964a) and uses "Rhythm" changes in B-flat, illustrates this point.[8] On hearing this example, Jaki Byard remarked:

> That's old, that's a riff, it's an old big band riff. . . . The main thing was swing, you know, and creating that intense feeling. (Byard 1990)

Note that Byard's riffs in bars 1 to 3 and 5 to 7 provide harmonic and rhythmic stability under the dissonant solo line of Eric Dolphy. Byard's

Musical example 4. *Continued*

line emphasizes a G diminished sonority that relates to the B-flat tonality of the tune through the pitch D♭ as a blue note.[9] The most stable tonal features of Dolphy's line also make use of this diminished seventh chord (see musical example 4, mm. 1–2 and 5–6).

Jackie McLean's "Fidel" provides an example of a riff figure in which the drums join the riff while the bass walks (McLean 1958). The dashed vertical lines in musical example 5 indicate where the drummer's accentuation matches the accentuation of the riff played by Sonny Clark on the piano. Donald Byrd solos against this rhythmic background without directly responding to it as a rhythmic figure. Michael Weiss made the following observations about this riff style of comping:

> One of the aspects of [Sonny Clark's] comping style is
> he—depending on the tempo—likes to riff and will incite
> the drummer and bass player to play this figure along with
> him, which is something I like very much. . . . What he's
> doing is really independent of Donald Byrd. . . . I like that
> kind of accompaniment in a way because it's still fulfilling
> the role of being an accompaniment but it's like a second-
> ary melody, a rhythm as opposed to not having any indi-
> vidual identity of its own. . . . I like that type of comping
> because I trust that the soloist has enough strength of his
> own to maintain his dominance . . . and not be side-
> tracked by a secondary rhythm or melody going on.
> (Weiss 1990)

Musical example 5. Riff style comping.
"Fidel." (*Jackie's Bag.* Blue Note CDP 7 48142 2.
Recorded: New York, 18 January 1959.)

Musical example 5. *Continued*

Weiss continued by saying that some soloists prefer the type of comp Sir Roland Hanna talked about, one that fills in gaps without disturbing the line, while others enjoy the intensity provided by a more intrusive style.[10]

Pianists, in addition, have expectations about what the bass player should be able to hear:

> A bass player in particular should be able to recognize the sound of many standard jazz voicings on the piano and respond to that . . . be well versed in all the different possibilities of chord substitution . . . on a number of different standards . . . so he knows—when he hears a piano player playing a certain variation or a certain voicing—he immediately knows what's the most suitable bass note to play. (Weiss 1990)

In addition to the technical knowledge described by Weiss, players become familiar with individual bass styles, especially those of musicians with whom they frequently work. In talking about his relationship with Richard Davis, Roland Hanna explained why things are particularly musical when the two of them play together:

> When you're talking about having been around somebody for thirty years . . . you're close to the way they think. Now maybe I don't know exactly . . . the way he thinks, but I am close enough to what he has been thinking in the past to have an idea of what he *might* play from one note to the next. If he plays a C at a certain strength, then I know he may be looking for an A-flat or an E-flat or whatever direction he may go in. And I know he may be making a certain *kind* of a passage. I've heard him enough to know *how* he makes his lines. So I may not know exactly what note he's going to play, but I know in general the kind of statement he would make, or how he would use his *words,* you know, the order he would put his words in. . . . There's a curious thing about musicians. We train ourselves over a period of years to be able to hear rhythms and anticipate combinations of sounds before they actually happen. (Hanna 1989)

This developed and empathetic sense of listening that enables pianists to anticipate the harmonic and rhythmic direction of a bass player results in moments of unison such as measure 64 of musical example 3. To an observer unfamiliar with this tradition, the rhythm section climax of Hubbard's solo on "Blues for Duane" may appear to have been planned in advance. This ability to anticipate musical ideas and respond to musical events in the ensemble is the product of a shared sense of musical style that includes a notion of the appropriate rhythmic, harmonic, and melodic responses to given musical events. Ultimately it is experience and knowledge of repertory as well as sensitivity toward other musicians that inform this sensibility, a theme that looms large in the broader discussions taken up in later chapters of this book.

Like most instrumentalists, many pianists feel that their instrument is arguably the most important within a band. Roland Hanna explained:

> The piano in jazz is like three instruments. It's the chord instrument, it's the rhythm instrument, and it's the bass instrument at the same time. Then it's enhanced by the drums, the bass, and the guitar. (Hanna 1989)

In other words, Hanna suggests that the role of the other instruments is to amplify functions already taken care of by the piano. While acknowledging that the bass and drums can occupy a central place in a jazz ensemble, Michael Weiss argued that in certain situations the piano can lead like no other instrument:

> The piano is in a very sort of pivotal place. . . . Let's say there's a situation where somebody gets lost or not everybody is sure they're in the same place, let's say in a fast tempo, very fast tempo tune. When the piano player plays a chord deliberately on a certain beat, everybody will respond to that more than almost anything else. And will react to that, so in that respect . . . the piano player can have a dominant role in the rhythm section. (Weiss 1990)

Bassists, as we have seen, frequently mentioned their central importance within a band: "We are the foundation on which everything is built" said Bowler (1989); "The bass player is the captain," commented McBee (1990). Added Jerome Harris (1989), *Everyone* in the band is affected if the bass player isn't on the case." Drummers spoke similarly of their role. Although such passages on one level express an instrumental chauvinism on the part of players, self-centeredness is not really at their core. Rather, these passages underscore the fundamental interdependence of the musical roles fulfilled by the instruments. Each instrument may feel like the most important because it handles certain musical situations uniquely. Players of each instrument can effectively signal or initiate musical events according to these unique abilities and honestly feel that their role in certain situations is the most crucial. In the end, however, it is the balance of these complementary musical roles that contributes to ensemble cohesiveness.[11]

The Drummer

The drummer is generally the member of the band most underrated by the audience and least discussed in the jazz historical and analytical literature. Since drummers don't play harmonies and melodies in the same way as the other instrumentalists, audience members and even some musicians have a tendency to deprecate the musical knowledge of the person sitting behind the drum set. Many mistakenly assume that the drummer just plays rhythm and therefore doesn't participate in the melodic and harmonic flow of the music. From an interactive perspective, however, the drum set represents a microcosm of all the interactive processes we have discussed, including harmonic and melodic sensitivity.

The drum set is, after all, an ensemble in its own right. A standard jazz kit includes a ride cymbal, a hi-hat (or sock cymbal), a bass drum, one or two mounted tom-toms, a floor tom-tom, and one or more crash cymbals. The single most important event in the development of the modern drum set, according to Theodore D. Brown (1976), was the development of the bass drum pedal, which occurred during the latter half of the nineteenth century. In 1909 the Ludwig Drum Company patented an all-metal, toe-operated pedal that enabled drummers to play more than one percussion instrument at once.[12] The second most important innovation from the modern drummer's perspective was perhaps the foot-operated hi-hat cymbal pair, introduced in approximately 1927 (Brown 1976, 310–11). The foot-operated bass pedal (usually played by the right foot among right-handed players) and hi-hat (usually played by the left) enabled the drummer to use all four limbs of the body in providing the rhythmic foundation of the jazz ensemble. Four-way coordination among these limbs is essential to modern jazz drumming technique, and it often mystifies audience members and other musicians alike. As Michael Carvin explained:

> You can actually have four different parts [on the drum set], which is a quartet. And if you practice and get the right amount of discipline, you can actually develop those parts to where it *is* a band within itself. . . . I can hear a melody against a melody against a rhythm against a rhythm. And that's why I feel that the drummer *is* the band. (Carvin 1990)

Carvin stressed that the drummer has musical interaction among his or her four limbs that can be just as polyphonic as the interaction among the drummer and the other instruments in the band. The pianist also has an interaction taking place between his or her hands that may add another layer to rhythmic tensions in the band.

To the concept of good time must be added the idea of *playing time,* a particular specialty of drummers. One or more of the drummer's limbs generally remain stable and are said to be playing or keeping time; the remaining limbs often play freely "against" the time.[13] Musicians call the different styles of playing time—each of which implies a different set of ensemble rhythms—rhythmic feels or grooves. These styles of playing time establish the rhythmic framework against which improvisation takes place. A particular feel played by the drummer signals the bassist that certain bass lines are appropriate and others are not. Likewise, a particular groove tells the pianist that certain types of comping are expected and others are not. These relationships work in reverse as well. A certain style of comping, or a certain bass line, will tell the drummer which time feel would be most appropriate. Musicians listen carefully for musical details such as these.

For the time being, we'll focus on the most typical jazz time feel and how it's played on the drums: swing time, in its bebop-and-after version. It's the groove that musicians are likely to play when given no further specification than to "play time." Swing time can be seen as a version of the shuffle family of rhythms, which Jerome Harris defined as triplet-based rhythms that give a "12/8 feeling" to a piece. While shuffle rhythms are generally notated as triplet rhythms in 4/4, the subdivision of units into three is a central component of a swing feeling

Musical example 6. The shuffle family of rhythms.

that could just as—perhaps more—easily be expressed in 12/8. Musical example 6 illustrates several variations of this type of rhythm. Shuffle grooves can be slow or fast, articulate all of the subdivisions (as in 6a and b), drop the middle eighth note in each group (6c), or alternate unsubdivided beats with subdivided ones (6d). The last rhythm, of course, is the standard ride cymbal rhythm (variously notated in 6e, f, and g).

When bass lines are added, however, a musician can inflect the shuffle rhythm (generally played on ride cymbal or hi-hat) in the direction of R&B, jazz, or gospel. In musical example 7, Harris sang the bass line while patting the shuffle rhythm in musical example 6c, which inflected the groove toward R&B. The standard ride rhythm can be found extensively in R&B as well as in jazz but with different bass lines

Musical example 7. Jerome Harris singing R & B bass line with the shuffle.

Musical example 8. Jerome Harris singing walking bass line with ride cymbal beat.

and comping styles. The bass line in musical example 7, for instance, tends to evoke a two-beat dance feeling, while the four-beat line in musical example 8 is equivalent to a basic jazz walking bass line. If the shuffle rhythm in musical example 6h is played over a slow walking bass line, a groove common to gospel and blues emerges.

The Ride Cymbal

Since the time of Kenny Clarke and Max Roach, the primary time-keeping rhythm in a swing feel has been played on the ride cymbal, the large suspended cymbal that the drummer plays with his or her dominant hand. This rhythm known as the *ride cymbal beat,* can be played and represented in a variety of ways (see musical example 6d–g).

The character and timbre of a drummer's ride cymbal beat, as well as the length of the short note in beats 2 and 4, are among the most identifying features of a drummer's style. Kenny Washington explained:

> That cymbal beat is the most important thing that you
> have. There have been drummers in the history of jazz
> who didn't have fantastic chops [technique], but they had a

great feeling, they had a great cymbal beat. (Washington
1990)

He characterized many drummers in terms of their cymbal beats:

> Shadow Wilson is another *master* of the cymbal beat. Billy
> Higgins in another one. . . . He's got a certain kind of feel-
> ing and he's got one of them big *wide* cymbal beats. Like if
> you listen to Lee Morgan records, like that tune "Hocus
> Pocus," like on the *Sidewinder* record [Morgan 1963]. Lis-
> ten to that man, he's got a big, big *wide* cymbal beat.[14]
> (Washington 1990)

The hi-hat often participates in keeping time as well by articulating
beats 2 and 4 against the ride cymbal rhythm. Drummers since the late
1950s and early 1960s have experimented with other ways to play time,
sometimes avoiding playing beats 2 and 4 on the hi-hat continually or
shifting the primary time-keeping function from the ride cymbal to
another limb.

Michael Carvin likened the time-keeping rhythmic parts to the state
of being "solid" and the freer rhythmic parts to being "liquid." The
four limbs integrate solid and liquid aspects of rhythm, so "we can
have something floating and something solid—instead of having all
solid . . . or all liquid." Carvin explained:

> See, a drummer has to give the band one limb. It can be
> any one that he chooses to. If we go back to 1920 with Sid
> Catlett and Baby Dodds . . . the limb that they gave was
> the bass drum. (Carvin 1990)

In the early swing era, drummers such as Cozy Cole, Gene Krupa,
and Dave Tough played the bass drum on all four beats of the bar;
what we now think of as the ride cymbal beat came to be played on
the hi-hat, a trend led by Jo Jones. The reason for continual quarter
notes in the bass was not entirely rhythmic, however. Since the acoustic
bass was not amplified in that time period, Carvin explained, the bass
drum helped support the harmony.

> But all those guys played that bass drum [pats his hand in
> quarter notes]. You could hear it through the whole song.
> Because the bass didn't have an amp. So the cat would try
> to tune his bass drum close to the sound of the bass so he

could help make the bass player sound stronger, so the changes would be stronger. (Carvin 1990)

By the late thirties, Count Basie's drummer, Jo Jones had shifted the primary time-keeping function from the bass drum to the hi-hat, thereby freeing his bass drum for *dropping bombs,* the term bebop musicians would later use to describe irregular accents played on the bass drum. Jo Jones was cited by several musicians, including Roy Haynes (1990), as the most important precursor to the development of bebop drumming. Kenny Clarke and Max Roach built upon Jo Jones's use of the cymbals to keep time by transferring the time-keeping rhythm to the ride cymbal. In an oral history interview conducted by the Smithsonian Institution (Clarke 1977),[15] Kenny Clarke explained that his primary motivation in transferring the time-keeping rhythm to the ride cymbal was to free his left hand. Recalling his thoughts in the late 1930s, Clarke remarked, "There has to be a better way, because if I play the sock cymbal [for time], then I can't use my left hand, you know" (91). Since the hi-hat was on the drummer's left side and the time-keeping rhythm was played with the right hand, the options available to the left hand were limited by the right arm's position across the snare and the drummer's body. Michael Carvin cited the timbral advantages of playing time on the ride cymbal:

> By the cymbal being bright and the bass being dark. Now you have a nice sound as far as keeping the time for the band. (Carvin 1990)

The basic rhythmic *hookup,* or synchronization between the drummer and the bass player, in this sense is a function of how well the walking bass line locks or is in the pocket with the ride cymbal rhythm. A drummer's preference for working with particular bass players is often a function of how easily and naturally this hookup occurs. Different musical factors may be at work in this relationship. Drummers report adjusting their playing according to whether the bass player plays on top of or behind the beat. These terms suggest that the pulse of the bass player may be perceived as located in the center of, ahead of, or behind the beat. If a bassist plays behind the beat, the drummer may compensate by pushing ahead of the beat. Both the location of the pulse and the bassist's phrasing style are factors affecting the compatibility of the drummer and the bassist (Cole 1991).[16]

The principle of limb choice also stands behind Carvin's explanation

Musical example 9. Michael Carvin singing Tony Williams-style ride cymbal beat.

of the variable ride rhythms played by innovative modern drummers such as Tony Williams.

> Now Tony Williams, when he was with Miles Davis. The limb that he gave to Miles was the hi-hat . . . and he would dance [play freely] on his [ride] cymbal. . . . Tony confused a lot of drummers because when they heard Tony Williams, they knew that you were supposed to keep time on the ride cymbal. . . . But what they didn't understand about Tony's playing was that that wasn't the limb that he was giving to the band. That wasn't the limb keeping time . . . because Tony would say, [see musical example 9 for notation], but his foot was talking about [straight quarters]. So now you hear all these young drummers today and they can't keep time on the cymbal. (Carvin 1990)

It is important to note that this idea of one limb carrying a solid, repeating rhythmic pattern that other rhythms are played against has strong continuities with both West African drum ensembles and the Caribbean percussion sections they have influenced (Gerard 1989). The function of the ride cymbal in bebop drumming is analogous to that of the bell pattern played by the gankogui in Ewe drum ensembles (Brown 1976, 5–6; Locke 1987, 16). This repeating pattern is the reference point against which the remaining percussion instruments orient their parts. The timbale part, which is an elaboration of an underlying clave pattern not always directly played, often fulfills this function in Afro-Cuban music (Gerard 1989, 24–26). The difference is that in the jazz drum set, one player coordinates the multiple rhythmic parts, which in turn must hook up or interlock with the remaining instrumental layers of the ensemble.[17]

The Left Hand

While the time-keeping function of the drummer's ride cymbal hand synchronizes directly with that of the bass player's walking bass line, many drummers think of their left hand as linked to the piano.[18] Kenny Washington, for example, said:

> For me, besides the bass player, the first person I'm a look at when I get on the bandstand is the piano player. Because I'm always listening to how he comps, the kinds of voicings he uses and his rhythm, because that affects what my left hand is gonna do. (Washington 1990)

Washington, in fact, viewed jazz history through the lens of piano and drum relationships:

> For me there's certain piano and drum hookups throughout the history. Vernell Fournier and Ahmad Jamal, instant hookup. Wynton Kelly and Jimmy Cobb, Sonny Clark and Philly Joe Jones.[19] (Washington 1990)

Roy Haynes also spoke of the importance of connecting to the piano:

> I need the piano; when I play I listen to the [piano]—I need that. (Haynes 1990)

Pianists such as Michael Weiss often concurred with this association as well:

> The piano player has to respond harmonically to what the soloist is doing and what the bass player is doing, complement the soloist and also respond rhythmically to the soloist and—within the rhythm section—to the drummer. I often liken the pianist's rhythmic role with the drummer's left hand, the types of accents and figures he plays on the snare drum and the bass drum. Comping rhythms, as you will. (Weiss 1990)

If we recall that Jaki Byard emphasized the relationship of his bebop comping style to the riffing and shout chorus passages of big bands, Michael Carvin's characterization of his left hand as a brass section makes intuitive sense:

> I really feel my left hand is more brass . . . like in a big band, the brass section is playing the shout parts. And I

hear a small group as big band. And before I let the music get stale, I play a riff. . . . But I hear the left hand as brass. Short, staccato, spurts or like a boxer, jabbin', jabbin', always keeping something happening. (Carvin 1990)

Ralph Peterson Jr. likened his entire drumming style to comping:

Well, it's important to me as a drummer to be a musician and to always deal in the context of *music* and not in the context of drumming. And as far as accompanying a soloist, that means comping as opposed to playing time. (Peterson 1989b)

Whether likened to the piano or to brass, the left hand plays quite independently of the right. Roy Haynes commented:

The left hand is not supposed to let the right hand know what it's going to do. The right hand's not supposed to let the [left hand know], you know. The hands don't know . . . and I don't know. (Haynes 1990)

The drummer's left hand plays rhythms that are more liquid than the solid ride-cymbal rhythm. At any given moment, the drummer can choose to direct the attention of the left hand to other members of the ensemble—the pianist or the soloist—or to asserting an independent rhythmic line that may or may not influence what other ensemble members play. The left hand provides variety against the relatively more static function of the ride cymbal.

Like other members of the ensemble, drummers exercise musical options beyond playing time. At various points in a performance, drummers break the time to play two-handed interjections called *fills*. These are distinguished from the left-hand interjections already mentioned, since the drummer temporarily suspends playing the ride cymbal rhythm while executing them. Fills can serve a variety of musical functions: they might be melodically interactive, provide a seamless comping rhythm, or lead the ensemble from one structural section of a tune to the next. They might be one or two beats or several measures in length. The drummer often plays a large role in intensifying the musical energy at important structural points such as the beginning of sections or choruses.

The fill usually directs the rhythm toward an arrival point of some kind. The drummer may end a fill with the strong articulation of the

Musical example 10. Simple drum fill.

downbeat of the measure it leads into or on an offbeat that anticipates the new section. Players may emphasize this articulation by playing it on a crash cymbal or by punctuating the resumption of the ride rhythm with a strong "1" on the bass drum. The first beat of measure 2 of musical example 10 illustrates punctuation of the downbeat with the crash cymbal and bass drum. This punctuation of arrival points often coincides with harmonic arrival, frequently featuring faster harmonic rhythm. It is not unusual to hear drummers speak of harmonic motivations for their playing choices, since they must be sensitive to the harmonic flow if they are to provide the most thoughtful accompaniment to a soloist.

Melody, Harmony, and Timbre

> It comes back to people's ideas or perspectives of the *role*
> of the drummer, you know, and only being able to relate to
> drums rhythmically. You know a lot of things I play, I play
> from a chordal, melodic standpoint . . . and the reason I
> play a lot of things I play have more to do with what's
> played harmonically and melodically than rhythm.
>
> (PETERSON 1989b)

Every drummer spoke to me about exploiting the timbral resources of the drum set. Although indefinitely pitched, the trap set includes tonal and timbral contrast within its musical resources.[20] The drums—bass, tom-toms, and snare—array pitch from low to high. Cymbals, which contrast timbrally with the drums, also include an array of pitches from low to high—ride, crash, hi-hat (sock), and splash. These tonal and timbral contrasts form an integral part of how a drummer hears his or her instrument(s).

When drummers speak of playing melodically, at the most basic level they are referring to melodic rhythms—either those that imitate the melody or the soloist's line or those that form thematic ideas developed by being played at different pitches and timbral levels around the drum set. In addition, great musical variety can be achieved by playing a given rhythmic idea between two or more parts of the drum set tuned in contrast to each other.

Drummers are aware of the tonality and harmonic progression of a tune, and this awareness may help them keep their place in the time cycle. When Kenny Washington spoke about the way he listens to a piano player in an ensemble, among the things he cited were the voicings played by the pianist. While the harmonic sensibility of a drummer may not be as specific as that of a piano or bass player, the player's reasons for choosing to play on certain parts of the drum set at particular points in the music include harmonic ones. For example, when I was playing along with the Count Basie recording of "Shiny Stockings" in my drum lesson, my teacher Michael Carvin and another drum student in the room commented approvingly when I played a figure on the floor tom at the point in the music when the pitch of the tom happened to closely match the tonality of the musical passage. When playing another tune in a contrasting key, I noticed that playing a similar figure on the tom did not feel as right as it had in the first passage. Although drummers do not retune their drums for particular keys, many have a clear sensibility about which of the array of pitches in the drum set fits best with the tonality of a particular piece. When playing fills under such circumstances, they may choose to play on the drum that most enhances the tonal environment.

Ralph Peterson Jr. had his cymbals specially made based on tonal considerations.

> What I requested from the cymbal maker was to make
> sure that the overtones matched. . . . Each cymbal is an ex-
> tension of one partial or another from the fundamental of
> the largest cymbal. So therefore, if you play the correct
> area of the cymbal, you can play melodies, because each
> section of the cymbal brings out certain overtones in the
> series. (Peterson 1989b)

Peterson plays actual melodies on these cymbals in performance. Not all drummers go to such lengths in the tuning of cymbals, but Peterson's comments about wrong and right "colors" to play with certain passages are echoed by many other drummers:

> What I'm hearing a lot of times is the harmony in the cym-
> bals, you know. I mean, if a certain color is played, I know

what cymbal to play. And it's automatic. . . . A lot of times
if I set my cymbals up in a different sequence, I'll strike
the wrong cymbal. If I get lost in the music and forget I
have an abbreviated setup, I'll play the wrong color. It's
nothing that stands out to anybody who's not really aware,
other than myself. . . . It's something I spend a lot of time
thinking about. . . . I don't really talk to many people
about it. (Peterson 1989b)

Michael Carvin has names for his cymbals that reflect their timbral
color:

It comes from the sound. See, when the sun kisses you, it's
warm but it's very soft. That's my ride cymbal. I grew up
in hurricane country, so thunder is lightning striking it—
dark. Thunder is strong and black. So I have Thunder,
that's my crash cymbal. . . . Then my little cymbal that I
use is called Puddin' . . . because in the South all little girls
when they're first born are called Puddin'. So that [one] is
like the baby, so I call her Puddin'. . . . So I don't relate to
my cymbals as cymbals because if I did I wouldn't play
them the way I play them. (Carvin 1990)

In this context, the drum set should not be viewed as providing an
exclusively rhythmic function. It is clear that professional drummers
think about melody, harmony, and timbre, just as the other members
of the jazz ensemble do. They are not interested in timbre and tone
merely as decorations for their primarily rhythmic function either, for
they see that rhythm, pitch contrast, and timbre interact in interesting
ways in building a performance. Billy Higgins's cryptic comment about
the relationship of sound and swing illustrates this point:

What I try to do is not rely upon *one* part of the instrument. It's to integrate them all. Play them so they balance
out. . . . There's more about sound than anything else. A
certain sound is more palatable to human beings than others. The sound is what gets to the person. Even the swing.
Swing is not the swing. Swing is the sound. (Higgins 1990)

Higgins's assertion that "swing is not the swing" may at first sound
obscure, but to anyone who has experienced the intensely pleasurable
feeling of finding timbral variety in the cymbal, it makes a great deal

of sense. The location and touch of a drummer's stick can produce widely constrasting timbres that themselves help lock the time-keeping rhythms. Once the artist's basic time feel is solid, a great deal of drum artistry can be expressed by getting just the right timbre to color the time. This timbral fit can then energize everyone around it. Higgins, for example, has an easily identifiable cymbal sound. When asked why he uses a sizzle cymbal for his ride, he explained:

> Because it does a lot of work itself, without you having to do it. . . . It adds a certain picture. While you can do the rest of the stuff it sustains.[21] (Higgins 1990)

It is amazing to watch Higgins interacting with a band of young musicians, as I did when he was playing with the up-and-coming Roy Hargrove (trumpet) and Javon Jackson (tenor sax) at Bradley's on 5 August 1990. The young horn players started out sounding very good, but not particularly in the pocket. As he played with the timbres of his instrument, Higgins watched them constantly with his well-known big smile. During the three sets, the ensemble's performance slowly but inexorably intensified as Higgins, bassist David Williams, and pianist Larry Willis established a groove that made it difficult not to pat one's feet. It had a similar effect on the young horn players, for they went from playing competently to totally swinging over the course of the evening. During the interview after the performance, I asked Higgins what he did to get a soloist's attention if it seemed as though that player was not listening very well. His response surprised me: "I always feel like it's my fault" (Higgins 1990). His fault?, I thought; Billy Higgins's fault? His view of the drummer's job clearly includes the *obligation* to inspire musicians into playing their best.

More than bassists and pianists, drummers tend to stress their coordinating and psychological function in the ensemble. Higgins continued:

> It's something about reading everybody individually, you know. You have a slot in your mind for certain people; you have a slot in your mind for other people. So the drums are supposed to be that kind of instrument where you can make everything fit, and that's the whole challenge of it all. (Higgins 1990)

This emphasis on fit is also reiterated by Roy Haynes:

> I would play with Stan Getz. I would play different with
> him than I would play with John Coltrane, because it
> doesn't really fit, you know. There's a saying of Moms
> Mabley, the comedienne. She had a saying: "If it don't fit,
> don't force it."[22] (Haynes 1990)

Kenny Washington echoes both Higgins's and Haynes's theme of adjusting to individuals:

> When you listen to jazz, you have to go beneath the sur-
> face, you know. You have to go beneath all that and find
> out *why* the drummer is playing like he's playing. . . . The
> way I look at it, like all these different people that I play
> with, they're all personalities. They all have different per-
> sonalities and you have to play differently with each one
> of them. Like every piano player I play with, they play
> differently, and the thing about it is that you have to know
> their styles and know what to do and what not to do.
> (Washington 1990)

Perhaps the most extensive elaboration of this interpersonal and musical theme is in Michael Carvin's explanation of why Kenny Clarke once said that the drum is a woman. I thought that I was about to get a sexual explanation, but the topic came up when he likened jazz to a family.[23] I quote Carvin's explanation at length to convey the storytelling style in which it was presented:[23]

> It is a family. That's why you say a drum is a woman.
> That's what Klook [drummer Kenny Clarke] was talkin'
> about. That's what Prez [tenor saxophonist Lester Young]
> was talking about. He say, "Man, the drum is a woman,
> man." And I say, "Klook, what you mean by that?" He
> say, "Well, you take a woman that has four kids, and all
> four of them come home from school together. One of
> them made an A; he's very happy. One made an F; he's
> very sad. One caught a cold today; he's upset. And one
> lost his jacket and he's *very* upset. Now when they hit the
> house, all four of them is hittin' the mother at the same
> time. The one that got an A'll say, "Mommy, look I got an
> A," and he's excited; and the one that got an F, say [crying

tone of voice], "Oh mommy, I got an F"; the one that got
a cold, "Mommy, I'm catching a cold," but she have to, at
the same time, deal with *all* of them at the same time and
cool each one of them out for the energy level that they
are *dealing* with. And that's why they say the drum is a
woman . . . cause that's the same thing a drummer has to
do. You come to the gig, [pace of speaking increases] the
trumpet player's *up,* boy he feel like playing it. The saxophone, you know, he don't feel too good. The piano player
say, "Aw, man, I shouldn't have ate so much, man, I'm feeling a little sluggish." It's the same thing. And . . . they all
coming to you at the same time, so you're getting the news
from all four of them at the same time. Right? Cause
you're the bandleader, right? And you have to say, "Aw,
man, damn you ate too much? [high tone of voice] Why,
man, you big as a house." And you got to try to get him
happy and the other guy that's *already* stretching, then
you want to kind of cool him *down,* cause he's stretching
too much. He got too much energy. And then the guy that
is not feelin' so good, then you got to [give him] a pep talk
. . . before you go play. And they never ask you, "How do
you feel?" But when the four kids came in the house, they
didn't ask mommy. Right? . . . But mommy had to go right
into her motherhood and cool them out. That's why
Klook said a drum is a woman.[24] (Carvin 1990)

On one level, Carvin was speaking metaphorically about being a
bandleader, a role shared by other players; on another he was describing a coordinating and nurturing role specific to the drummer. If a
drummer's right hand coordinates with the bass, the left hand with
the piano or soloist, and the legs in a manner that may emphasize
connections with either the bass or the piano or soloist (solid or liquid
functions), the drummer is coordinating, or cooling out, the energy of
these instruments within his own body. If the soloist, bassist, or pianist
is out of phase with the rest of the band, a drummer can subtly (or not
so subtly) influence the errant musician to get back on track by pushing (or restraining) him or her with the playing of one or more limbs.
The nurturing or enabling aspects of the drummer's role have been
expressed by other musicians as well. Roy Haynes remarked that as a

drummer, "you're supposed to make everything sound good" (Potter 1986, 20), and Billy Higgins's willingness to take the blame for a disappointing performance draws attention to the importance of the drummer's enabling functions.

Carvin's use of mothering as an image to describe the nurturant and interpersonal aspects of the drummer at first seems at odds with the cultural coding of the drum set as a masculine instrument requiring both physical strength and endurance. As a familial image, however, mothering fits right in with the conception of sociability prevalent in jazz performance and within the community of jazz musicians. Billy Higgins, for example, likened jazz as a genre to a family: "The first thing that I'm thinking about is that I'm able to play music and be a link in the chain. Jazz is a family. It's a blessing just to be in that link and be a part of it. . . . It's a big family" (Bernstein 1983, 74). There are families within the greater family as well: groups of musicians who are more compatible with some family members than with others. Joanne Brackeen, for example, spoke in familial terms of the enjoyment of playing in an ensemble:

> It's certain people who are into the energy in the same
> kind of way that I am . . . you know, and, of course, two is
> more fun than one. Three is more fun than two . . . and so
> on and so forth, just like conversation. You know, you can
> have a complete conversation with two people, but it's re-
> ally nice when you add a third thing, just as long as the
> thing—its people—are free in the energy in the same kind
> of way. . . . It's like people born in a family sometimes will
> be close to that family, not necessarily so . . . but there's
> families of musicians, you know, things that work best to-
> gether. (Brackeen 1989)

The Ensemble as a Whole: Grooving as an Aesthetic Ideal

There is an inherent tension within the jazz ensemble between the individual and the group. On the one hand, the aesthetic of the music is centered on the inventiveness and uniqueness of individual solo expression; on the other, climactic moments of musical expression require the cohesiveness and participation of the entire ensemble. In an improvisational music, such as jazz, the interaction between group and individual greatly affects the ultimate composition and development of the music. Since the ensemble is divided into soloist and rhythm section, it should be noted that there are two levels on which this individual-versus-group tension operates: the relationship of the soloist (who may be a rhythm section member) to the rhythm section, and the relationship of each individual to the remainder of the rhythm section. Cecil McBee described how this tension arises in the context of a performance and how a musician must be prepared to face the uncertainty of the situation:

> We are all individuals. . . . When we approach the stage
> . . . we are collectivized there. . . . I mean history is about
> to take place, right? When . . . the band begins to play, his-
> tory is going to take place. This energy proceeds to that
> area and it says, "All right, I'm here, I will direct you and
> guide you. You as an individual must realize that I am
> here. You cannot control me; you can't come up here and
> say, 'Well, I'm gonna play this,'" unless you're reading. . . .
> You can't go there and intellectually realize that you're go-
> ing to play certain things. You're not going to play what
> you practiced. . . . Something else is going to happen . . .
> so the individual himself must make contact with that and
> get out of the way. (McBee 1990)

Just as the ride cymbal provides stability and unity to the multiple rhythms played on the drum set, the notion of the groove supplies underlying solidity and cohesiveness to freely interacting, improvising musicians. We've already encountered *groove* as a noun when we talked about rhythmic feels—those particular sets of rhythm-section parts that combine to produce particular rhythmic patterns. Jerome Harris's description of a groove as a "rhythm matrix" illustrates this usage. Harris's comments also remind us that although *groove* is most centrally a rhythmic term, the flow of harmony, rhythm, and timbre affects how a groove feels in a particular performance. Since a tune is played within a particular groove, the bass and piano fulfill their rhythmic function by playing harmonic and melodic parts appropriate to that groove or feel.[25]

Groove is also an aesthetic term, and in this capacity it is usually used as a verb. It is synonymous with a number of other terms found with varying frequency in the jazz community: *swinging, burning, cooking, putting the pots on* (Davis 1989). When I asked musicians to define the term *groove,* I tried to phrase the question in a way that left it open to each musician to select the noun or verb meaning, but most musicians chose the latter.[26] Most also described grooving as a rhythmic relation or feeling existing *between* two or more musical parts and/or individuals. Don Byron, for example, described grooving as "a euphoria that comes from playing good time *with* somebody" (Byron 1989).[27] Michael Weiss explained it as a type of personal and musical chemistry:

> Every bass player and drummer [and] piano player sort of
> feels the rhythm their own way, and some are more sensi-
> tive or flexible than others. . . . It's not . . . different than
> when you meet somebody and you find a compatibility of
> personalities that's just there.[28] And it's not something that
> you have to try to do. And sometimes it just isn't there
> and it's nobody's fault. (Weiss 1990)

The use of the term *feeling* as a synonym for *groove* underscores the emotional and interpersonal character of groove—something negotiated between musicians that is larger than themselves. Good time in this sense produces not only the physical patting of the feet but an emotional response as well. Phil Bowler called it a "mutual feeling of agreement." Both Richard Davis and Kenny Washington emphasized the interpersonal aspect of groove by comparing it to "walking down the street" with someone. Davis's description likened groove to a romantic or familial relationship, Washington's to walking "arm-in-arm" with someone.

Once established, there is something inexorable about groove as well. Kenny Washington talked of the feeling that the "instrument is playing by itself." Michael Carvin compared it to a "trance" in which you experience "being out of yourself." He also spoke about musicians being "so relaxed that they weren't forcing anything out." The physical pleasure of being in a groove is captured in Carvin's image of soaking in a bathtub and feeling, "Oh, that's what I needed," as well as in Don Byron's comment that "it's about feeling like time itself is pleasurable."

Two more points deserve to be emphasized. Michael Weiss commented that "a lot of times it's a matter of just hitting the right tempo."[29] Although other musicians did not state this explicitly, I doubt that they would disagree. Informally, I heard musicians comment that certain tunes or time feels just don't groove if they are played too quickly or too slowly. The association of tempo with swing or groove is long-standing. Count Basie's guitarist Freddie Green, for example, credited Basie's tempos for the achievements of the legendary rhythm section of Basie, Green, Jo Jones, and Walter Page: "Basie was the greatest tempo setter . . . that I ever ran into" (Green 1977). Second, musicians stressed that grooving is an aesthetic ideal that cannot be premeditated (Carvin 1990) and that in its fullest form is achieved only rarely (McBee 1990).

If the groove (in the nominative sense) is to the ensemble what the ride cymbal (or stable limb) is to the drum set, moments of deviation from the predictable flow of rhythmic energy are comparable to the functions of the drummer's other limbs. Continuing his familial imagery for the drum set, Michael Carvin told me to think of my ride cymbal and hi-hat (which I was playing on 2 and 4) as the "father and mother" and my left hand and bass drum as the "children." I should "let the children play," while the mother and father kept time. At another time he told me that I should allow my snare and bass drum to "have a conversation." If for a moment we think of the jazz ensemble as a drum set writ large, the groove is a collectively produced sense of time against which the children play or the musicians converse. The fundamental sociability of improvisation as a musically creative process is underscored by this anthropomorphic imagery, a topic introduced here but explored more fully in the next chapter.

The Soloist

I have left the role of soloist for last to emphasize that it is in relation to this complex musical sociability that a musician organizes his or her improvised solo. The role of soloist is one that every member of the ensemble is expected to fulfill.

Trumpets, trombones, saxophones, flutes, and other instruments not generally used in the rhythm section are often referred to collectively as *horns* or *the front line*. The latter term derives from the typical spatial arrangement in jazz performance that places the reeds and brass instruments in front of the rhythm section. Using the term *horn* for any single-line melody instrument collapses instrumental differences into a particular musical role played by a soloist who is accompanied by the full rhythm section. The horn player is in a position to exploit most fully the accompanimental resources of the jazz ensemble, as he or she is not required to sustain the groove during the solos of other ensemble members. Unlike pianists, who as soloists frequently comp with their left hand while playing melodic lines with their right, horn players can devote their full attention to phrasing against the relatively fixed rhythmic environment created by the rhythm section. Even so, comments about horn soloists apply in a general sense to rhythm section soloists as well, although at least one accompanimental role is missing when the bass player or the drummer plays a solo.

If we return to the image of the drum set writ large, the soloist's phrasing functions analogously to the drummer's left hand in a general sense. The requirement that the soloist sustain melodic, harmonic, and rhythmic interest, however, creates significant differences between actual phrases occurring in the drummer's left hand and the horn player's solo.[30] What the two have most in common is a rhythmic independence characterized by offbeat phrasing. The musical excitement of the phrasing derives from the juxtaposition of this independence with a relatively stable background.

The fact that some musicians describe a particular musician's style by reference to the character of the eighth note is germane here. Since the second half of a pair of eighth notes is particularly flexible, the way in which the second note is emphasized greatly affects the offbeat feeling of a musician's phrasing style. Clarinetist Don Byron noted:

> Different cats have different eighth note concepts, man.
> [Steve] Lacy, man, that's the closest thing to like a Monk
> eighth note on the piano. . . . It's like real punchy . . . "I
> play with my thumbs too much" type of thing like Monk
> plays. (Byron 1989)

We are now in a better position to understand the prioritization of rhythm expressed by Cecil McBee and Ralph Peterson earlier in this chapter. The harmonic and melodic expertise of the soloist, which is essential to competent jazz improvisation, must be expressed against the rhythmic flow generated by the musically sociable rhythm section. Those who take for granted their competence in the harmonic and melodic dimension commonly discuss pitch selection in relationship to rhythm. Don Byron commented on tenor saxophonist Wayne Shorter in this manner:

> I mean, note choice is just the way you tend to color the
> rhythm. . . . I feel that when I hear Wayne. It's those

groups of five and seven and thirteen notes. There's always some odd number. It's always starting on some odd off-beat.... And ... where you get his mind working is [in] what color he's going to put on each note. The drama of his playing to me is which one of them notes that he's going to color it with is going to be right and which one is going to be wrong,[31] cause he can place them all right ... it's obvious that he's got *that*. So *where* he's going to put the note that's a half-step away from where it ought to be, that's the drama in *his* playing. (Byron 1989)

An improviser's pitch choice during the course of a lengthy solo can augment and intensify rhythmic development as well, a point that underscores the interdependence of musical dimensions. Jerome Harris spoke about tenor saxophonist Sonny Rollins's abilities in this regard:

You might be able to get the same mileage out of working in a restricted range harmonically. ... Then when you bring in the alterations they have a context ... because what's gone before is different than what you're introducing. ... Sonny's *real good* at this sort of thing. You won't really ... notice it, but he'll be hanging out in a certain pentatonic or six-note ... place ... through a substantial amount of a tune. *Then* he'll bring in ... some notes that aren't *in* that key ... which are more chromatic alterations and you really *feel* the change going to a new [place]. (Harris 1989)

If we return to the tension between the group and the individual, the role of horn soloist in some ways is both the most independent and the most dependent in the ensemble. The soloist's ability to float on top of the rhythmic energy generated by the rhythm section is an independence that the members of the rhythm section do not as fully share.[32] This musical independence is perhaps a factor in the high prestige accorded to horn soloists in the jazz tradition. At the same time, the soloist's ability to be an effective voice requires considerable support from the rhythm section. The horn player, for example, cannot define a change in groove as clearly as a rhythm section member, nor can he or she as fully accompany another soloist. Nevertheless, the role of soloist is the most prestigious in the jazz ensemble. To be a jazz musician, one must be able to play solos as well as fulfill the ensemble responsibilities of one's instrument.

The basic instrumental roles (bass, piano, drums, soloist), musical functions (keeping—or suspending—time, comping, soloing), and interactional alternatives open to jazz musicians (imitation, call and response, walking, riffing, playing pedal points) present only a basic tool kit for improvising band members. How musicians deploy these resources over extended performances and how musical decisions during improvisation combine to mold the large-scale musical shape and texture of a performance are topics that reappear in subsequent chapters. For the moment, however, I would like to step back and consider the cultural implications of jazz improvisation as a sociable musical process. I wish to examine how cultural meanings become associated with musical resources and forms, how musical processes themselves shape cultural meaning, and how heterogeneous conceptions of cultural and musical processes are necessary to make sense of a musical genre that has at every historical point been improvised against the inexorable groove of racial politics in the United States. The view from the bottom of the band emphasizes the collective character of jazz improvisation as well as the heterogeneity of cultural experience. These conceptual issues deserve to be at the very center of thinking about jazz, not at the margins.

chapter three
music, language, and cultural styles: improvisation as conversation

Paul Berliner's monumental *Thinking in Jazz* (1994) has demonstrated beyond any doubt the centrality of the musical perspectives of professional jazz musicians in rethinking our understanding of improvisation. Berliner describes how jazz musicians acquire and develop improvisational expertise through interaction with an ever-changing community of musicians functioning as a learning environment, a musical process that defies explanation by traditional musical analyses of self-contained works. Berliner found that many musicians used the metaphor of conversation to describe aspects of the improvisational process, as have I.[1] In fact, several metaphors about language and music appeared in the interview materials I compiled from my discussions with musicians: jazz as a musical language, improvisation as musical conversation, and good improvisation as talking or "saying something." In this chapter, I undertake a close examination of these metaphors and several others as pathways into a deeper understanding of the relationship between musical practice and cultural meaning.

On one level, the image of conversation has structural affinities with interactive improvisational process; on another, the stylistic and affective aspects of conversation raise the issue of music and cultural style. Since jazz musicians have been nearly as famous for their talk—their so-called jargon, the subject of much stereotyping since the swing era—as for their music, the linking of music and language in issues of cultural identity seems especially germane. The ironic, double-edged predicament of African American cultural practices is everywhere in evidence: linguistic and musical practices that have been the cause of cultural celebration and valorization since the 1960s retain their power to stereotype when they are not situated within the history of ethnic interaction and politics in the United States.

The informal, sociable, and metaphorical modes of speaking about music favored by many jazz musicians challenge traditional presumptions about both the nature of the musical object and the definition of musical analysis. In their differences from and overlaps with traditional Western musical theory, the commentaries of professional musicians suggest that musical theories developed for the explication of scores are not fully appropriate to the elucidation of improvisational music making. This is not to say that Western analytical tools are completely inappropriate, only that we need to be aware of their limits. I argue here that meaningful theorizing about jazz improvisation at the level of the ensemble must take the interactive, collaborative context of musical invention as a point of departure. This context has no parallel in the musical practice of Western classical composers of the common practice period, and it should not be surprising that jazz musicians choose to talk about music making in different terms.

In the following two chapters, I develop a perspective on these various linguistic metaphors (especially improvisation as conversation) and on the more general issue of music as a cultural discourse that considers both close analysis of the music and cultural analysis of how improvisation has been part of the construction of meaning, identity, and critique in twentieth-century African American and American society. If musicians are saying something, by what musical and cultural processes do they succeed?

Music and Language

Translating musical experience and insight into written or spoken words is one of the most fundamental frustrations of musical scholarship. Charles Seeger (1977) called this dilemma the *linguocentric predicament*—no matter how elegantly an author writes, there is something fundamentally untranslatable about musical experience. The relationship between music and language, however, has been a continual source of speculation for music theorists and ethnomusicologists and a part of everyday metaphors about music in many cultures.[2] Seeger viewed music and language as two principal means of auditory communication, fundamentally linked through sound but differentiated in their cognitive perception of reality. If language emphasized the "intellection of reality," music stressed its "feeling" (35). Steven Feld has also spoken of music as a "special kind of feelingful activity," but he has not shared Seeger's pessimism on the impasse between speech and music. Seeger, in his view, concentrated too heavily on the referential functions of language and too little on the figurative capacities of both language and music. For Feld, the way in which people talk about music—especially their metaphors—contributes a "parallel stream" of figurative information regarding the conceptualization and interpretation of sound and mediates between speech and music as feelingful activities (Feld 1984).

In discussing the Kaluli of Papua New Guinea, Feld (1981) has placed particular emphasis on the role of metaphor in encoding musical theory. Feld noted the way in which metaphors recur in semantic fields from contrasting cultural domains (22–23) and discussed music itself as a metaphoric process (Feld 1982, 38–43; 1984, 14–15). He argued that "an analysis of musical theory . . . relies in part on understanding linguistic mediation of concepts of the musical system" (1981, 23). This linguistic mediation then becomes a means for thinking about the cultural aesthetics of Kaluli society. In a consideration of how to extend this perspective to jazz, the differences between a small, relatively isolated cultural group such as the Kaluli and the heterogeneous musical, cultural, and linguistic systems of urban North America are obvious. Most professional jazz musicians have great proficiency in aspects of Western musical theory—particularly in harmonic and melodic analysis—and can speak its language with great fluency when they choose. Like other African Americans, jazz musicians may speak at one moment in the styles of everyday African America and at another in white, middle-class, school English. The ability to draw from both worlds, which W. E. B. Du Bois long ago termed *double consciousness,* is arguably one of the most significant aspects of the culture of Africans in America (Du Bois 1969). In the community of jazz performers, non–African American musicians must also become familiar with both worlds, for the leadership in this musical tradition has always flowed most heavily from the African American side. How these worlds collide, intersect, and overlap, and what implications these culturally as well as musically interactive processes have on the way in which jazz is perceived and understood as a cultural force, are questions that underlie the following discussion.

Metaphors and Tropes

Anthropologists, too, have long recognized the importance of figurative tropes in cultural interpretation, including those of metaphor, metonymy, synecdoche, and irony. As James Fernandez (1986) has argued, "the analysis of metaphor seems to me to be the very nature of [anthropological] inquiry" (6). Metaphors point to similarities between contrasting cultural domains or activities, while metonyms suggest part-to-whole (contiguous) relationships within cultural domains. Ironic tropes, on the other hand, assert incongruity, especially between apparent meaning and deeper ironic reversal of that meaning. While cultural theorists have devoted their attention mainly to the metaphor, recent work on the theory of tropes has emphasized the relationships among these figurative ways of speaking in cultural practice. Terence Turner (1991) has augmented Fernandez's discussion of metaphor by presenting a theory of the relationships among metaphor, metonymy, and synecdoche. In brief, Turner argues that a metaphor (such as "improvisation is conversation") links cultural domains by selecting an attribute in one domain (improvisation as part of music) similar to an attribute from another (conversation as a part of language). Turner argues that a metonymic (part-to-whole) relationship is therefore implicit in any metaphoric association. The metaphoric association of contrasting domains may in turn construct a more encompassing, higher-level category that "assumes the essential character of its parts," or becomes an example of synecdoche (Turner 1991, 148). Charles Seeger's (1977) view of music and language as subsets of aural communication provides an example of one such larger whole.[3] To return to the metaphor we're examining, if improvisation is like conversation (subsets of music and language), then sociable, face-to-face communication (subset of communication) may be the larger category at stake.

Recall Richard Davis's description of an imitative exchange during improvisation: "That happens a lot in jazz, that it's like a conversation and one guy will . . . create a melodic motif or a rhythmic motif and the band picks it up" (Davis 1989). This association could be taken as either a structural or a textual metaphor in Fernandez's definition of the terms:

> In the case of structural metaphor the translation between
> realms is based on some isomorphism of structure or simi-
> larity of relationship of parts. By textual metaphor we
> mean an assimilation made on the basis of similarity in
> feeling tone. (Fernandez 1986, 12)

There are structural aspects of the music (the trading of different musical voices) and textual aspects (the feeling or tone of sociability) united
in Davis's image. The utility of thinking about these two aspects of the
metaphor of conversation lies in the links that can be clarified between
music in the moment of performance and the cumulative construction
of cultural feeling and tone over time, which Steven Feld (1988) terms
an "iconicity of style." Chapter 3 of this book focuses primarily upon
the structural affinities in performance and chapter 4 upon the accu-
mulation and communication of cultural feeling. The latter also engages the broader issue of how instrumental music conveys cultural
meaning, cultural critique, and—most important—communities of
emotional feeling and moral sensibility. While these two chapters separate the performative aspects from the historical and referential aspects of improvisation for purposes of narrative clarity, it is important
to keep in mind that the two actually occur simultaneously.

Musical Affinities with Conversation

While sitting in the Gibralter Transmission garage in Machito Square
in November of 1989, I played a tape for drummer Ralph Peterson of
his composition "Princess" (Peterson 1988). Pianist Geri Allen soloed
with the accompaniment of Peterson and bassist Essiet Okon Essiet.
Peterson's accompaniment was very dense, and there were several in-
stances in which Allen and Peterson traded ideas with each other. After
one rhythmic exchange I remarked, "Salt Peanuts!" since Geri Allen's
piano figure (musical example 11, mm. 9–11) reminded me of Gillespie's famous riff (musical example 12). Peterson commented:

> Yeah! "Salt Peanuts" and "Looney Tunes"—kind of a
> combination of the two. Art Blakey has a thing he plays.
> It's like: [he sings measures 1 and 2 of musical example
> 13]. And Geri played: [he sings measures 3 to 5 of musical
> example 11]. So I played the second half of the Art Blakey
> phrase: [he sings measures 3 and 4 of musical example 13].

Musical example 11. Excerpt from Geri Allen's piano solo on "Princess."
Ralph Peterson. (*Triangular*. Blue Note CDP7 92750 2.
Recorded: New York, NY, 21–22 April 1988.)

Peterson then offered this interpretation:

> But you see what happens is, a lot of times when you get
> into a musical conversation one person in the group will
> state an idea or the beginning of an idea and another per-
> son will *complete* the idea or their interpretation of the
> same idea, how they hear it. So the conversation happens
> in fragments and comes from different parts, different
> voices. (Peterson 1989b)

In associating the trading of musical ideas with conversation, Peterson stressed the interpersonal, face-to-face quality of improvisation.
The circulation of the Art Blakey rhythm was not only a significant
musical moment but an instance of musical dialogue between Peterson

Musical example 11. *Continued*

Musical example 12. "Salt Peanuts." Kenny Clarke.
      (*Groovin' High with Dizzy Gillespie*. Savoy SV-0152.
      Recorded: New York, NY, 28 February 1945.)

"Salt Pea– nuts,   Salt   Pea– nuts"

Musical example 13. Ralph Peterson Jr. singing Art Blakey rhythm.

dink dink   dink dink   dink dink di dink   dink   dink   ah

and Allen. The exchange of the idea not only established an abstract succession of sounds and rhythms but linked Allen and Peterson as musical personalities (with some experience playing together) at a particular moment in time. At the time I interviewed him, Peterson particularly enjoyed working with Allen because spontaneous moments of musical communication such as this one just seemed to happen without a lot of effort. Peterson felt Allen's contribution to his group was "pivotal," even to the point of saying that if Allen couldn't make a performance, "I'd rather have another instrument. I feel that strongly about her playing" (Peterson 1989a).

These moments of rhythmic interaction could also be seen as negotiations or struggles for control of musical space. One player's interjection, for example, might be experienced by another as an interruption or a challenge. Peterson told me that there were times when Allen felt uncomfortable with some of his interjections and that they had discussed the difference between enhancing a solo and obliterating it (Peterson 1989b). In the "Princess" example we have been discussing, Peterson's Art Blakey rhythm could potentially be perceived as an intrusive rhythmic idea, but Allen's quick reaction communicates that she is strong enough to respond to almost anything he can put forth. In other words, Peterson's completion of the Art Blakey rhythm in measures 7 and 8 (musical example 11) could be seen as an interruption of Allen's phrase that begins in measure 6. His interjection could have caused her to abandon the completion of her melodic idea in measures 7 and 8. Once he has completed his idea, however, she immediately asserts a new and forceful one of her own (m. 9), to which he responds in measure 12. There is a great deal of give and take in such improvisational interaction, and such moments are often cited by musicians as aesthetic high points of performances.

The indivisibility of musical and interpersonal interaction underscores the problem of thinking about jazz improvisation as a text. At the moment of performance, jazz improvisation quite simply has nothing in common with a text (or its musical equivalent, the score) for it is music composed through face-to-face interaction.[4] Musicologists familiar with the eighteenth century will counter that contemporary writers also referred to the conversational and rhetorical aspects of music making. Friedrich Wilhelm Marpurg spoke of subject and answer in his description of the baroque fugue (Mann 1986, 154–55), while Heinrich Christian Koch likened the relationship of antecedent and consequent in periodic phrasing to the subject and predicate of a sentence (Ratner 1956, 441). Language metaphors are in fact extremely common in many musical periods and many cultures.[5] An eighteenth-century score, however, is far more like a novel in Mikhail Bakhtin's (1981) sense than a conversation: if a novel portrays multiple characters and points of view all refracted through a single author's pen, a musical score presents multiple musical lines, instruments, counterpoints, textures, and harmonies coordinated by the composer. Performance of these musical texts—transformation of the notation into sound—includes multiple participants, but in Western classical music performers are generally not allowed to alter or (in some repertories) even embellish this musical notation.

In jazz improvisation, as we have seen, all of the musicians are constantly making decisions regarding what to play and when to play it, all within the framework of a musical groove, which may or may not be organized around a chorus structure. The musicians are compositional participants who may "say" unexpected things or elicit responses from other musicians. Musical intensification is open-ended rather than predetermined and highly interpersonal in character—structurally far more similar to a conversation than to a text. Herbie Hancock put it this way when talking about his experience with the Miles Davis Quintet in the early 1960s:

> We were sort of walking a tightrope with the kind of experimenting that we were doing in music. Not total experimentation . . . we used to call it "controlled freedom" . . . just like conversation—same thing. I mean, how many times have you *talked* to somebody and . . . you got ready to say, make a point, and then you kind of went off in another direction, but maybe you never wound up making that point but the conversation, you know, just went somewhere else and it was fine. There's nothing wrong with it. Maybe you *like* where you went. Well, this is the way we were dealing with music. (Obenhaus 1986)

When musicians use the metaphor of conversation, they are saying something very significant about musical process.

Sociolinguists define *conversation* as talk occurring between two or more participants who freely alternate turns (Levinson 1983, 284). The process of turn taking builds larger units of talk that Marjorie Goodwin calls *participant frameworks.* Arguments, storytelling, instigating, and a gossip dispute process called "he-said-she-said" are among the types of participant frameworks Goodwin identified for African American children in Philadelphia (Goodwin 1990, 9–10). In their conversations, participants situate themselves in relationship to other participants through language or depict a party (present or absent) as a character within the discussion (10). Through close analysis of conversational interactions, Goodwin observed that during turn taking, individuals display their own interpretation of the talk in which they participate.

> Participants in conversation have the job of providing next moves to ongoing talk which demonstrate what sense they make of that talk. It therefore is possible to see how group members themselves interpret the interaction they are engaged in. (6)

From these ideas it is apparent that the jazz ensemble, with its rhythm section and soloist roles, is itself a musical framework for participation. This framework balances the relatively fixed rhythm section roles against the freer role of improvising soloist. Composer Olly Wilson has argued that this division into what he calls "fixed" and "variable" rhythmic groups is characteristic of African music:

> Though musical ensembles in African cultures follow a variety of different formats, a general principle appears to govern the division of a musical ensemble into at least two functional groups. The first is one that I refer to as the "fixed rhythmic group," so called because its instruments maintain a fixed rhythmic pulsation throughout the duration of the composition with little variation. The group has a time-keeping or metronomic function; it is frequently manifest in a relatively complex rhythmic form and serves, according to Nketia, as the "time line." The second is the "variable rhythmic group," so named because the rhythms performed by these instruments change. (Wilson 1992, 331)

There is a considerable degree of flexibility even in the relatively fixed instrumental roles of the jazz rhythm section, but the primary function of the rhythm section is nevertheless to provide the timeline

against which the soloist can interact and build. The quality of swinging or grooving is itself produced by this dynamic tension between the
relatively fixed and variable elements of the ensemble. Samuel Floyd
has suggested that musicians who swing are "Signifying on the timeline" (Floyd 1991, 273). Soloists often change the character of what
they play from chorus to chorus, and sensitive rhythm sections change
the character of accompaniment in response.

   A look at Freddie Hubbard's six-chorus solo on "Blues for Duane"
illustrates this situation (see musical example 3 in chapter 2). In the
first two choruses, Hubbard leaves much space in his solo, which Davis
fills with melodically oriented bass lines. Brackets 1 and 2, which are
highlighted in this example, point to particularly notable examples of
this in the bass part. The triplet character of Davis's bass line in bracket
2 (mm. 7–8) is clearly a response to Hubbard's triplets in the preceding
bar. Under bracket 3 (mm. 23–24), it can be seen that Hayes's drum
roll collaborates with Richard Davis's half notes to lead into chorus 3
(m. 25). Perhaps in response, Hubbard begins chorus 3 with an increased level of rhythmic subdivision, while Davis plays a more rhythmic bass line that lays down the time and harmony very clearly: four
beats to the bar (bracket 4, mm. 25–28). Bracket 5 (mm. 35–36) shows
the interaction between drums and piano that sets up the top of chorus
4, in which Hubbard takes over part of the time function by playing a
two-bar repeating riff figure. This assumption of a rhythm section–like
role by the soloist frees the rhythm section to interact more among
themselves. The piano becomes more prominent, Davis takes more lib-
erty with the harmony than in the preceding chorus, and Louis Hayes
sets up more cross-rhythms.

   In reacting to the continuous changes in an improviser's solo,
rhythm section members display their hearings of the musical events
and their understandings of appropriate musical responses. Their responses also indicate what musical events they take to be most significant. Musicians who miss opportunities to respond to or enhance their
accompaniment (such as those taken by Davis, Hanna, and Hayes in
"Blues for Duane") are often said to be "not listening" to what is going
on in the ensemble. In other words, it is not enough for a musician to
play through a tune with only its melody and harmonic structure in
mind, as many jazz pedagogy books would have us believe; the player
must be so thoroughly familiar with the basic framework of the tune
that he or she can attend to what everyone else in the band is doing.

Nearly every musician who talked to me mentioned the importance of listening in good ensemble playing. Listening in an active sense—being able to respond to musical opportunities or to correct mistakes—is implicit in the way that musicians use this term. It is a type of listening much like that required of participants in a conversation, who have to pay attention to what is transpiring if they expect to say things that make sense to the other participants. Listening affects what musicians decide to play at a particular moment, which is why Cecil McBee was so sure that in good jazz performance, "you're not going to play what you practiced. . . . Something else is going to happen" (McBee 1990). This spontaneity is absolutely central in the jazz improvisational aesthetic.

To say that a player "doesn't listen" or sounds as though he or she is playing "something he or she practiced" is a grave insult. Such a musician may play ideas that fulfill the minimal demands of the harmony or chorus structure but fail to respond well to the other players in the band. Don Byron commented:

> I hate hearing them bands where like . . . one cat's playing some shit that he practiced. Another cat's playing some shit that he practiced. Everybody's playing some stuff that they practiced. . . . On a certain level there's like a feeling, "Well, I like playing with you," but I mean, what does that mean? . . . You know, we didn't play shit together. We didn't do nothing together. I played my stuff, you played your stuff, we didn't screw up the time. (Byron 1989)

Good jazz improvisation is sociable and interactive just like a conversation; a good player communicates with the other players in the band. If this doesn't happen, it's not good jazz.

The importance of communicativeness and the ability to hear is underscored by another type of language metaphor used by musicians: "to say" or "to talk" often substitutes for "to play." In explaining what Tony Williams plays for a ride cymbal beat, Michael Carvin stated:

> That wasn't the limb keeping time . . . because Tony would say, [see musical example 9 in chapter 2], but his foot was talking about, [straight quarters]. (Carvin 1990)

Aesthetic evaluations frequently include this usage. To suggest that a soloist "isn't saying anything" is an insult; conversely, to say that he or she "makes that horn talk" is very high praise. The perception of musical ideas as a communicative medium in and of themselves can be most effectively understood against the background of aural recognition of elements of musical tradition, which is the principal topic of the next chapter. A secondary meaning of the talking horn image relates to the ability of horn players to mimic a vocal quality through articulation, attack, and timbre. A very literal imitation of arguing voices can be heard on Charles Mingus's "What Love" (1960). Eric Dolphy on bass clarinet and Mingus on bass sound as though they are having a very intense verbal argument. The musical image of the talking horn personifies the horn, once again refusing to separate the sound from the person who makes it.

A third type of metaphor uses the term *language* to mean "musical style and syntax." When Jerome Harris (1989) explained that he went through periods in which he was less interested in his own instrument than in what trumpeters and sax players and pianists were doing because "the language seemed to be more developed there on those instruments," and Sir Roland Hanna spoke of being able to anticipate Richard Davis's musical "words" (Hanna 1989), they were distinguishing jazz as a unique musical and aesthetic system from other musical genres. This type of language metaphor occurs in a broad spectrum of music traditions throughout the world.

The salience of language metaphors in talk about jazz is clear at this point in our discussion. It is important to realize that there is a coherence among the three types of musical language metaphors as well. Saussure used the terms *langue* and *parole* to distinguish generally between ideas about language as a system and language as it is performed (Saussure 1986). When musicians speak of the "jazz language," they are talking about a musical and aesthetic system that contrasts with others—a usage comparable to *langue*. When they refer to playing music as "talking," they emphasize communication through the act of performing music—a usage akin to *parole*. When they compare performance in the ensemble to "conversation," they refer to a specific genre of musical talk that requires listening carefully to the other participants.[6] The interpersonal character of this process is emphasized very clearly by the conversation metaphor, for what could be more social than a musical or verbal conversation?

I am certainly not the only writer who has noted the pervasiveness of language images in African American music. Ben Sidran, for example, entitled his book on jazz *Black Talk* (1986). Lester Young used of the image of storytelling to describe improvisation (Daniels 1985; Porter 1985b, 34), as have many of the musicians who used the metaphor of conversation. Pianist Roland Hanna, for example, talked about technique from this perspective:

> Technique is a living process. . . . It's a kind of storytelling
> that utilizes everything in your life up to that moment.
> (Stix 1978)

Drummer Roy Haynes put it this way:

> I like to paint some sort of picture . . . you know, tell a mu-
> sical story according to how I feel. (DeMichael 1966, 19)

A great deal of the most recent work on African American music has also drawn upon the pervasiveness of these images in African American cultural life (Floyd 1991; Hartman 1991).

African American literary theorists have likewise emphasized an ethos of communication in recent years: bell hooks entitled a collection of essays *Talking Back* (hooks 1989), and the work of Henry Louis Gates Jr. has inspired many to take the African American notion of signifying as a point of interpretive departure (Gates 1988). Prior to the work of Gates, academic discussion of this concept was confined primarily to the literatures of sociolinguistics, folklore, and linguistic anthropology. Among the contributors to this literature are Claudia Mitchell-Kernan (1986), Thomas Kochman (1981, 1983, 1986), William Labov (1969, 1972), Geneva Smitherman (1977), and Roger Abrahams (1970). In the earliest academic literature, most of the attention was focused on the genres of verbal dueling, variously termed *sounding, woofing, playing the dozens, marking,* and *jiving.*[7] Claudia Mitchell-Kernan was among the first to include along with genres of verbal dueling what sociolinguists term *indirect modes of discourse:*

> A number of individuals interested in black verbal behav-
> ior have devoted attention to the "way of talking" which is
> known in many black communities as *signifying.* Signi-
> fying can be a tactic employed in game activity—verbal
> dueling—which is engaged in as an end in itself. . . . Signi-
> fying, however, also refers to a way of encoding messages
> or meanings in natural conversation which involves, in
> most cases, an element of indirection. This kind of signi-

fying might best be viewed as an alternative message form, selected for its artistic merit, and may occur embedded in a variety of discourse. (Mitchell-Kernan 1986, 165)

Signifying as a speaking style defined in this manner includes both formal verbal games and individual statements in which two-sided or multiple meanings are embedded. Often these are statements that indirectly tease, provoke, or potentially insult one or more addressees, who are then challenged to respond in a way clever enough to save face. The difference between these two aspects of signifying corresponds roughly to Bakhtin's distinction between external and internal dialogism. Externally dialogical discourse is compositionally marked—that is, structured like actual dialogue between two or more individuals (Bakhtin 1981, 279, 283). The notion of internal dialogism, by contrast, involves two issues: (1) multiple semantic meanings that vary according to and are defined in relationship to one another and the sociocultural context in the present and (2) the temporal context in which ideas are expressed and defined in relation to a history of competing social or cultural discourses. The second sense of internal dialogism is often glossed as *intertextuality* in literary circles.[8] In recent years, the common use of the term *signifying* in studies of African American literature has stressed these internally dialogic aspects of intertextuality and double-sidedness. What is lost sometimes in the extension of this metaphor to texts with a single author is a sense of how signifying as an aesthetic developed from interactive, participatory, turn-taking games and genres that are multiply authored. The particular logic of turn taking in the construction of participatory verbal and musical frameworks is something I wish to stress. Their entextualization through "writing down" or recording is a separate but related matter.

Face-to-Face Verbal and Musical Interaction

Sociolinguist Thomas Kochman described the interactional strategy in the verbal dueling genres of sounding, woofing, and playing the dozens (all of which Gates includes in the idea of signifying) as "indeterminate strategic ambiguity" (Kochman 1986, 156). He observed that whether a particular statement in a verbal duel is taken as a serious insult depends more on the receiver's reaction than on the sender's intentions. From this perspective, the interaction between the speakers is more important than any pre-existing strategic intention in determining whether a given statement leads to play or fighting (157–59). In fact, fighting might ensue only when one party is unable to keep up with the invention of creative responses. One of the chief functions of such verbal exchanges is to sustain the sociability as long as possible. The challenge of the verbal game, as it were, is to keep the interaction at the highest possible pitch of creative intensity.

From an African American perspective, the essence of a "cool" or "hip" response includes reacting with poise and balance to these potentially unsettling verbal teases and challenges. Work by Goodwin (1990) and Morgan (1991) has shown that the sociolinguistic issues Kochman discusses also apply to African American women and children—not just to men, as the work of Kochman, Labov, and Abrahams has implied. The non–African American unfamiliar with these norms of interaction might interpret such teases and challenges as rudeness. This is precisely the type of situation Gumperz had in mind when he suggested that differences in discourse norms and contextualization cues are more likely to be interpreted as attitudinal than linguistic (Gumperz 1982, 132).

In musical aesthetics informed by African American cultural aesthetics, the idea of response is just as important as in verbal communication. Referring to the imitative passage between trumpet and bass back in musical example 2 (see chapter 2), Richard Davis commented:

> Now what occurred to me at the moment was responding
> to what I heard the leader voice doing. And then the drum-
> mer might pick it up and it might be a whole thing of trip-
> lets going back to the second eight; you never know where
> it's going to go. Sometimes you might put a idea in that
> you think is good and nobody takes to it. . . . And then
> sometimes you might put an idea in that your incentive or
> motivation is not to influence but it does influence. It's a
> very subtle, ESP kind of thing going with people who have
> traditionally created a ethnic kind of music. (Davis 1989)

The response of musicians is clearly crucial to whether a particular musical idea is picked up on, developed, or ignored. Samuel Floyd has recognized the critical importance of this principle in African American music and suggested that it be named *call-response,* the equivalent of Gates's signifying as a "master musical trope" for black music (Floyd 1991, 276). I am interested here in its particular realization in the context of jazz improvisation, where it is a crucial component in the large-scale momentum of improvised performances. It is a fundamentally social, conversational, and dialogic way to organize musical performance. Frequently an exchange will begin with the repetition of a particular musical passage or a response with a complimentary musical interjection, although these are certainly not the only possibilities. I want to underscore the importance of repetition here, since it has been something Western classical music commentators have often disparaged in jazz improvisation and African American music more broadly. The function of repetition in creating a participatory musical framework against which highly idiosyncratic and innovative improvisation can take place has often been lost upon otherwise sympathetic commentators.[9]

Goodwin (1990) has discussed the function of repetition in face-to-face verbal interaction. She notes in her study that a participant in an argument will frequently make use of the sentence structures of the opposing party in responding to and transforming an exchange. She calls this process *format tying* (177–88). In the following example,

> *Billy, who has been teasing Martha about her hair, has just laughed.*

> Martha: I don't know what you laughin' at.
> Billy: I know what I'm laughin' at. Your head.

Goodwin points out that "Your head" would be a sufficient response if all that were needed were an informational reply to Martha's question. "I know what I'm laughin' at" reiterates Martha's sentence structure but transforms it into a reply that escalates the interaction—in effect, using her words against her. This transformative reuse of material is something that Gates emphasizes in his definition of signifying: "repetition with a signal difference" (Gates 1988, 51). Structurally, Goodwin's idea of format tying is very much like the musical process occurring in the rhythmic exchange between Ralph Peterson and Geri Allen in musical example 11. The rhythmic redundancy is used to construct a reply and to reassert the leadership of the soloist. The repetition emphasizes the face-to-face character of the musical interaction.

Goodwin also articulates the relationship between sentence structure and the social action it accomplishes:

> While it is possible to escalate an argument with a subsequent action whose structure is unrelated to that of the ac-

> tion being dealt with, the utterances [she previously cited]
> . . . display their status as escalations of prior actions . . .
> by making use of the talk of the prior speaker and trans-
> forming it to their advantage; in essence, they turn the
> prior action on its head. Indeed there is a very nice fit be-
> tween the social activity of escalating a sequence and chal-
> lenging a prior move, and the syntactic structure of these
> utterances, in which the prior move becomes an embedded
> subcomponent of the sentence used to answer it. (Good-
> win 1990: 180–81)

Goodwin emphasizes here the dialectic between the microcommand of language structures and their employment for interactional competitive or cooperative purposes, which are both social and aesthetic in character.

This relationship between formal linguistic devices and their practical use in social interactions offers us an important point of comparison to the relationship between formal musical structures and their emotional, aesthetic, and cultural feeling. In the process described by Richard Davis, the same set of musical details (an imitative passage) functions both to create a formal musical shape and to establish a playful dialogue between the soloist and the bassist. The process by which that communication takes place—the choice to pick up on a particular musical opportunity or not—effectively fuses the social and the musical in the same interactive moment. As Cecil McBee emphasized, a process of collectivization occurs when musicians walk out on stage: the interdependence of the members of the ensemble ensures that each individual must adjust to the presence and activities of the other band members.

Feeling and Tone

The metaphor of conversation directs our attention not only to the structural aspects of interactive music making but also to the feeling and tone of particular styles of conversation. Because the musical leadership of jazz has been primarily black, African American cultural sensibilities and ideas of sociability have defined the ideal social and interactional values within multi-ethnic performing and listening communities. In this context, it is not surprising that many non–African Americans in the jazz world have emulated and deeply identified with these musical and social ideals.

During the mid- to late 1930s, popular magazine articles about jazz and swing music began to include definitions of the terms supposedly used by jazz musicians (Chapman 1935; Harvey 1936).[10] An article appearing in *Esquire* magazine in 1936 (Poling 1936, 92) attempted to explain to the reader the meaning of terms such as *breaks, licks, riffs,* and *groove.* That these published definitions are not entirely reliable is apparent when the writer defines *in the groove* as "to play in a dull, unimaginative rut" (92)—certainly the opposite of the term as used by the musicians. In 1938 *Life* magazine pondered the definitions of *jitterbugs, cat,* and *ickey* ("Speaking of Pictures" 1938). In November of that year, *Metronome* reprinted an editorial that had appeared in the *Tulsa Tribune:* "We're getting pretty sick of 'swing,'" it says, because "there is very little that is new about swing except the name and the bewildering vocabulary which accompanies it" ("They're Killing Swing" 1938).

The focus on jazz terminology seems to have come with the swing era, a time when African American–based dance music was popularized on a mass scale by white big bands. To non–African Americans who had little familiarity with African American speaking norms, these terms were amusing, confusing, fascinating, and exotic—not at all what they had expected.[11] This fascination with African American speaking styles was sometimes accompanied by a deprecation of African Americans and their fellow travelers who spoke in this manner. Sociological writings from the 1950s and early 1960s are perhaps the worst offenders in this regard. William Cameron described jazz musicians as "non-literate," "non-verbal," and "totally unable to translate their most important feelings into more generally conventional symbols" (Cameron 1954, 180). Merriam and Mack wrote that the jazz musician "remains illiterate with respect to the verbal expression of his own art" (Merriam and Mack 1960, 216).

That the verbal inventiveness of African American speakers could be interpreted as nonverbal is highly ironic in view of the tremendous efforts undertaken by some white jazz musicians to learn how to speak as cleverly as black musicians. Leonard quotes alto saxophonist Art Pepper in this regard:

> I used to stand around and marvel at the way [African American musicians] talked. Having really nothing to say, they were able to play those little verbal games back and

forth. I envied it but was too self-conscious to do it. What
I wouldn't give to just jump in and say those things. I
could when I was joking to myself, raving to myself in
front of the mirror at home, but when it came time to do
it with people, I couldn't. (Leonard 1987, 92)

This combination of fascination with black verbal and musical inventiveness and deprecation of the intelligence and knowledge necessary to produce it has proved to be a tenacious feature of the American
reaction to African American presence in society more generally. The
presumption that indirect, multisided, and metaphorical modes of
speaking require less development of the mind reflects a Western cultural ideology about language that prefers the nonambiguous and non-
playful delineation of ideas in intellectual discourse as well as the separation of these ideas from emotions (Lutz 1988, 53–80). In the Western
classical music tradition, this preference has manifested itself in the
long tradition of separating musical theory from practice, which is
perhaps fitting for a musical tradition in which composition has in
principle been separated from the moment of performance. In improvisation, composed through face-to-face interaction, however, the separation of sounds from the human beings who produce them makes
far less sense. What Christopher Waterman has argued in the case of
Yoruba musicians deserves exploration with reference to jazz musicians:

The tendency in Western analytical thought to divorce
structure from content finds its counterpart in musicological approaches which presume a radical distinction between reified musical structures (forms, scales, melodic
and rhythmic modes) and qualitative parameters such as
timbre, texture, gesture, and flow. This is not a meaningful
distinction for Yoruba musicians and listeners. The experi- ·
ential impact of the base metaphor "good music is good
consociation" depends upon the generation of sensuous
textures. (Waterman 1990a, 376)

Jazz musicians stand in a particularly betwixt and between relationship to standard musical analysis. Most are quite able to talk about
harmony, scales, melodic ideas, and rhythmic precision in terms familiar to students of Western music theory; many, in fact, have had extensive training in classical music and music theory. When describing the

effective deployment of these musical resources with other musicians in the context of jazz performance, however, they often prefer metaphorical description for its ability to convey the more intangible social and aesthetic dimensions of music making. The analytic vocabulary of Western musical theory seems "soulless" to many.

Waterman's commentary refers to the equivalent of the groove in neotraditional Yoruba music and emphasizes the idea that "good music is good consociation." The aesthetics of jazz improvisation, as we have seen, also uphold this idea. Since groove is a concept that simultaneously refers to interdependent musical structures and an aesthetic ideal larger than any one individual, it is not surprising that social metaphors figure prominently in musicians' definitions of groove: "playing good time *with* somebody" (Byron 1989); "walking down the street with somebody" (Davis 1989; Washington 1990); "when you meet somebody and you find a compatibility of personalities" (Weiss 1990); "a mutual feeling of agreement on a pattern" (Bowler 1989). The importance of human personality and individuality is conveyed through metaphors that unify sound and the human beings who make the sound through collaborative musical activity.

When Michael Carvin likened groove to "getting into a bubble bath" (Carvin 1990) and Phil Bowler said that the bass is "like the earth—you walk on the earth" (Bowler 1989), each selected a vivid image with which to compare a particular musical process. Such images tend to be personal and individual. In Carvin's case, the image of "hot water around your body" communicates relaxation, which he later cited as an essential component for the establishment of groove. Bowler's comment highlighted through images from nature two essential musical functions of the bass: contributing the bottom of the harmony and providing a walking bass line. Drummer Michael Carvin also spoke of his left hand:

> But I hear the left hand as brass. Short, staccato, spurts or like a boxer, jabbin', jabbin', always keeping something happening. (Carvin 1990)

"I always speak in parables," Carvin added, because it "helps for people to understand" (Carvin 1992). There is nothing inarticulate or analytically vague about these statements; metaphorical images are in many cases more communicative than ordinary analytical language.

Sociability and Competition

While the musicians I interviewed tended to emphasize positive aspects of musical communication and sociability, Richard Davis did point out that things aren't always perfect:

> But you'll find, just like any other relationship—man and wife, child and parent, friend and friend—[musicians are] not always on the same level all the time. You have fights, you hate each other, you love each other . . . you scream at each other . . . but all that is part of the natural ingredients that come out of the music. (Davis 1989)

Sometimes things can even be hostile:

> That's why I won't make music with people that I don't like. . . . I'd rather starve to death than play with a son of a bitch that I don't like. Because then I ain't gonna make no music.[12]

Because sociability includes the possibility for discord, the bandstand is an arena in which jealousies and competition—as well as harmony and brotherhood—can occur. A pianist who doesn't respect the musicality of a bass player, for example, may feel frustrated when the bass player doesn't pick up on the harmonic direction the pianist would like. A drummer might find that a particular pianist is always rushing and in an attempt to hold the pianist back must limit his or her musical ideas in the interest of rhythmic cohesion. A usually reliable player may have an off night, causing frustration for the rest of his or her band mates.

Musicians sometimes feel that other musicians are not sufficiently worthy to play with them. An "unworthy" musician can transform this image by performing well, which may include responding well to the potentially confusing musical interjections of other musicians. Such interjections challenge the soloist in much the same way as an opening insult in a verbal duel. An improviser can choose to respond to or ignore these musical ideas, but some of the most magical moments in jazz have occurred when the soloist is, as clarinetist Don Byron has put it, "poised enough to do something about them" (Byron 1987). This poise is essential for defending and defining one's reputation within the fiercely competitive world of professional jazz. The positive feelings musicians report for their peers generally occur between play-ers who respect one another professionally. Musicians are constantly being evaluated both by one another and by audience members.

As we have seen, the interaction between the rhythm section and the soloist has often been likened to a communicative dialogue between musicians and their audiences. The interactive sociability of the ensem-ble can be expressed in other images as well. Richard Davis, for ex-ample, compared the sociability of the jazz ensemble to that occurring in African American churches:

> It's like sayin' that you all are talking about the same
> thing. And no matter what you might be concentrating on,
> which in a lot of cases is the melody, you hear the overall
> picture as if it's one person playing. So that happens on
> the bandstand without any announcement. This is to me
> just part of the jazz language and part of the congrega-
> tional impact, you might say, and compare it to a church
> service. (Davis 1989)

Davis was referring to the participatory framework of the African American Christian church service, as found in Baptist, African Meth-odist Episcopal, Apostolic, and Holiness congregations, among others. As African American clergyman Henry H. Mitchell (1970) com-mented, unlike the more restrained modes of participation typical of the European American church, "The Black worshipper does not merely acknowledge the Word delivered by the preacher; he talks back! Sometimes the Black worshipper may shout" (Mitchell 1970, 44).[13] Mitchell also spoke of the preacher's relationship to the audience:

> [Black preaching] has been shaped by interaction with that
> audience—hammered out in dialogue with the Black
> Brothers and Sisters. If the Black preaching tradition is
> unique, then that uniqueness depends in part upon the
> uniqueness of the Black congregation which talks back to
> the preacher as a normal part of the pattern of worship.
> (Mitchell 1970, 95)

Interjections from congregants such as "Tell it," "That's right!," "Uh-huh," and "So true!" have direct counterparts in the frequently heard responses of jazz audience members to memorable passages of improvisation: "Yeah!," "Um-huh," and "Right." Composer Olly Wilson (1990) has suggested calling such passages *soul focal points,* a term that underscores the connection between musical climaxes and African American ideas of spirituality. These soul focal points somehow manage to project attitude and feeling in a way that sets them apart from less inspired moments.

In Davis's metaphor, the soloist is likened to a preacher and the accompanying musicians—not the audience—to a responsive congregation. Davis applied the metaphor at the level of the ensemble, I would argue, because this is where musical development is hammered out in dialogue with interacting musical personalities. Davis continued:

> The leader . . . instigates an idea, and a response comes
> from the leader's idea. The leader not necessarily has just
> to be the guy who's playing the melody . . . but it could
> come from anything that happens in any part of the con-
> gregation or combo. (Davis 1989)

We have moved in this chapter from the structural aspects of the metaphor of conversation to the social ethos of jazz talk in music and words. The importance of interaction in jazz improvisation and the reasons why musicians have found language metaphors so attractive in their theorizing should be clear. In the next chapter, we will deepen our examination by looking at the questions of how such musical moments manage to project attitude and feeling to audience members, what African Americanness means in a highly diverse American society, and how cultural influences and borrowings occur.

chapter four
intermusicality

We have seen that the conversation metaphor used by jazz musicians operates on two levels: it simultaneously suggests structural analogies between music and talk and emphasizes the sociability of jazz performance. This metaphor also includes a temporal dimension. In this chapter I develop the idea of intermusicality, which is something like intertextuality in sound, as a way to begin thinking about the particular ways in which music and, more generally, sound itself can refer to the past and offer social commentary. In so doing, I am interested in how music functions in a relational or discursive rather than an absolute manner, and I foreshadow a theme taken up in a later chapter: the limits of the metaphor of language in thinking about music. The topic of interest here is the musical quotation or allusion, which embodies the conflict between innovation and tradition in jazz performance as well as the larger question of how instrumental music conveys cultural meaning.

When jazz musicians learn traditional repertory, quote a particular musician's solo, play a tune with a particular groove, or imitate a particular player's sound, they reveal themselves to be very aware of musical history. It is important to note that the sonic features that allude to prior musical performances include dimensions beyond harmony, rhythm, and melody. The use of a plunger mute by a trumpet player, for example, can invoke the legacy of Cootie Williams and Bubber Miley among those familiar with the repertoire. For many listeners, the use of a harmon mute immediately brings Miles Davis to mind.

The style of a groove can also invoke musical tradition. When a drummer plays the rhythm in musical example 6h (see chapter 2) on the ride cymbal, both blues and gospel repertoires are brought to mind—for example, Big Mama Thornton's rendition of "Ball N' Chain" or Aretha Franklin's version of "What a Friend We Have in Jesus" (Thornton 1967; Franklin 1972).[1] This type of groove is frequently described by the feeling or association it evokes and implies: "bluesy," "downhome," or "church."

Playing a particular composition can also immediately point to a prior performance, especially when the tune is a jazz standard. Recordings of "Body and Soul" (Green and Heyman 1930), for example, invite comparison with Coleman Hawkins's performance on 11 October 1939 (Hawkins 1939). John Coltrane's recording of this piece on 24 October 1960 (Coltrane 1960a) transforms several dimensions of the tune at once: the groove, the harmony, and the melody. But merely hearing this tune played on the tenor saxophone causes the historically aware listener (whether he or she is a musician or an audience member) to compare the present version to prior respected performances. This evaluation depends on the listener's response to multiple elements of the sonic texture—melody, harmony, rhythm, phrasing, groove, texture, timbre, and tempo—in the present and over historical time.

Bakhtin, Du Bois, Cakes, and Signifying

> Music is music, you know . . . regardless of what [style]
> you're playing.
>
> (BYARD 1990)

Jazz musicians and listeners draw upon knowledge of many different types of music in interpreting and perceiving performances. It is not unusual to hear people remark on affinities that particular jazz performers have with rhythm and blues, gospel music, classical music, Latin jazz, or rock and roll. These different musical styles, to be sure, are not neatly bounded.

Mikhail Bakhtin developed a theory to talk about similar situations in the sphere of language. The diversity of language styles he called *heteroglossia,* and the tensions between an overarching category (music, in our case) and the particularity of social styles (jazz, R&B, classical, rock and roll) he called respectively the *centripetal* and *centrifugal forces of language* (Bakhtin 1981, 263, 272). On the centripetal side are forces of centralization, unification, authoritativeness (hegemony), and standardization; on the centrifugal are those of decentralization, disunity, and competition among multiple social voices. Bakhtin sees these forces intersecting in any particular speech utterance, which has aspects that affirm the general category and those that are highly particular to the moment. Bakhtin's more abstract prose on the subject is worth citing in full.

> Every utterance participates in the "unitary language" (in its centripetal forces and tendencies) and at the same time partakes of social and historical heteroglossia (the centrifugal, stratifying forces).
>
> Such is the fleeting language of a day, of an epoch, a social group, a genre, a school and so forth. It is possible to give a concrete and detailed analysis of any utterance, once having exposed it as a contradiction-ridden, tension-filled unity of two embattled tendencies in the life of language.
>
> The authentic environment of an utterance, the environment in which it lives and takes shape, is dialogized heteroglossia, anonymous and social as language, but simultaneously concrete, filled with specific content and accented as an individual utterance. (272)

It is Bakhtin's idea of *dialogism*—that categories are "contradiction-ridden, tension-filled," unstable unities caught between the general and the wholly specific—that I wish to underscore in approaching the problem of boundaries, both in music and in the broader culture. The idea that the centripetal and centrifugal are dependent upon each other for their mutual definition in ways that vary over time is an important part of the story.

Thirty-eight years before Bakhtin developed these ideas, W. E. B. Du Bois wrote about the intertwined relationship of things black and white in American history: "It is two worlds separate yet bound together like those double stars that, bound for all time, whirl around each other separate yet one" (Du Bois 1985, 49). In an often cited passage from *The Souls of Black Folks* (1969), Du Bois developed this idea into his notion of African American *double-consciousness,* the "twoness" of experiencing oneself as an American and an African

American—"two warring ideals in one dark body" (Du Bois 1969, 45). Less often mentioned are Du Bois's observations on the effects of racial polarization on "The Souls of White Folks."[2]

> High in the tower where I sit beside the loud complaining of the human sea I know many souls that toss and whirl and pass, but none there are that puzzle me more than the Souls of White Folk. Not, mind you, the souls of them that are white, but souls of them that have become painfully conscious of their whiteness; those in whose minds the paleness of their bodily skins is fraught with tremendous and eternal significance. (Du Bois 1910, 339)

Du Bois's metaphor of doubleness summarizes the encounter between Africans and Europeans in America by constructing an image that includes two separate worlds clearly demarcated yet inextricably entwined, a concept with affinities to Bakhtin's dialogism. The vernacular gloss, which sets "the black way" against "the white way," simplifies a long historical process of cultural confrontation that has resulted in a cultural landscape in which African American and non–African American worlds remain distinct but partially overlapping.

Du Bois's concept of doubleness has resonated in the thinking of African American intellectuals, including most recently Henry Louis Gates Jr., who speaks of a "two-toned heritage" (1988, xxiii), and poet Elizabeth Alexander, who has proposed the term *collage* to describe the multiplicity of voices that coexist in African American identity. Alexander (1992) explicitly moves away from a dichotomous opposition of black and white to a perspective that includes multiple voices. She rejects the notion that African Americans speak from a "state of spiritual and cultural schizophrenia and self-division" in favor of a conception that "maps a theoretical space in which the myriad particulars of identity can reside." And in an anthropological assessment of Du Bois's early writings, Nahum Chandler has argued further for "a generalization and therefore radicalization of Du Bois's notion of 'double-consciousness' as the process by which social identity in general is constructed" (Chandler 1992, 16). Chandler reminds us that the self-consciousness of non–African Americans is also affected by the doubleness or multiplicity of co-existing cultural voices.

Despite such insights, the process of categorizing musical types and voices continues. Michael Carvin spoke of this process from the perspective of a jazz insider:

> So there are all kinds of cakes. But they're all cakes. A symphony is to me a plain cake. But a lot of people like plain cake. . . . Upside-down cake with brown sugar, now that's improvisation. . . . You cook it upside down but you eat it right side up. Now *that's* improvisation. . . . But it's still a cake. It's all music. . . . That's one thing that really pisses me off [parody of pretentious tone of voice]—"Well, this is more of a jazz; well, this is more of a rhythm and blues." No, it's music. That's what it is. "Well, this is more of a Beethoven; well, this is more of a Ravi Shankar type of . . ." No. It's music. And that's all it is. (Carvin 1992)

A lot of musicians don't like the word *jazz.* Michael Carvin even went so far as to say, "Don't use the word *jazz.* . . . Don't pigeonhole the thing" (Carvin 1992). When musicians say this, they aren't arguing that there is no difference between jazz improvisation and other types of music; they are recognizing the social significance of labeling. The music that is labeled, they realize, is somehow the one that carries less prestige, the one that is considered less universal. Musicians who "play the music called jazz" (as Carvin prefers to put it) have noticed, for example, that what universities mean traditionally when they talk of a "music department" is a "Western classical music department." This form of music, which has typically been accorded the highest status in intellectual circles and American institutions, is thus made to stand metonymically for all music. When musicians who play the music called jazz talk about "the music," they are turning this usage on its head—like the upside-down cake with brown sugar mentioned by Carvin. Within jazz communities, "the music" means jazz and other African American musical genres. This usage inverts the hegemonic presupposition that Western classical music can stand for all music, setting African American varieties on an equal footing with other forms and asserting pride in an aesthetics of improvisation that expects those who come within its orbit to interact on its terms.

In the twenties and thirties, the term *jazz* was not widely used by musicians, either black or white (Peretti 1992, 133–34). The title of Eddie Condon's memoirs reminds us, *We Called It Music* (1947). Jaki Byard views jazz as a term that comes from "the world of enterprise," while Sidney Bechet states more bluntly that jazz is "a name the white people have given to the music" (Peretti 1992, 133). Byard prefers to describe the music as "the art of improvisation, usually associated with the term *jazz*" (Byard 1991).

The use of the word *jazz,* however, is somewhat unavoidable in this manuscript, for the contexts within which "the music" communicates the equivalent of what it does within African American communities can't be provided for readers whose idea of music might be Javanese Gamelan, Western classical, Eastern European dance, or neotraditional Yoruba music. Despite the obvious problems with the term, the word *jazz* remains widely used among musicians, the music industry, and fans of the music. Like many other categorical labels, it is useful within limits, glossing meaningful distinctions in musical style and audience that can serve to locate the general subject matter.

In this context, a further discussion of the categories I am employing is due. When I speak of black and white, African American and European American, African American and non–African American, I am mobilizing a variety of terms that draw attention to the fact that race has been a particularly salient category in American history in general and jazz music in particular. My intention has been to explore the ambiguities, indistinctness, overlaps, and variety within racial and musical categories and to look especially at the ways in which improvising musicians say something about them through music. I have tried to avoid reifying these categories into monolithic and unchanging entities while at the same time recognizing that, as Cornel West has argued (1993), "race matters." It has deeply affected the material, historical, ideological, political, and cultural positions of all Americans, even (or especially) when it is not mentioned. What Toni Morrison has argued for literary discourse is important to keep in mind more generally:

> One likely reason for the paucity of critical material on
> this large and compelling subject is that, in matters of
> race, silence and evasion have historically ruled literary dis-
> course. Evasion has fostered another, substitute language
> in which the issues are encoded, foreclosing open debate.
> The situation is aggravated by the tremor that breaks into
> discourse on race. It is further complicated by the fact that
> the habit of ignoring race is understood to be a graceful,

even generous, liberal gesture. To notice is to recognize an already discredited difference. To enforce its invisibility through silence is to allow the black body a shadowless participation in the dominant cultural body. (Morrison 1992, 9–10)

In music, it is particularly important to talk about the relationship of African American aesthetics to the "dominant cultural body," because music is an arena in which the taken-for-granted hegemonic presumptions about race have been turned upside down by the leadership of African American music and musicians in defining and influencing the shape of American popular music. The zeal with which white Americans have taken up black musical styles in the twentieth century while at the same time failing to address the cultural implications of this process is a striking American cultural paradox.

Michael Carvin's image of the upside-down cake also provides an example of what Henry Louis Gates Jr. would call signifying. As mentioned in chapter 3, Gates drew upon the sociolinguistic literature on African American language to extend this concept beyond its exclusive association with African American verbal dueling genres by making explicit its relationship to literary discussions of transformation and intertextuality. African American literary aesthetics, in his opinion, transform and frequently invert the sense of mainstream literary and linguistic conventions:

Signifyin(g) is black double-voicedness; because it always entails formal revision and an intertextual relation. . . . I find it an ideal metaphor for black literary criticism, or the formal manner in which texts seem concerned to address their antecedents. Repetition with a signal difference, is fundamental to the nature of Signifyin(g), as we shall see. (Gates 1988, 51)

This notion is similar to the definition of parody proposed by literary theorist Linda Hutcheon:

Parody, then, in its ironic "trans-contextualization" and inversion, is repetition with a difference. A critical distance is implied between the backgrounded text being parodied and the new incorporating work, a distance usually signaled by irony. But this irony can be playful as well as be-

littling; it can be critically constructive as well as destruc-
tive. The pleasure of parody's irony comes not from humor
in particular but from the degree of engagement of the
reader in the intertextual "bouncing" . . . between complicity and distance.[3] (Hutcheon 1991, 32)

Signifying, for Gates, is about the valorization of figurative modes
of expression that mark the "two discursive universes" of black and
white (1988, 75–76). It is not so much a matter of what is said as of
how it is said: "One does not signify something; rather, one signifies
in some way" (54). The transformation of the language uses of the
"white" discursive universe into the expressive modes of the "black"
discursive universe underlie Gates's notion of repetition with a signal
difference. At the most general level, Gates uses the term *signifying* to
mean any transformation that employs African American modes of
figurative expression. More specifically, Gates is interested in "repetition and reversal" (63), the kind of transformation that includes the
ironic "critical distance" Hutcheon mentions in her definition of parody. Reversal, incongruity, and recontextualization are the hallmarks
of irony as defined in both literary and anthropological usages
(Hutcheon 1991, 32; Fernandez 1986, 268).

Transformation of existing genres is also a well-known feature of
African American musical expression. The transformation of Isaac
Watts hymns into African-American Christian songs, of march forms
into ragtime, and of musical theater tunes into jazz standards have all
been important signs of African American creativity and originality.
Indeed, synthesis and transformation of musical elements from both
African and European origins have long been noted in scholarly discussions of jazz history (Schuller 1968, 3–62). It is this transformative
quality of jazz improvisation that Gates has in mind when he comments that "there are so many examples of signifyin(g) in jazz that one
could write a formal history of its development on this basis alone"
(Gates 1988, 63–64).

The salience of irony in the expression of cultural identity was noted
by Don Byron when asked what he thought were the most important
elements of African American musical aesthetics.

There's irony *all over,* irony everywhere. . . . It's definitely
that balance . . . between totally opposing aesthetics . . .
the conflict between being serious and avant, and just play-

ing swinging shit . . . a polar pulling between cleanliness
and dirtiness, between knowing rules very well and breaking them. There's a certain kind of pull between opposite
impulses that you . . . see in any good black anything . . . a
certain kind of inventiveness outside of . . . what is accept-
able. And I think that comes from being in the society in
that role . . . just the fact that you're not quite an accepted
member of society gives you a certain distance from the
way things usually go. (Byron 1989)

Byron's discussion is organized around a series of oppositions: being
serious/playing swinging shit; cleanliness/dirtiness; rules/the breaking
of rules; and the confrontation of "opposing aesthetics," which he interpreted as "black" and "white." One might at first see Du Bois's idea
of two warring ideals deeply embedded within this entire chain of association, yet a close examination of the musical embodiment of these
oppositions reveals, if anything, a far more complicated situation. The
tensions that this musician cites co-exist and often are emphasized selectively in one direction or another according to context. This is more
like the dialogic situation described by Bakhtin than an irresolvable
conflict.

The topic of irony has, of course, long been important in African
American studies.[4] Imamu Amiri Baraka's commentary on the cakewalk is emblematic of the issues contained in the examples of irony in
music explored here:

If the cakewalk is a Negro dance caricaturing certain
white customs, what is that dance when, say, a white theater company attempts to satirize it as a Negro dance? I
find the idea of white minstrels in blackface satirizing a
dance satirizing themselves a remarkable kind of irony—
which, I suppose, is the whole point of minstrel shows.
(Baraka 1963, 86)

The idea that there is the *potential* for cultural irony in interpretation
underlies the musical examples in this chapter. Since listeners and performers from divergent backgrounds potentially produce multiple interpretations of the same event, I do not mean to imply that an ironic
interpretation of a musical moment is the only one possible. In the
following musical examples, consequently, irony is one of several possible intents and perceptions, depending on an individual listener's or

musician's perceptions, interpretation, and social situation. Intentionality in any particular case is in fact a moot issue. We know from historical accounts that jazz musicians have intended to convey social and cultural criticism in many aspects of their musical practice, for they have talked about it openly (Gillespie and Fraser 1979, 141–42, 208–9, 287–91).

I will now discuss four examples of musical irony or parody in jazz, two of which are cross-cultural and one of which is intracultural. The first example presents musical irony conveyed by the transformation of a European American popular song into a vehicle for jazz improvisation; the second example makes reference to a particular classical composer in an ironic style; and the third and fourth examples make humorous allusion to styles within the mainstream jazz tradition. Many more examples of each type could easily be cited for these cases represent practices that quite literally pervade jazz improvisation. In part, it seems, African American music makes use of the doubleness of the African American position in American society through allusions to divergent musical repertories.

"My Favorite Things"

In October of 1960, John Coltrane recorded the selections that would appear on three very well known Atlantic recordings: *My Favorite Things, Coltrane Plays the Blues,* and *Coltrane's Sound* (Coltrane 1960c, 1960b, 1960a). *My Favorite Things* included all standards: Richard Rodgers and Oscar Hammerstein's "My Favorite Things" (1959), Cole Porter's "Everytime We Say Goodbye" (1944), and George Gershwin's "Summertime" (1935) and "But Not for Me" (1930). As has already been noted, jazz versions of Broadway musical tunes form one very important part of a jazz musician's repertory. The remaining selections on the three albums recorded in October were all originals, with the exceptions of "Body and Soul" (Green and Heyman 1930) and "The Night Has a Thousand Eyes," which were included on *Coltrane's Sound.* Atlantic Records made the decision to market *My Favorite Things* as an album of standards, a decision that paid off commercially. During the first year of release, the album sold fifty thousand copies, five times the number expected for a reasonably successful jazz album (Thomas 1975, 133). The title track was also released as a 45 rpm single, and it became Coltrane's most popular tune (Priestly 1987, 42).

"My Favorite Things" was not widely known at the time, for the Broadway show *The Sound of Music,* for which it was originally written, had only been in production for approximately one year.[5] A song plugger supplied the sheet music to the Coltrane quartet while they were performing at Joe Termini's Jazz Gallery in New York in 1960 (Thomas 1975, 133; Kernfeld 1988, 2:278). McCoy Tyner reported that he was not very enthusiastic about the tune at first, but Coltrane was. One of the things about it that appealed to audiences, according to Tyner, was that it was in triple meter (3/4) at a time when very few jazz tunes ventured beyond duple meter: "The audience really liked it, the way we played it in three-quarter time. It was probably the only jazz waltz they'd ever heard since Sonny Rollins' 'Valse Hot.' So John decided to record it on his next album" (Thomas 1975, 133).

In live performance, "My Favorite Things" became a vehicle for extended improvisations by Coltrane and his group, and these often fueled the criticism of jazz critics that Coltrane played "too long" (DeMichael 1962, 21). In time, Coltrane's versions of the tune became a symbol of an increasingly open direction in improvisational aesthetics and an example frequently cited by musicians and audience members who wished to emphasize the way in which jazz versions of standards surpass the originals in musical power. Henry Louis Gates Jr. used it to illustrate his ideas of repetition and reversal:

> Repeating a form and then inverting it through a process
> of variation is central to jazz—a stellar example is John
> Coltrane's rendition of "My Favorite Things," compared
> to Julie Andrews's vapid version. Resemblance thus can be
> evoked cleverly by dissemblance. (Gates 1984, 291)

Coltrane's rendition predates the film version of *The Sound of Music,* of course, and it was Mary Martin who sang the song in the original stage production (Rodgers and Hammerstein 1959). But Julie Andrews's version from the 1965 film remains the most widely known to general audiences and consequently is the version that many post-1965 listeners have in mind when they make the comparison.

There are many transformations and reversals in Coltrane's 1960 version of the tune that deserve close attention. I would like to emphasize that the effect of ironic reversal, or transformation of a "corny" tune into a vehicle for serious jazz improvisation, is communicated by multiple musical parameters and depends upon the "the degree of en-

Introduction	A	Interlude	A	Interlude	A	B	Coda
	E minor	E minor	E minor	E major	E major	E minor	G major
4 (bars)	16	2	16	2	16	16	4

Figure 2 Formal plan of Broadway version of "My Favorite Things"

gagement of the reader [listener] in the intertextual 'bouncing' . . . between complicity and distance" that Linda Hutcheon mentioned (Hutcheon 1991, 32).[6] I will focus upon transformations of form, harmony, and groove in "My Favorite Things" to illustrate the contrast between the Broadway and Coltrane versions of this tune.

To begin with, the Coltrane version does not use the chorus structure of the tune to frame its improvisational structure. The formal plan of the Rodgers and Hammerstein tune is shown in figure 2. It includes three A sections and a B section, each of sixteen bars' duration. In this version, each of the first two A sections is followed by a two-measure interlude. The three A sections also include tonal contrast: the first two A's are in the minor mode, the third in the parallel major. The B section modulates from the minor mode to the relative major and is followed by a four-measure coda of the same character as the first two interludes (but in the relative major). The full AAAB form with interludes occurs twice, the first time sung by Maria in the key areas of em/G major and the second time sung by the Mother Abbess in fm/A♭ major. This version concludes with both characters repeating the B section, modulating a full step upward to gm/B♭ major. The key changes underscore the theme of the lyric: triumphing over hard times by remembering one's favorite things (minor to major).

> A (minor): Raindrops on roses and whiskers on kittens,
> Bright copper kettles and warm woolen mittens,
> Brown paper packages tied up with strings,
> These are a few of my favorite things.

> A (minor): Cream-colored ponies and crisp apple strudels,
> Doorbells and sleighbells and schnitzel with
> noodles,
> Wild geese that fly with the moon on their
> wings,
> These are a few of my favorite things.

Introduction	Vamp 1	A	Vamp 2	A	Vamp 2	A	A
8	8 e minor	16 e minor	8 e minor	16 e minor	24 E major	16 E major	16 E major

Vamp 2	Piano solo . . .
16 e minor	

Figure 3 Formal plan of Coltrane version of "My Favorite Things." *My Favorite Things.*
New York: 21 October 1960. Atlantic SD 1361.

A (major): Girls in white dresses with blue satin sashes,
Snowflakes that stay on my nose and eye-
lashes,
Silver white winters that melt into springs,
These are a few of my favorite things.

B (minor to major):
When the dog bites, when the bee stings,
When I'm feeling sad,
I simply remember my favorite things and
Then I don't feel so bad!

Figure 3 illustrates how different the Coltrane version is. Most notably, the interludes are expanded into two-chord extendable vamps—
e-9–f♯-9/e for the minor section and EM7–f♯-7/e for the major section.
Where the original version used one chord (the first of each pair), the
Coltrane quartet uses two. Second, the Coltrane quartet plays only the
A sections of the melody. The B section is not heard until the reprise
of the tune at the very end of the performance, when Coltrane abbrevi-
ates the thematic statement to a major A section followed by the B
section and the minor vamp. Coltrane's B section does not modulate
to the relative major.

In the Coltrane version, soloing occurs over the vamp sections, not
over the chord structure of the composition, as in a more typical jazz
usage of a musical theater tune. The vamp sections vary in length at
the performer's discretion, and the bassist plays a tonic pedal point
throughout. The soloist indicates an impending change of mode or an
end of the solo by playing the melody and the harmonic changes of

Melody	Vamp	Melody	Vamp	Melody	Vamp	Melody
e minor	e minor	e minor	E major	E major	e minor	e minor
16	32	16	148	8 + 8	32	16

Figure 4 Formal plan of McCoy Tyner's solo on "My Favorite Things." *My Favorite Things.* New York: 21 October 1960. Atlantic SD 1361.

the A section. McCoy Tyner's solo on the 1960 version, for example, is illustrated in figure 4. There are three improvisational sections over the vamp (two in minor and one in major) interspersed by the playing of the melody of the A section. The middle solo section over the major vamp is by far the most extended—148 measures as opposed to 32. Coltrane reported that the length of the minor and major solos was "entirely up to the artist," not predetermined (DeMichael 1962, 21).

The vamps also set the character of the rhythmic feel or groove. The accompaniment in the Coltrane version consists of three independent yet interlocking parts played by the drums, piano, and bass. Musical example 14 presents a rhythmic transcription of the Coltrane (1960c) version. (I have limited my transcription of the drum part to the principal time-keeping rhythm articulated by Elvin Jones on the ride cymbal and occasional interjections on the snare and bass drum.) The first vamp section begins in measure 9. Note that Elvin Jones, McCoy Tyner, and Steve Davis all play different but interlocking two-bar rhythmic patterns. Elvin Jones's ride cymbal rhythm is particularly infectious given the timbre and accentuation with which he plays it—something not visible on the transcription itself. The repetition at two-measure intervals gives the vamp sections a strong metric feel in six. By contrast, in the A sections of the melody, the rhythm section plays rhythms that repeat at one-measure intervals, giving these sections a rhythmic feel in three. Tyner's rhythmic riff figure that begins in the vamp section started at measure 33 becomes something of the home comping rhythm, and the interlocking of his part with the bass tonic pedal point produces the hypnotic feel often mentioned in contemporary accounts (DeMichael 1962, 21). In vamp 2, the piano, bass, and ride cymbal parts come together on the downbeats of the two-measure pattern and on the "and" of 1 in the second measure (mm. 33–34) while at the same time playing three distinct rhythmic figures.

Against this syncopated and interlocking rhythmic and harmonic framework for participation, it would be almost impossible to play the

Musical example 14. Coltrane version of "My Favorite Things."
(*My Favorite Things*. Atlantic SD 1361.
Recorded: New York, 21 October 1960.)

melody as squarely as it is written in the sheet music (musical example 15). Coltrane instead articulates a highly syncopated version of the melody, providing a fourth independent part to the complex, interlocking texture (musical example 14, mm. 17–33). Upon first hearing, it is the dramatically different groove that stands out to the listener. It sets the basic tone for the entire piece and is strong, firm, and infectious. This is the foundational quality to a good rhythmic feel that underlies Michael Carvin's claim that "the groove is the point of departure for ALL improvisational music" (Carvin 1992). It is also one of the most important means for transforming music from other repertories into an African American improvisational sensibility.

As innovative and strikingly different as the Coltrane quartet's rhythmic feels are, they nonetheless demonstrate continuities with firmly established African American musical conventions. The inter-

Musical example 14. *Continued*

textual engagement that Hutcheon talks about is especially important in the appreciative listener's reaction. Jerome Harris, for instance, cited "My Favorite Things" as an example of a new sound drawing on African American musical tradition and a model for the way in which a rhythm section might think about its roles.[7]

> You think of Coltrane's "My Favorite Things" and what McCoy Tyner's playing on piano there. I mean it's a repetition riff [sings comping part], you know. I mean that's a

Musical example 14. *Continued*

time-honored part of tradition and part of what a rhythm
section can do. You get into the details of whether the piano is going to be the one that's playing the riff . . . and
the bass and drums are going to be freed up to dance
around that. Or if the bass player is going to be playing
the ostinato-type line and the drums and the comping instrument are going to be free. Or whether the bass and
drums are going to be together. And it can change from
section to section. That's just another resource to use.
(Harris 1992)

Musical example 14. *Continued*

By contrast, the rhythmic framework of the Broadway version is in simple waltz time. This arrangement supports the sung melody with an accompaniment that alternates pizzicato rhythmic figures with sustained harmonies in the strings (musical example 15, mm. 5–20). The rhythmic figure in the interlude is the "um-pah-pah" typically associated with the waltz (mm. 21–22), and it provides the main accompaniment for the second and third A sections of the tune (see figure 2). Musical contrast is generated through the alternation of short and sus-

Musical example 14. *Continued*

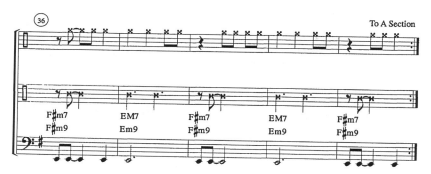

tained instrumental sonorities and through change in dynamics. Unlike the case of a jazz version, there is no need to set up a musically
interactive situation that supports improvisation. The arrangement instead supports the clear articulation of the text with an unsyncopated
rhythmic framework appropriate to the musical theater context for
which it is intended.

Jazz listeners generally view the transformations of Broadway tunes
by jazz musicians as considerably "superior" to the original materials.
In such evaluations an African American musical aesthetic is the
taken-for-granted standard against which the Broadway version is
judged. I wish to emphasize my awareness that the African American
versions are not "better" inherently but relative to a particular aesthetic, which many non–African Americans share as well. Most notably, these tunes are made to swing by the addition of jazz grooves;
they make use of more complex harmonies than are present in the
sheet-music versions; and they are vehicles for improvisational invention. In "My Favorite Things," the rhythm section of Elvin Jones on
drums, Steve Davis on bass, and McCoy Tyner on piano provides a
multi-leveled musical context against which Coltrane's transformation
of the melody, harmony, and rhythm of the tune interacts. There is no
doubt that in terms of the improvisational aesthetic standards of jazz,
the Coltrane version is a vast improvement upon the original.

Max Roach makes explicit this feeling about the superiority of the
jazz versions that many musicians and audience members of many ethnic backgrounds share: "The only reason that the music of the Gersh-
wins and all these people lived during [the 1940s] was because all the
black people, the Billie Holidays, Ella Fitzgeralds, Dizzy Gillespies,

Musical example 15. Broadway version of "My Favorite Things."
(*Sound of Music Selections*. Columbia LP 5450.
Recorded: New York, NY, 1959.)

Charlie Parkers, the Monks, the Coleman Hawkinses projected this music, used this music and kept it alive" (Gillespie and Fraser 1979, 208). Don Byron also mentioned that he thinks the only reason certain standards are remembered is because some "black cat played the hell of them" (Byron 1992).

This transformation of "My Favorite Things," or what Gates would term signification upon the tune, inverts the piece on nearly every level. It makes the interludes, not the verse, the subject of the performance; it transforms waltz time into a polyrhythmically textured six-feel;

Musical example 15. *Continued*

and it transforms a sentimental, optimistic lyric into a vehicle for a more brooding improvisational exploration. Since the lyrics would have been on the sheet music the song plugger brought to the quartet, Coltrane would have been well aware of the emphasis on white things in the lyric—girls in white dresses, snowflakes on eyelashes, silver white winters, cream-colored ponies. In 1960—a year of tremendous escalation in the Civil Rights movement and a time of growing politicization of the jazz community—there was certainly the possibility that Coltrane looked upon the lyrics with an ironic eye.[8] Even if he didn't, however, the potential for an ironic interpretation on the part of his listen-

Musical example 15. *Continued*

ers and fellow musicians is clearly present. One factor in the symbolic importance of "My Favorite Things" within the community of musicians and core audience members is these multiple levels of potential irony.

Another possible inversion has to do with Coltrane's version beating the European American musical standards at their own game, and this is where the idea of irony at a cultural level becomes important. Coltrane's quartet turns a musical theater tune upside down by playing with it, transforming it, and turning it into a vehicle for the expression of an African American–based sensibility that even many non–African

Musical example 15. *Continued*

Americans prefer to the original. In so doing, it invokes some of the standards of European classical music against European American musical theater songs. The simple setting of the Broadway version of "My Favorite Things" works well within the context for which it was intended—a musical theater performance. In addition, the performance is well played by musical theater standards: the string and singer(s) are in tune, observe dynamics, and keep a steady tempo. Under the evaluative standards of Western classical music, however, the tune and arrangement would perhaps be described as "unsophisticated," "simple," or "too obvious." By contrast, the four-part contrapuntal texture generated by the musicians in the Coltrane quartet is certainly "more complex" than that of the Broadway version when measured by these standards (compare musical example 15, mm. 5–12; musical example 14, mm. 17–24). Jazz musicians, in this sense, are able to invoke selectively some of the hegemonic standards of Western classical music in their favor.[9]

At least part of the pride many African American jazz musicians take in their versions of standards lies in their ability to thus upstage the European American versions of the tunes—something acknowledged by audiences both black and white. In asserting a musical superiority, even when measured against the white hegemonic standard, musicians make ironic the presumption of racial inferiority. Not only does the Coltrane version of "My Favorite Things" stand out in comparison to the Broadway version within some standards derived from the European American world, it does so while at the same time articulating an independent improvisational aesthetic that draws on African American cultural sensibilities and is the taken-for-granted standard against which non–African American music is evaluated.

Jean and John Comaroff's discussion of ideology is helpful in thinking about this issue and in considering the role of assertion and cultural critique in the musical practice of jazz improvisation. Ideology, in the Comaroffs' conception, draws upon Raymond Williams's definition: "an articulated system of meanings, values and beliefs of a kind that can be abstracted as [the] 'worldview'" of a particular group" (Comaroff and Comaroff 1991, 24). The emphasis here is upon articulation. If hegemony rules by silence and "taken-for-grantedness," ideology is spoken and asserted. To borrow a linguistic analogy, hegemony is the unmarked category, ideology the marked. The hegemonic and ideological thus stand in interdependent and dynamic relationship. Once something formerly hegemonic becomes contested and articulated, it enters the realm of the ideological and can no longer be taken for granted. As the Comaroffs put it,

This follows a very common pattern: once something
leaves the domain of the hegemonic, it frequently becomes

a major site of ideological struggle. Even when there is no well-formed opposing ideology, no clearly articulated collective consciousness among subordinate populations, such struggles may still occur. But they are liable to be heard in the genre of negation—refusal, reversal, the smashing of idols and icons—and not in the narrative voice of political argument. (Comaroff and Comaroff 1991, 27)

It is from this vantage point that we can begin to understand the deep significance of irony and doubleness in the articulation of a jazz musical aesthetic. The cross-cultural and intracultural musical allusions through which jazz musicians assert irony can be interpreted as both cultural and ideological. The signs and practices through which musicians construct and represent themselves and others in musical terms are extremely powerful in African American music in general and jazz in particular. The fact that music has been an arena in which African Americans have not only asserted an independent cultural identity but have had non–African Americans acknowledge their leadership in the form of emulation is deeply significant in the constitution of American musical culture more broadly, and it underlies the tremendous symbolic importance of music for African Americans. For in jazz, European American musicians have indeed been painfully conscious of their whiteness, unable to take the superiority of things white for granted—the hegemonic made ideological, at least in part.

"Rip, Rig, and Panic"

Rip means Rip Van Winkle [or Rest in Peace?]. It's the way people, even musicians are. They're asleep. Rig means like rigor mortis. That's where a lot of people's minds are. When they hear me doing things they didn't think I could do they panic in their minds.

(KIRK 1965, liner notes)

Roland Kirk's commentary illustrates what the Comaroffs mean when they speak of the hegemonic being made ideological, the sense of panic that ensues when people do not fit properly within the categories that have been assigned to them by social convention, stereotype, and practice. Kirk's "Rip, Rig, and Panic" (1965) also provides a sec-

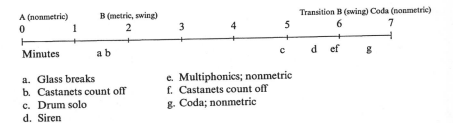

a. Glass breaks   e. Multiphonics; nonmetric
b. Castanets count off   f. Castanets count off
c. Drum solo   g. Coda; nonmetric
d. Siren

Figure 5   Formal plan of "Rip, Rig, and Panic"

ond example of musical irony, in this case an example created by specific references to the works of a particular classical composer—Edgard Varèse. Kirk cites Varèse as an inspiration in the liner notes to
the album, referring most directly to Varèse's *Poème électronique*
(1958b) and *Ionisation* (1958a).

Figure 5 provides a diagrammatic representation of Kirk's performance of "Rip, Rig, and Panic." The opening section of the piece (labeled A) is an out-of-time section that is freely improvised. At the end
of the A section, a breaking glass—which emulates sounds produced
electronically by Varèse in *Poème électronique*—signals the band to
stop. In the transition section and coda, both of which are out of time,
Kirk evokes the electronic sonorities of Varèse by simultaneously playing several instruments at the same time—something for which Kirk
was widely known.[10] Toward the end of Elvin Jones's drum solo, a siren
is sounded, mimicking an effect that is prominent in Varèse's *Ionisation*. The count-off into both B sections—an up-tempo swing melody
that is itself an AABA form—is also an opportunity for irony. Kirk
cued this uptempo 4/4 swing section by counting the band in with castanets (1, 2, 3, rest) rather than by using the voice or a drum cue, as
would be more usual in jazz performance. The light sonority and ex-
posed character of the castanets, which imitate "refined" classical percussion parts, create an ironic incongruity between the supposed seriousness of avant-garde classical music and the silliness of counting in
the band with castanets.

Don Byron, in fact, selected "Rip, Rig, and Panic" as a particularly
good example of a piece that embodies an African American musical
aesthetic. He broke into uproarious laughter at the breaking of the
glass and the sound of the castanets when he played this recording for
me, and he said that Kirk was "buckwild," an admiring term to de-

scribe the willingness to go, as he said, "outside of . . . what is accept-able" (1989). An admiration for irreverence, particularly toward the decorum and perceived stiffness of the Western classical music tradi-tion, is another way in which a cross-cultural sense of irony can be projected in jazz improvisation. Note that Kirk is not necessarily ridi-culing Varèse; rather, he probably admired Varèse's sense of humor and adventure, since the classical composer was himself marginal and not fully accepted in the world of "serious" composition. In this sense, Kirk could be expressing a solidarity with Varèse as an outsider. It is unlikely that the favor would have been returned, however, as Varèse did not like jazz (Bernard 1987, 9).

Kirk ultimately makes use of the citation of Varèse for his own pur-poses: to demonstrate that his virtuosic multi-instrument technique can make fun with music from an unlikely source. This act functions on many levels simultaneously—paying homage to the source (Mur-phy 1990), playfully teasing, critiquing the source, and making artistic assertions beyond it. By referring to Varèse, Kirk also demonstrates his knowledge of music beyond jazz and other African American tradi-tions. Many European Americans in his audience might presume that a jazz musician such as Kirk would not know about Varèse, but by skillfully quoting and parodying his work, Kirk demonstrates (to an audience with enough cultural knowledge to recognize the allusion) that he does. In similar fashion, Charlie Parker often cited fragments from the classical compositions of Wagner, Bizet, and Stravinsky (Kernfeld 1988, 2:288).

"Parkeriana"

The perception of transformation, irony, and humor depends on a lis-tener's aural familiarity with the musical repertories and conventions upon which the allusions turn. This, again, is what Hutcheon (1991) means when she speaks of "the intertextual 'bouncing' . . . between complicity and distance" that results in the pleasure of perceiving par-ody. Listeners who are familiar with the mainstream jazz repertory, for example, often recognize tunes that are based on the harmonic progression to George Gershwin's "I Got Rhythm" (1930). The humor and delight that listeners take in Eric Dolphy and Jaki Byard's perfor-mance of "Parkeriana" (Mingus 1964a) turns on this ability to recog-nize "Rhythm" changes, as musicians call them (see chapter 2, note 8).

Musical example 4 in chapter 2 is taken from near the midpoint of Eric Dolphy's solo in this tune. The dissonant character of the solo over consonant "Rhythm" changes signals a level of incongruity that causes smiles among those familiar with the solos traditionally associated with this progression. When Jaki Byard plays a big band riff against Eric Dolphy's line, an additional layer of intertextual irony is added. On the one hand, the rhythmic conventionality of the big band riff figure is a stabilizing influence; on the other, its dissonance (even though more consonant than the solo) highlights its distance from more conventional uses of the rhythmic riff. In ways such as this, performers engage those listeners who have enough experience to understand allusions and their possible humor and irony. These qualities are thus co-constructed by the performers and the listeners (who, remember, also include the musicians themselves), and there is always the potential for disjunctions between performers' intentions and audiences' interpretations.

Direct quotations or indirect musical allusions may also be made for reasons of homage and respect (Gates 1988, xxvii; Murphy 1990). For example, Coltrane's turn to the soprano saxophone, which he plays on "My Favorite Things," was partially in response to the death of Sidney Bechet in 1959 (Priestly 1987, 42). In some cases, audience members may interpret allusions to past styles as ironic and humorous when the musician playing them is doing so as an act of homage. Generational differences are also a factor: an older musician may play a passage from an older style that younger audience members find humorous but older musicians and listeners do not view as parody. Nevertheless, in the jazz aesthetic, homage and respect are not incompatible with humor, and listeners may respond to the recognition of homage with laughter.

To laugh at a musical allusion during a jazz improvisation is, after all, a token of admiration, not scorn. The laugh acknowledges the cleverness of the musical moment or citation and draws attention to the fact that the listener has understood the musical argument in the context of the jazz tradition. The appreciation of musical humor in the African American tradition conflicts with the preference in Western classical music for more "serious" means of musical expression.[11] In jazz, humor and artistic seriousness are not incompatible. Jaki Byard is, in fact, insulted when people think his music is less serious because it contains humor:

My music *is* serious. I might do it with humor, but it's still serious because I mean what I'm doing. (Brown 1979, 16)

"Bass-ment Blues"

Jaki Byard's performance on "Bass-ment Blues" (Byard 1965)—which includes Byard on piano, George Tucker on bass, Alan Dawson on drums, and Joe Farrell on flute—provides yet another example of humorous allusions to musical styles likely to be known to jazz listeners. Here the sense of irony and humor derives from transformed references to recognized stylistic devices *within* the jazz big-band tradition: Byard plays traditional shout-chorus riffs but with very dissonant cluster voicings in an avant-garde approach to the blues. Knowledgeable listeners laugh when they hear Byard go into the twisted and transformed big band riff clichés, for much as Kirk did in his citation of Varèse, he adapts the musical allusion to his own clever purposes. Byard himself laughed at this passage when I played it for him during the course of an interview; he liked it so much he even asked me to play it for him twice. The point for our broader discussion is that cross-cultural allusions are often used in ironic passages in jazz, but allusions need not be cross-cultural to be ironic. We will take a closer look at this performance in the next chapter.

Intermusicality

What a given audience member can recognize in a jazz performance depends on that person's age, experience, attention, memory, timbral sensitivity, and aural ability, among other factors. Each individual has a personal listening world that intersects to a greater or lesser degree with those of other participants in a particular musical tradition, but no two people are likely to have exactly the same sound worlds. Some jazz listeners know more repertory than others, which comes as no surprise. This audience stratification by aural familiarity creates groups of people sharing musical bonds that are denser at the center than near the edge of any particular category. This is precisely the type of tension between centrifugal and centripetal tendencies that Bakhtin (1981) was talking about, and it helps reinforce the idea that categories such as the jazz community, African American musical aesthetics, European American musical aesthetics, and so forth are significant but not clearly bounded. There is much room for overlap and difference between any two individuals within and between categories.

Recordings heavily mediate the aural transmission of style in jazz.[12] Jazz performances are not musical texts in and of themselves (in that they are negotiated between multiple improvising participants), but when such performances are recorded and disseminated through LPs, CDs, and cassettes, they become texts. Musicians may use them as resources for learning tunes, solos, harmonic substitutions, timbral sensibility, or rhythm section styles. Kenny Washington suggested that listening to records was particularly important for rhythm section players whose parts are minimally notated on written charts, or lead sheets. Verbal instructions to play a certain groove or feel, plus a chart with the song form and harmonies, may be the only guidance given to rhythm section players. Their aural knowledge of the appropriate accompanimental styles is therefore often heavily informed by familiarity with particular recordings. This is another aspect to the "conversation over time" that we have been talking about.

Older musicians generally know more repertoire (tunes and records) than younger musicians. Kenny Washington—who is young himself—complained that younger musicians do not do enough listening:

> But you know, what [successful ensemble playing] comes from is . . . the amount of listening . . . that musicians—especially rhythm section players—do. Problem nowadays is not enough guys *listen,* and when I say listening I'm talking about, do their homework. (Washington 1990)

Since music from around the world is widely available in the form of recordings, the personal sound horizons of any individual are unlikely to be restricted to the music of one tradition. Jazz musicians are often familiar with a broad spectrum of musical styles ranging from R&B, gospel, bebop, and Western classical music to Indian classical music, West African drum ensembles, Brazilian music, Afro-Cuban music, and reggae. Musicians may choose to incorporate into their playing and compositional styles elements from any of the musical traditions with which they are familiar. The question of how audiences and fellow musicians react to and evaluate these borrowings and influences returns us to the subject of boundaries, the articulation of cultural identity in music, and the idea of categories that are denser at the middle than around the edges. Often the style of groove in which these influences are incorporated is an important factor in whether or not the resulting music is considered jazz.

As noted earlier, all four examples presented in this chapter employ musical allusion in one form or another to communicate the ironic play of difference. The important point is that a chain of associations is set off that engages the listener and unites her or him with a community of individuals who share a similar musical point of view. A reference may be as specific as a melodic quotation from a particular piece or as diffuse as a timbre or style of groove. It might be from within or outside of mainstream jazz repertory. Quotations are only the most obvious examples of the thick web of intertextual and intermusical associations to which knowledgeable performers and listeners react. Theoretically, almost any musical detail or composite thereof could convey a reference, as long as a community of interpreters can recognize the continuity. The key here is the community of interpreters (which includes both performers and audience), for a sonic detail becomes socially meaningful and actionable only in a context that is at least partially shared.

The semiotic modes of signaling implicated in this process combine aspects of the indexical and iconic in Charles Peirce's tripartite framework: an aural passage conveys to those with the sociocultural knowledge to recognize and interpret it a relation between a past performance and a present one. The quoted musical detail indexes or points to another performance, placing the two in a socially interactive dialogue (Hanks 1990, 1–15). At the same time, this indexing works by virtue of the iconic resemblance, or mirroring, between the two passages. In the examples of irony in jazz improvisation presented here, the crucial point is that the iconic moment is not simply resemblance but a transformation of the thing resembled. In the case of "My Favorite Things," the transformation of the tune simultaneously communicates the resemblance between the two versions and the vast differences between them—Gates's signifying "repetition with a signal difference."

In jazz improvisation, aural references are conveyed primarily through instrumental means—that is, without words. While it is possible to speak of these references as the intertextual aspect of music, I prefer to call them intermusical relationships to draw attention to a communication process that occurs primarily through musical sound itself, rather than words. The word *intermusical* is best reserved for aurally perceptible musical relationships that are heard in the context of particular musical traditions. Associations carried primarily through song lyrics would be primarily intertextual; musical relationships observable only with the aid of a score might best be called intertextual musical relationships.[13] The complicated relationship between written and aural modes of musical knowledge, it seems to me, must be carefully distinguished. While the more generalized usage of the term *intertextual* in literary studies can include music as a specific mode of textuality (Hanks 1989), it seems that musical scholars have had sufficient difficulty distinguishing cultural meaning conveyed by text, music in its written aspect, and music in its aural aspect so that a specifically musical term would be useful.[14] The intertextual aspects of music are in this sense more complicated than those in the realm of language.

Intermusical relationships are not merely of theoretical interest; they are also an important aspect of how musicians talk and think about communicating in music. In chapter 3, for example, we talked about the structural affinities between improvisational musical process and conversation in the context of drummer Ralph Peterson's comment that "the [musical] conversation happens in fragments and comes from different parts, different voices" (Peterson 1989b). Peterson's comment came after I had mentioned that a particular passage sounded like a reference to Dizzy Gillespie's "Salt Peanuts." The phrase that reminded me of "Salt Peanuts" (musical example 11, mm. 9–11) was contained in Geri Allen's response to Peterson's Art Blakey rhythm. When I mentioned "Salt Peanuts," Peterson knew exactly which musical passage I had in mind, but he focused on a different set of details to explain his musical thinking. The shared but different musical association was not merely fortuitous since there is a musical relationship between the Gillespie riff and the Art Blakey rhythm: the rhythmic accentuation of "Salt Peanuts" (musical example 12, m. 1) corresponds to the accentuation pattern in measures 3 and 4 of the Art Blakey rhythm (musical example 13). My point is that intermusical relationships need not be exact or unambiguously shared in order for them to be communicative. The fact that we both had intermusical associations with this passage is what made it a topic of discussion.

The ability of some musicians to pick up on one another's ideas, to find chemistry in their musical affinities, seems in part the result of this intermusical component of musical perception. According to

Peterson, "In time, through playing together, what you develop is the ability to play the same; to be *thinking* the same phrase" (Peterson 1989b). Sir Roland Hanna made this point too when he observed, "There's a curious thing about musicians. We train ourselves over a period of years to be able to hear rhythms and anticipate combinations of sounds before they actually happen" (Hanna 1989). The idea that intermusical associations are part of the musical communication process during performance highlights the practical—and not merely theoretical—implications of the ideas of intermusicality. Peterson and Hanna in effect explain that recognition of familiar rhythmic, melodic, harmonic, textural, or gestural ideas (the intermusical conversation over time) underlies a social process of developing musical ideas between individuals in performance (the conversation in the present) and underscores what an intimate experience jazz improvisation can be for its players. This combination of reference and interactive musical responsiveness is something particularly characteristic of improvisational musics.

Traditional accounts of the relationship between music and language have interpreted the ability to anticipate musical ideas as syntactical rather than social (Meyer 1956). My emphasis on intermusical, intertextual, and cultural aspects of musical interpretation in part aims to correct what I see as an artificial opposition between these two components, the formal and the social. Form never exists without its social component, its dialogic relationship to the other forms of discourse in its social world, both in the present and over time. The improvisational process in jazz underscores this point in a particularly vivid manner: the shape of a musical performance is the product of human beings interacting through music both in time and over time. While more textual or novelistic forms of musical creation (such as scores written by single authors) also have intermusical aspects, improvisational music-making processes raise these issues more directly, demanding that musical scholars rethink some of their analytical presumptions.

Intercultural Relationships

As we have seen, jazz improvisation frequently draws upon repertories outside of African American music, often signifying upon them in the assertion of an African American musical aesthetic. In this context, intermusical relationships may be intercultural relationships as well.

The cultural knowledge of African American musicians includes familiarity with both "black" and "white" music, and it is upon *all* of this
knowledge that a musician draws in the act of performance. This is
what I mean when I say that music making is an active participant in
cultural discourse. What Kobena Mercer recently argued in the case
of African American hairstyles applies to the situation in African
American music as well:

> Black practices of aesthetic stylization are intelligible at
> one "functional" level as dialogic responses to the racism
> of the dominant culture, but at another level involve acts
> of appropriation from that same "master" culture through
> which "syncretic" forms of diasporean culture have
> evolved. (Mercer 1990, 257)

In much jazz historical literature, an essentialized concept of African American culture has been mapped onto an essentialized concept
of musical detail: here we find jazz writers such Hugues Panassié
(1942) speaking of the black rhythm and white harmony, black talent
and white knowledge. As one of the musicians I interviewed remarked
in passing, "If a black man knows some shit, that's talent. If the white
guy knows the same shit, he's smart." At the heart of the problem is
the inability to recognize that the heterogeneity of musical elements
found in jazz improvisation is deeply related to the heterogeneity of
African American cultural experiences. The jazz experience has always
been more varied and cosmopolitan than many of the narratives that
have been written about it.

It is no accident, then, that the double consciousness of which Du
Bois wrote has inspired several recent African American cultural critics. bell hooks remarked on the problem of "authentic" African American identity in describing her experience as the only black student in
a writing class.

> Whenever I read a poem written in the particular dialect
> of southern black speech, the teacher and fellow students
> would praise me for using my "true," authentic voice, and
> encouraged me to develop this "voice," to write more of
> these poems. From the outset this troubled me. . . . It
> seemed that many black students found our situations
> problematic precisely because our sense of self, and by
> definition our voice, was not unilateral, monologist, or

static but rather multi-dimensional. We were as at home in
dialect as we were in standard English. (hooks 1989,
11–12)

The "opposing aesthetics" that Byron mentioned are examples of
divergent cultural knowledges that coexist in particular individuals.
The ways in which individuals choose to take action with this knowledge are highly variable and change from context to context. The extensive jazz literature devoted to categorizing what in the music is
"white" and what is "black" is fundamentally flawed from this perspective. The question that has animated these discussions must be
reformulated: instead of asking which components belong to an essentialized category of "black" or "white," we must ask, In what way do
jazz musicians draw upon multidimensional cultural and musical
knowledge in the articulation of particular aesthetics and ideological
positions in music? How do we then draw boundaries (however flexible
and contested) around a particular aesthetic, which may include participants from many ethnic and racial groups? It seems to me that
the polymusicality of many jazz musicians—and by this I extend
Mantle Hood's term to mean the ability to play in multiple musical
styles (Hood 1960)—should not be seen as a liquidation of cultural
identity but rather as an important component of the cultural identity
of a cosmopolitan group. The aesthetic and value system by which all
these heterogeneous musical and cultural elements are integrated and
evaluated form the analytical level at which one can begin to speak of
cultural identities.

At a time when scholars in the fields of anthropology, ethnomusicology, and cultural studies are radically rethinking the very idea of culture, it seems to me that this close reading of the musical and human
aspects of jazz improvisation has a great deal to offer the rethinking
of these basic concepts. As I have tried to stress in this chapter, there
is an ongoing tension between the general and the particular (Bakhtin's
centripetal and centrifugal) that plays out in specific ways in jazz improvisation, the music industry, and the larger context of racial relations in the United States.

Some anthropologists have called for the complete dismantling of
the concept of culture, arguing that to identify differences between self
and other is necessarily to place the two in a hierarchical relationship
(Abu-Lughod 1991). Recall Toni Morrison's observation (cited near

the beginning of this chapter) that the denial of difference might be taken as a "generous, liberal gesture," but in the context of American society it has resulted in a "shadowless participation in the dominant cultural body" by African Americans. The denial of difference in a cultural field such as jazz, in which African Americans have always been dominant, has often resulted in a failure to acknowledge the influence of African American cultural sensibilities on American society more broadly. To make a fetish of the differences between African Americans and non–African Americans, however, is equally problematic.

We turn now to bringing these various conversations back together, relating the intercultural to the intermusical to the interactive within the context of a more extended musical example.

chapter five
interaction, feeling, and musical analysis

These lines in terms of what's *pure* jazz are not necessarily as hard and fast as some folks would want to believe.

(HARRIS 1992)

By the way, I don't think that anybody has the right to tell anyone else what jazz is. You know what I mean? Like what some motherfuckers say: "Well, that ain't jazz, the one over here is jazz." Anybody who says that about anybody is *fucked up.*

(BYRON 1989)

Despite Harris's and Byron's observations about the boundaries of jazz, the historical literature has by and large attempted to prove the opposite—that jazz is a distinctive, "pure," autonomous, strictly defined genre that can be distinguished from the musics surrounding it.[1] The chapter titles to Gunther Schuller's classic *Early Jazz* (1968) illustrate the teleological framework that has informed much historical discussion about jazz: "The Origins," "The Beginnings," "The First Great Soloist," "The First Great Composer." The music progresses from "simple" to "complex," from collective improvisation to solo improvisation, from elaborating the melody to elaborating a chord progression, from a folk music to an art music, from a music with fuzzy, eclectic beginnings to a clearly bounded art form. The object of many such accounts was to construct a narrative history of jazz that would legitimate the music in terms of elite American cultural and aesthetic values. As Scott DeVeaux has emphasized, metaphors of growth, evolution, and organicism pervade these accounts (DeVeaux 1991, 535, 541).

Schuller's *Early Jazz* (1968) exemplifies this aspect of jazz historiography and its paradoxes. This work provided the most musically detailed and insightful account of jazz history to that date. Schuller's account of Louis Armstrong's achievements illustrates the critical framework he brought to the music:

> The clarion call of *West End Blues* served notice that jazz had the potential capacity to compete with the highest order of previously known musical expression. Though nurtured by the crass entertainment and night-club world of the Prohibition era, Armstrong's music transcended this context and its implications. This was music for music's sake, not for the first time in jazz, to be sure, but never before in such a brilliant and unequivocal form. The beauties of this music were those of any great, compelling musical experience: expressive fervor, intense artistic commitment, and an intuitive sense for structural logic, combined with superior instrumental skill. By whatever definition of art—be it abstract, sophisticated, virtuosic, emotionally expressive, structurally perfect—Armstrong's music qualified. (Schuller 1968, 89)

Schuller's line of reasoning presupposes an omniscient perspective from which a hearer might assess whether jazz meets the modernist criteria of "real art." The values he cites—expressive fervor, artistic commitment, structural logic, virtuosity—are all criteria derived from ideas of German romanticism and modernism about absolute and autonomous music and the artist as genius. Ethnomusicologists have long remarked that these supposedly "timeless" artistic values actually articulate a culturally specific notion of musical art, not an objective, universal framework. Musicologists are also increasingly recognizing the cultural and historical construction of aesthetic forms and values. The criteria cited by Schuller were hegemonic in Western classical music circles at the time Schuller was writing, but they have become contested in musical scholarship today.

The irony of the deeply intercultural dilemma in which African

American musical history is embedded is that there are many aspects of this Western aesthetic ideal that jazz improvisation and composition have embodied very well, as Schuller's praise indicates. His account of Armstrong's emergence as "the first great soloist" praises him for the "impeccable design" of his solos (Schuller 1968, 92), for expanding the role of solo improvisation, for leading an inchoate form into a "unified style" (99), for his "intuitive grasp of musical logic and continuity" (103), and for his "superior choice of notes and the resultant shape of his lines" (91).

That these same musical standards can be used in a more pejorative manner is illustrated by Schuller's often cited article "Sonny Rollins and the Challenge of Thematic Improvisation" (1986). While praising Rollins for his individual transcendence, Schuller deprecates the work of jazz artists who do not meet his "timeless" criteria.

> Simple or not, this kind of extemporization has led to a critical situation: to a very great extent, improvised solos—even those that are in all other respects very imaginative—have suffered from a general lack of over-all cohesiveness and direction—the lack of unifying force. . . . Successful exceptions have only served to emphasize the relative failure of less inspired improvisations. These have been the victims of one or perhaps all of the following symptoms: (1) The average improvisation is mostly a stringing together of unrelated ideas; (2) Because of the *independently* spontaneous character of most improvisation, a series of solos by different players within a single piece have very little chance of bearing any relation to each other . . . ; (3) In those cases where composing (or arranging) is involved, the body of interspersed solos generally has no relation to these non-improvised sections; (4) Otherwise interesting solos are often marred by a sudden quotation from some completely irrelevant material. (Schuller 1986, 87).

Schuller chose to focus on Sonny Rollins's "Blue 7" in this piece because he heard thematic continuities in Rollins's playing that he found absent in what he clearly considered to be "lesser," nonthematic jazz improvisations. In seeking to prove to classically oriented listeners that jazz improvisation is music of merit, he deprecates jazz improvisers who may not share his aesthetic criteria. In the passage that follows, he even goes so far as to insult the intellectual capacities of musicians who choose to play with a different aesthetic.

> I have already said that this [lack of thematic coherence] is not altogether deplorable (I wish to emphasize this), and we have seen that it is possible to create pure improvisations which are meaningful realizations of a well-sustained over-all feeling. Indeed, the majority of players are perhaps not temperamentally or intellectually suited to do more than that. (Schuller 1986, 88)

It is not that Schuller does not recognize the role of African American contributions to the music; he devotes the first chapter of *Early Jazz* to pondering African and European elements in jazz music, and he recognizes the timbral and rhythmic distinctiveness of African American music. But when it comes to critical evaluation, he looks first to the supposedly universal standards of Western musical analysis and cites them as evidence of the value of jazz music. As an outside observer, he feels entitled to evaluate the musical production of jazz musicians by these standards without asking whether these indeed are the sole—or even the most important—criteria to musicians and their audiences. The fact that these aspects of jazz can be partially explained by the musical preoccupations it shares with Western classical music (such as harmonic and melodic sophistication, notions of melodic development, cohesiveness, virtuosity, and the notion of genius) leaves unexplored the particular logic of improvisational music making.

I do not mean to single out Schuller as an individual; he is simply the most prolific and visible exponent of a larger intellectual trend in jazz historiography that has left the evaluative standards of Western musical scholarship relatively unquestioned (Owens 1974; Tirro 1974). My purpose here is to suggest that a communicative perspective in its broadest sense can provide a point of departure for exploring the relatively neglected—yet aesthetically central—interactive aspects of jazz improvisation. I wish not simply to criticize what has already been done but to offer a vision of a potentially productive direction for jazz scholarship.[2]

Recent scholarship, in fact, has done much to erode several persistent sociocultural myths in jazz historiography. Burton Peretti's carefully documented *The Creation of Jazz* (1992), for example, takes issue with the ideas that early jazz was a single, autonomous repertory (39), that early jazz musicians were "untutored" (103–7), and that the jazz community was a subculture in relation to mainstream American life (120–44). Peretti explores the difference in perspectives between black and white musicians and in so doing challenges the tenability of teleological ideas about jazz history—that jazz has progressed in some inexorable way from "simple" to "complex," from folk music to art music. Perhaps most important, however, Peretti recognizes that jazz history challenges traditional ideas about what is mainstream in American cultural life:

> The story of early jazz is unusual in American cultural history. Our historiographical tradition has invariably treated white history as the mainstream of the American past, but white jazz history is an appendix to an African-American mainstream. In creating jazz, black players exercised a kind of cultural leadership in America that has rarely been permitted or acknowledged. (177)

In Peretti's view, the tenacity of the idea that the jazz world is "deviant" and "exotic" is in part explained by the fact that observers have interpreted the musical world from a white cultural perspective. "As they observed swinging, colorful musicians," he writes, "what white Americans thought was a novel jazz subculture was often actually a group of professionals strongly influenced by the *African-American* mainstream" (130).

"Bass-ment Blues"

Into this context I drop a particular performance entitled "Bass-ment Blues," which I have mentioned in earlier chapters. This piece was recorded by the Jaki Byard Quartet on Thursday, 15 April 1965, at Lennie's on the Turnpike, a jazz club located in West Peabody, Massachusetts.[3] The band included Jaki Byard on piano, George Tucker on bass, Alan Dawson on drums, and Joe Farrell on flute. Recording engineer Dick Alderson and producer Don Schlitten of Prestige Records taped on Thursday and Friday nights, although the quartet began the engagement at the club on Monday (Gitler 1965, 1967; Byard 1990; Bruyninckx 1980). Two albums were created from these two nights of recording—*Live! Vol. 1, The Jaki Byard Quartet, and Live! Vol. 2, The*

Jaki Byard Quartet, which have recently been reissued on one CD (Byard 1965)—but only ten of the twenty-six tunes recorded were released (Bruyninckx 1980). Byard expresses a common frustration among musicians about unreleased recordings: "There's a guy in California's got tapes of it. They plan to put them out some day, as soon as they can get their act together. Some cats, boy, you know. That's the business" (Byard 1990).

When interviewing Byard in 1990, I played the opening of "Bassment Blues," since it embodied so well the interactive musical playfulness that I was interested in getting musicians to talk about. Byard's dissonant cluster voicings intertwine with George Tucker's bass solo, leading provocatively and humorously to an ensemble peak accented in the twelfth and thirteenth choruses by Joe Farrell's dissonant flute entrances and Alan Dawson's sympathetic drumming. Byard remembered the engagement at Lennie's on the Turnpike very well and was clearly pleased to hear the recording. I wanted to know what factors he saw as contributing to the excitement of the performance:

> Swing . . . that intensive feeling of producing rhythmic excitement . . . one of the most important parts of improvisation, especially when you're playing this kind of . . . music, which is supposed to provide swing and a beat. . . . It just gives you that feeling. (Byard 1990)

The feeling in the performance is overwhelming, despite the fact that the piano at Lennie's left a great deal to be desired:

> Oh, man, it was fantastic. And all the time the piano was going out of tune, out of tune, out of tune. So finally the cat [the club owner] bought a piano. Bought a brand-new piano. He said, "Well, the next time you come in here we'll have a new piano[!]" [pause] Lennie. Lennie's on the Turnpike . . . yeah, that was swinging. (Byard 1990)

Figure 6 is an intuitive schematic diagram of the intensification occurring over the course of the performance that provides a visual image of what music analysts might call *large-scale development.* The peaks that occur toward the end of the bass, flute, and piano solos illustrate that several climactic points occur during the performance. In analytic discussion of through-composed scores, the identification of such structural articulations and formal coherences has been among the

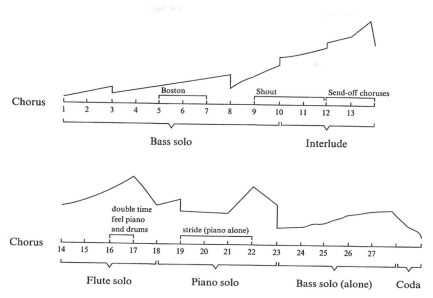

Figure 6   Musical intensification in "Bass-ment Blues"

most important criteria in defending the aesthetic and artistic merits of particular musical works. Jan LaRue (1970) has termed this level of style analysis "growth," which he distinguishes from "form." Growth, in LaRue's framework, includes the ideas of movement (motion created through micro-level musical activity) and shape (the larger-scale form that results from this musical activity). LaRue puts it more poetically: *"Musical Shape is the memory of Movement"* (115).

In rethinking analytic priorities for approaching the larger-scale dimensions of jazz improvisation, I would like to suggest that we not be content with identifying structural shapes alone; we should be concerned as well with the interactive processes by which they emerge. I am using *intensification* as a deliberately amorphous term that combines musical events internal to a particular performance that contribute to the feeling of musical climax (such as changes in dynamics, rhythmic density, register, timbre, melody, harmony, interaction, and style of groove) with intermusical aspects of performance (such as quotation, irony, and parody) that link it to issues of history and the African American sensibilities of "taking it to another level"[4] and grooving.

Musical example 16. Four melodic ideas in "Bass-ment Blues."

1. Measures 1–2

2. Measures 3–4

3. Measure 5

4. Measure 11–12

The following discussion of "Bass-ment Blues" attempts to capture this dual musical intensification as a product of the interactive relationships examined in the previous two chapters. The transcription of the first thirteen choruses of "Bass-ment Blues" makes visible the conversation in time, while Jaki Byard's musical history directs us to the conversation over time and its intermusical ramifications. It is my contention that much more than musical shape results from these interactive and communicative relationships in jazz improvisation.

The view begins with the bottom of the band and bassist George Tucker. In the first chorus of this twelve-bar blues in G, Tucker introduces four melodic ideas that are reused and transformed throughout the solo (musical example 16). These ideas amount to the head of the tune, for which Tucker and Byard share compositional credit. The first melodic/rhythmic figure emphasizes the fifth degree of the scale (d) in swing eighth notes and descends diatonically to the lower octave (mm. 1–2).[5] The second idea ascends and descends in triplets and chromatic passing tones through the range of a tenth (d2–f3–d2; mm. 3–4); the third idea repeats in triplets a chromatic ascent between the flat 7 and the tonic of the subdominant (C7) chord (b-♭2 and c3; m. 5).[6] The fourth melodic/rhythmic figure is characterized by repeated quarter-note triplets on the same pitch, two beats in length (mm. 11–12).[7]

Musical example 17. "Bass-ment Blues." Jaki Byard and George Tucker.
(*The Jaki Byard Quartet Live! Vol.2.* Prestige PR-7477.
Recorded: West Peabody, MA, 15 April 1965.)

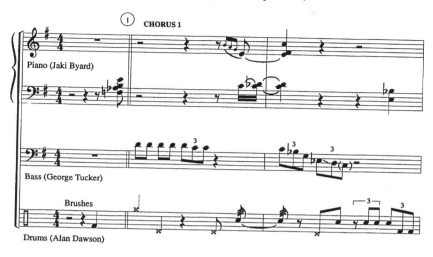

In musical example 17, Tucker establishes the pulse with the repeated eighth notes in the first three beats of measure 1, and Alan
Dawson plays time with brushes—a timbral choice that avoids over-
powering the bass solo. Jaki Byard comps sparingly, sustaining in diatonic clusters the harmonic extensions of the tonic chord (I 7 13) in a
relatively high registral position (for example, m3). His sustained
chords provide contrast to the swinging timeline established between
Tucker and Dawson in the first chorus.

Dawson anticipates and reinforces Tucker's continuing triplet
rhythms in measures 5 and 6 by playing a triplet-based fill between the
snare, tom-toms, and bass drum. Dawson's accentuation of every other
triplet eighth note in measure 6 creates two levels of rhythmic interest.
On the first, he reinforces the flow of triplet eighths in the solo bass
line; on the second, his accentuation on the snare articulates a quarter-
note triplet against this flow that pushes toward completion on beat
3 of this measure. Dawson could not have known for sure whether
Tucker would continue with eighth notes in measure 6 but correctly
anticipated that he would. A rhythmic unity that supports the completion of Tucker's solo phrase thus occurs between the parts in measure
6—certainly a less frequent location for a drum fill than measures 4,

Musical example 17. *Continued*

8, or 11 and 12 in a twelve-bar blues. The fact that these musicians
had played the tune several times earlier in the week at Lennie's no
doubt enhanced their sensitivity to each other's phrasing.

Musicians often describe such moments as "ESP," something that
"just happens," or a reflection on their musical and personal compatibility with another musician. While Dawson's decision to play triplets
in measure 6 might be predicted in a syntactic sense by the repetition

Musical example 17. *Continued*

of triplets in Tucker's line and the completion of a two-measure phrase in measure 6 of the blues chorus structure, there is nothing that could have predicted the *exact* choices made by these individual musicians. Such spontaneous, fortuitous moments of coming together or hooking up are highly prized by musicians.

Another example of a responsive moment occurs in measures 11 and 12 when George Tucker plays a turnaround figure and Dawson

Musical example 17. *Continued*

interjects a two-measure fill that leads into the top of the second chorus. In a blues, the final two measures of the twelve-bar structure is the standard location for such a figure. Tucker plays scale degrees 3̂, 6̂, 5̂ in a quarter-note triplet rhythm—a line that works effectively with the iii7–VI7, ii7–V7 harmonic progression, a typical turnaround progression in these measures. It is not surprising that Tucker played à turnaround pattern and Dawson played a drum fill in measures 11 and

Musical example 17. *Continued*

12 since these general events are expected at this location within the
time cycle. The relationship between the turnaround and the drum
part, however, most likely derived from Dawson's picking up on the
quarter-note triplets played by Tucker in measure 11. Dawson revealed
himself to be a responsive player, one who listens, when he incorporated a quarter-note triplet into his drum fill in measure 12 that responded directly to Tucker. He could instead have played many other

Musical example 17. *Continued*

rhythmic patterns that would have fulfilled the syntactic function of completing the two-measure fill.

An Invocation of Charles Mingus
In the second chorus (mm. 13–24), Tucker continues with a two-measure phrase in triplets that expands upon the descending portion of the second melodic/rhythmic idea in musical example 16. In mea-

Musical example 17. *Continued*

sures 15 and 16 he repeats the opening portion of this gesture but varies the second measure of the phrase in a manner that condenses the ascending/descending shape of this idea. He expands upon the third melodic/rhythmic idea from the first chorus in measure 17: the chromatic triplets ascending from b-flat to c. Against this figure Byard plays a direct quotation from the melody of Charles Mingus's "Fables of Faubus," beginning in the first subdominant measure of the chorus

Musical example 17. *Continued*

(m. 17). The melody of another composition here functions as an accompaniment.

It is not surprising that the melody of "Fables of Faubus" was in Byard's mind, for in 1965 he was finishing an intensive three-year stint with Mingus's band.[8] Approximately one month after the Lennie's engagement, Byard recorded his last session with Mingus (1965), who

Musical example 17. *Continued*

had a reputation for being exceptionally difficult to work for, both musically and personally. Byard may also have been complimenting
Tucker by suggesting musically that what he was playing was on the
level of Mingus. For listeners familiar with the Mingus tune, this moment stands out.

As Byard completes the phrase from "Fables of Faubus" in measure
19, Dawson intensifies his accompaniment by playing a triplet figure

Musical example 17. *Continued*

between the snare and hi-hat that reinforces Tucker's triplets. The pro-
ductivity of the communicative or call–response idea can be seen here
between the two accompanists as well as between each accompanist
and the soloist. While Byard presents the "Fables of Faubus" melody,
Dawson plays time very simply, but as Byard completes the phrase,
Dawson becomes more active. Byard in turn comps simply while Daw-

Musical example 17. *Continued*

son explores the triplet idea with Tucker, which leads to Dawson's apt fill into the third chorus in measure 24. The point to underscore here is that whether we think of these moments as conversation or as call–response, an interactive idea that is restricted to binary communicative pairs won't serve our purposes. The trading between soloist and accompanist, accompanist and accompanist—between relatively free

Musical example 17. *Continued*

and relatively stable musical ideas—permeates the entire ensemble. The accompanists can choose to play in a concerted fashion with or in counterpoint to the soloist, or in a more conversational manner among themselves and the soloist.

Time Cycles, or Getting On by Getting Off: Choruses 3–6

In the liner notes to the first volume of the Lennie's recordings, Ira Gitler emphasizes Byard's spontaneous arranging from the bandstand

Musical example 17. *Continued*

during the engagement: "You can hear Byard living his role of bandleader to the hilt: calling out for one musician to play here; another
to come in there; and routing the path of each number spontaneously.
Jaki is an imaginative arranger, and here Byard the bandleader calls
forth the services and talent of Byard the instant arranger" (Gitler
1965). What Gitler does not mention is that this band-leading style
requires great flexibility and responsiveness from the other musicians.

Musical example 17. *Continued*

"Bass-ment Blues" provides an extraordinary opportunity to document the way in which a band can collectively remedy confusions in performance while at the same time transcending them and generating an exceptionally rich musical texture. Paradoxically, as many musicians commented, "mistakes" in jazz improvisation not infrequently have as their consequence extraordinarily positive, spontaneous musical events. There are two such mistakes in "Bass-ment Blues," but

Musical example 17. *Continued*

it is apparent that the entire spirit of the evening was, as Byard re-
called, "out" and musically adventurous in a purposeful fashion (Byard 1991).

A glance at figure 6 illustrates the contrast in intensity in the third
chorus: while the first two choruses build up energy, the third subsides
to highlight George Tucker alone. Tucker begins the chorus with a

Musical example 17. *Continued*

melodic figure in quarter-note triplets that is related rhythmically to the fourth melodic idea in musical example 16. Dawson and Byard drop out, leaving Tucker to play completely solo. By the beginning of the fourth chorus (m. 37), Tucker is out of phase, with the twelve-bar chorus structure being kept by Byard and Dawson. There are multiple ways to explain what occurs between choruses 3 and 7. I have notated

Musical example 17. *Continued*

one of these, which suggests that Tucker adds two beats to the eighth measure of the third chorus (m. 32), but the situation is further complicated by the fact that when Tucker begins his fifth chorus, he is six beats ahead of where chorus 5 would have been had he maintained a consistent twelve-bar form. When Byard snaps his fingers at the beginning of what should have been chorus 4, we hear that he is maintaining the original chorus structure in his mind and is aware that there is a

Musical example 17. *Continued*

discrepancy between his time keeping and Tucker's. From this moment until a consistent chorus structure is reestablished at the beginning of chorus 7, the band's interactional challenge is to figure out how they are going to get back together, although this process of coordination is not easily audible to the listener. Indeed, Tucker's line is phrased so musically, Byard's comping so compelling, and Dawson's interjections

Musical example 17. *Continued*

so tasteful that I was not aware of the problem until I began working on transcribing choruses 3 and 4.

My explanation begins with what is obvious in the midst of the confusion in choruses 3 through 6: that Tucker articulates the harmonic structure of a twelve-bar blues beginning in measure 47, six beats ahead of where the original top of the chorus would have been and where Byard's chorus 5 does begin. In musical example 17, I have la-

Musical example 17. *Continued*

beled the harmonic progression above Tucker's line to indicate clearly where he hears his chorus. Byard and Dawson maintain the original chorus structure, just as any rhythm section would do. In general, rhythm section players are reluctant to make changes in the chorus structure, since in performances that use these structures as the basis of improvisation, the time cycle is the fixed element against which the

Musical example 17. *Continued*

entire performance is structured. When a soloist makes a mistake in keeping the form, the accompanying members will generally try to articulate the structure more clearly so that the soloist can get back on. When (as happens here) a soloist *remains* in a different spot in the time cycle over several choruses, however, a sensitive band will adjust to the soloist, even if he or she is technically incorrect within the context of

Musical example 17. *Continued*

the original time cycle. Although mistakes in keeping the form are not that frequent, the importance of the ability to recover from these moments is something that several musicians mentioned.

Bassist and guitarist Jerome Harris talked about an error in form that occurred during a sound check:

Musical example 17. *Continued*

We were playing this tune . . . in the sound check. . . . So,
the leader soloed a little bit, someone else soloed a little
bit, and the piano player soloed a little bit, and for some
reason the piano player just stayed in the A section of the
tune—did *not* go to the bridge *ever,* for his whole solo.
And he was like *into* it. . . . I wasn't playing bass, I was

Musical example 17. *Continued*

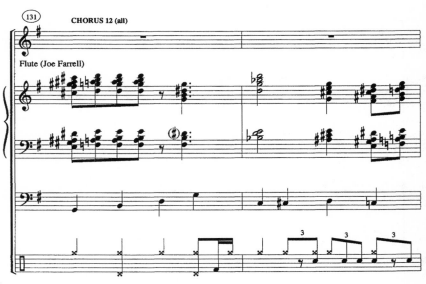

Musical example 17. *Continued*

Musical example 17. *Continued*

Musical example 17. *Continued*

Musical example 17. *Continued*

Musical example 17. *Continued*

playing guitar, at this particular time, . . . and the pianist
was so *into* what he was doing. . . . The bass player tried to
play the bridge, you know, for a minute, but it didn't matter. . . . He couldn't hear him well enough, or wasn't listening to him, wasn't paying attention—whatever. . . .
[There was] nothing we could do but just laugh and keep
playing that section and keep seeing—"Well, is he going
to go to the bridge now?" (Harris 1989)

Harris thus emphasized that keeping the band together was more important than keeping rigidly to the form in such circumstances. Ralph
Peterson concurred:

It's more musical to be wrong and go with everybody else's
wrong and make it right from that point . . . than it is to
stay *right* when everybody else is wrong . . . just to prove
that you know where you are. . . . That's actually a very ar-
rogant attitude . . . because in trying to show your knowledge you're really exhibiting your ignorance . . . in terms
of your musicianship. (Peterson 1989a)

By the beginning of his sixth chorus (m. 59), Tucker is aware that Byard and Dawson's chorus structure is different from his and that the accompanists are listening for an opportunity to get back into proper phase. Indeed, Byard's choice of a simple "Boston-style" accompaniment at the beginning of chorus 5 (m. 48) seems designed to promote the reestablishment of the chorus structure.[9] Had there not been a conflict in the time cycles, Byard may not have chosen to go into such a rhythmically and harmonically clear accompaniment style.

The adjustment occurs when Tucker plays an obvious two-measure turnaround (3̂6̂2̂5̂; mm. 71–72) after completing the twelve-measure chorus that began in measure 59. Byard and Dawson respond to the musical signal by adjusting to Tucker: they add two beats to the twelfth measure of their sixth chorus, and the three musicians establish the top of the seventh chorus together (m. 73). The musicality of these choruses despite the time discrepancy is worth noting. So convincing is the ensemble's out-of-phase playing that in measure 68 the audience's delight at the trio's musical punctuation is clearly audible. The poise that enabled Tucker to realize that something was amiss and correct it through a musical signal—as well as Byard's and Dawson's ability to respond to it—demonstrates the great flexibility and resourcefulness of these players. More inexperienced players would more likely have produced a train wreck under similar circumstances.

Once the time cycle is re-established, the accompaniment in chorus 7 becomes, not surprisingly, freer. Dawson, who throughout choruses 5 and 6 kept time with his hi-hat and punctuated with the bass drum, stops playing time and begins an accompaniment that resembles comping. Byard's offbeat chords in the upper register anticipate Tucker's phrasing in measures 73 through 76. In measure 74, Byard's chord matches Tucker's phrase ending on the second half of beat 2; in measure 75, Byard anticipates Tucker's eighth note on the second half of beat 4. Dawson's rhythmic figure in the first half of measure 76 responds to both Tucker's melody beginning in the second half of beat 4 (m. 75) and Byard's chord at the same location. In a similar fashion, there is an interplay between Tucker's phrasing in measures 76 through 78 and Byard's and Dawson's comping.

In chorus 8 (m. 85), the intensification that has built steadily since chorus 3 (see figure 6) subsides as Jaki Byard and Alan Dawson change timbres and stop articulating a time feel. Byard plays sparingly in sustained chords, and Dawson switches to a sizzle cymbal accompaniment

(m. 87). Byard's and Dawson's attacks tend to occur at the endings of Tucker's phrases (mm. 86, 88). In measure 91, Byard's attack matches the completion of Tucker's triplet figure (beat 1), another example of successful rhythmic anticipation.

In the last four measures of the chorus (mm. 93–96), Tucker plays a rhythmic line in strongly swinging eighth notes that signals to Byard Tucker's intention to continue the next chorus in a more swinging fashion. Byard picks up on this moment by playing a rolled riff-style piano accompaniment figure in measure 94. Tucker confirms this expectation in measure 95 by playing a quarter-note triplet figure in double stops, audibly related to the fourth melodic idea in musical example 16. The drive for intensification occurs in a syntactically expected position—the last four measures of the chorus—as the players push toward the beginning of the next chorus.

Call and Response: Chorus 9

By the beginning of chorus 9, the intensity level has increased considerably. Drummer Alan Dawson reacts to Tucker's triple-stopped call figure in measure 97 by interjecting a snare roll in the space Tucker leaves (m. 98). In measure 98, Byard plays a response phrase resembling a shout chorus–style riff figure. Byard and Tucker phrase their call and response in two-measure units, but note that both Tucker's and Byard's phrases are six beats in length: Byard's first two beats complete the second measure of the bass phrase, while his next four overlap the beginning of Tucker's second call phrase (m. 101). Dawson's drum interjections provide a third voice in this rhythmic interplay, with snare figures tending to come two beats before Byard's response (mm. 98, 100). Nevertheless, the interlocking call-and-response pattern between Byard and Tucker defines the intensified feeling of the chorus. In terms of the fixed/free, solid/liquid contrast we talked about in chapter 2, Byard articulates a relatively stable time-keeping figure that enables the remaining musicians to play more freely if they so desire. Dawson, for example, interjects more assertive snare figures than in the previous chorus.

On-the-Spot Arranging: Big-Band Shout Choruses

The interlude between George Tucker's bass solo and the beginning of Joe Farrell's flute solo illustrates what Ira Gitler meant when he called Byard an instant arranger. Byard saw these choruses as exemplifying a big band sound: shout-style riffs in thick, close voicing that resemble those used for the brass in arranged big-band shout choruses.[10] Byard directed the band in these choruses—for which he clearly had a plan—with verbal instructions in measure 103 to "walk it." Byard explained:

> I had asked for that type of thing. . . . I had told Alan . . . "Man, just play as many polyrhythms as you can, and if I ask you to walk backbeat or something like that, would you do it?" And he said yes. And if that person is . . . a cooperator . . . there's no problem. . . . There's some drummers that I might play with, or bass players that . . . I wouldn't ask . . . to follow my lead or to be sympathetic. (Byard 1990)

George Tucker gets off again by beginning a two-measure turnaround in response to Byard in measure 105, two measures earlier than its expected location. (Measure 105 is measure 9 of the chorus; the expected location would be measure 11.) This time Byard and Dawson decide to go with Tucker's turnaround: they respond by playing measure 107 as if it were the top of the chorus two measures after the beginning of Tucker's turnaround figure. Byard marked the change with a 7 ♭9 ♯9 ♯11 13 voicing of the tonic chord (m. 107)—the first change in the riff since measure 100. Dawson articulated this point as the top of the chorus in a particularly strong manner: he changed the groove to a shuffle, with strong backbeats on beats 2 and 4. His change was marked additionally by a switch from brushes to sticks, which increased the dynamic level significantly.

In measure 107, Byard shouts "One!" indicating that the band should take that measure as the top of the chorus. Tucker, however—perhaps afraid of causing a time-cycle problem again—plays a second turnaround in measures 107 and 108, which was the correct location for the turnaround in the chorus structure established in chorus 7. Tucker begins to walk solidly in measure 109, the top of what would have been chorus 10. In view of Byard and Dawson's adjustment, however, Tucker is two measures behind at this point; Byard and Dawson continue with considerable rhythmic intensity in the new chorus structure. I would like to emphasize that the problem with the chorus structure is not particularly audible to the listener; indeed, what is truly remarkable is how this second getting off prefaces an extraordinary musical climax that takes place in choruses 12 and 13.

Byard takes over at this point with thick cluster voicings, played in a register in which trumpets and saxophones might be voiced in a big band. To his shout chorus–style calls, he sings his own responses: "Huh, yeah," "Okay," "Oh yeah." The interplay between the dissonant, hornlike cluster voicings and his parody of the energetic bandleader lends an extraordinary playfulness to these choruses. What is not so obvious is that the spaces Byard leaves in the musical texture allow him to hear Tucker's out-of-phase location in the time cycle. Tucker remains two measures behind until the end of chorus 11, a situation made obvious by his playing a turnaround in measures 119 and 120, the location that would have been appropriate to the previous chorus structure. It is also confirmed by the progression that Tucker plays in measures 121 through 124 (I–IV–I–I)—the first four measures of a twelve-bar blues progression. Byard, however, confidently leads Tucker back into place by shouting "Four!" in measure 126, signaling him that the top of the chorus would occur four bars later. Byard and Dawson maintain the chorus structure they established in measure 107. Byard makes the lead into chorus 12 absolutely transparent by playing a three-measure dominant pedal point (mm. 128–30). Tucker joins him for the first measure of the pedal point and then plays a turnaround ($\hat{1}$, $\hat{6}$, $\hat{2}$, $\hat{5}$) to lead into chorus 12.

While listening to "Bass-ment Blues" with me, Byard said as we approached chorus 12, "Now dig this. This is a send-off" (Byard 1990). *Send-off* is a term from big band arranging that refers to an ensemble passage at the beginning of a chorus, leading into a solo that begins at some point after the top of a chorus. In typical big-band usage, the ensemble continues playing into the first or second measure of a chorus, and the soloist delays her or his entrance until the phrase is completed.[11] In "Bass-ment Blues," the send-off choruses (of which there are two) are four bars in length. The general structure for them was probably talked about before the performance: the piano, bass, and drums play the first four measures of each chorus (mm. 131–34; 143–46) and set up Joe Farrell's flute entrance in the subdominant (fifth) measure of the chorus.

In chorus 12, Alan Dawson reinforces the preparation of the soloist by intensifying drum activity (mm. 133–34). Byard, however, is apparently not fully satisfied by the intensity level, for as they approach the end of this chorus, he shouts, "Here we go again," indicating to the band members that he wants to repeat the structure of the previous chorus. Byard wants more energy, and this time he gets it. George Tucker switches from a walking bass line in quarter notes to a repeating triplet figure related to the third thematic idea in musical example 16 (mm. 143–45). Alan Dawson plays a drum figure between the snare and the bass drum that reinforces the triplet figure in the bass during the same measures. Byard hammers loud tremolos in the upper register, forming a relatively stable background that allows the lower parts to continue their rhythmic development. These first four measures culminate in a drum roll that crescendos and terminates just before the flute entrance—the climax of the first five minutes of the performance (mm. 145–46).

Gitler's comments regarding the entire Lennie's recording date might just as well have been written about this passage: "Even when they go 'outside'—and Jaki knows what he is doing when he is 'out there'—they are always under firm control of the leader who is able to bring everything and everyone back 'inside' to a logical, satisfying conclusion." So impressed was Gitler that he proclaimed, "This is one of the most important records of the last five years" (Gitler 1965).[12]

Musical Trust, Musical Face

Musicians must be able to trust the musical abilities of other band members in performance, especially if they are taking musical risks. They want to be able to rely on another musician's marking of the time cycle, for example, should they momentarily lose it themselves. George Tucker would not likely have lost his place in chorus 3 if he hadn't been playing unaccompanied. In chapter 1, Michael Carvin used the words "solid" and "liquid" to describe the contrast between the relatively fixed and free rhythmic elements played on the drum set. Many musicians who participated in this study also suggested that within the rhythm section as a whole, at least one member must function on the solid side. Ralph Peterson talked about this issue:

> Another thing about bass players that's very important is
> their ability to *concentrate* when I or another member of
> the ensemble moves away from the basic pulse beat—and
> start playing against the time, if you will. It's not always
> the best idea . . . —when somebody else starts playing

against the time—to hear that and go with them, because
somebody has to stay grounded. . . . When a bass player
has the ability to concentrate and . . . the wisdom to know
when to . . . play against the time and leave *me* as the centerpoint, that's very important and it's not anything that I
would want to have to *teach* anyone. . . . It's something
that *has* to be there . . . the ability to absorb large amounts
of rhythmic variants without being thrown. (Peterson
1989a)

Published interviews with many jazz musicians also raise the issue
of trust between band members. Bassist Ron Carter, for example, has
spoken of the musical trust between him and pianist Herbie Hancock
and drummer Tony Williams: "It's a very special relationship and it
continues to grow and prosper over the years because we all maintain
our trust in each other" (Milkowski 1988, 130). About playing duets
with guitarist Jim Hall, Carter has commented:

It's the kind of situation that in order for it to succeed
each guy has to trust the other guy's sense of it all. If I
play a note, Jim has to know that I mean that note to be
there. If he plays a chord, I know he expects me to find a
note to enhance that chord because I know he means that
chord to be there. And without this level of trustworthi-
ness, in spite of talent, it's not going to be successful musically (130).

That musicians rely upon one another to orient and reorient themselves—especially when playing against the time—is apparent in the
following story about lack of trust relayed by one of the participating
musicians.[13] He described a concert in which the drummer was un-
happy with the reliability of the bass player. The bassist didn't have
very good intuition about when to provide a centerpoint and when to
play more freely. After the performance, the drummer complained
about the bass player to the musician telling the story. This person
explained the drummer's position to me:

Cause [this drummer] wants the option of not even having
to pay attention to the bass player, and come back and
have the shit be right [in the time cycle]—which means he
has to trust somebody. And he just didn't, he just didn't

trust [this bass player]. If [this bass player] had come in
kicking ass it would be another story. . . . But you know,
[this bass player] plays [himself]. . . . His strength is just
not playing real straight-ahead shit.

In rectifying the mistake that occurred in measures 107 and 108 of
"Bass-ment Blues," Tucker had to rely on the other musicians to guide
him to the new chorus structure. Jaki Byard's leadership in choruses
10 and 11 was essential in this process. Byard was able to transform
great uncertainty into a means of intensifying further; he simply would
not back off from the rhythmic intensity already generated. A lesser
musician may have faltered, but Byard's musical experience and
knowledge enabled him to respond to an unexpected situation with
great resourcefulness and musicality. In turn, Tucker and Dawson ral-
lied to support the musical direction of choruses 12 and 13 and played
an integral part in the intensification. What Ralph Peterson told me
about mistakes is germane here:

It's not what you play when you're playing, but what you
play *after* you fuck up that really counts, you know. It's
not *that* you fuck up, but how you clean it up that matters,
because a lot of times those are the most musical moments, because the desire to compensate for the . . . mistake . . . often leads to a special moment in music where
everybody begins to come to the support. (Peterson
1989b)

These choruses from "Bass-ment Blues" illustrate just such a moment, but I do not mean to imply that such intensifications are particularly the product of errors, only that taking the music to another level
is an interactive and collaborative affair. To the extent that performers
take risks and push one another, they also risk making mistakes. The
repair of these moments—having the poise to take problems and make
aesthetic virtues of them—is one of the most highly prized skills of
an improviser.[14]

When I emphasized in chapter 3 that interacting musical parts are
simultaneously interacting personalities, the human and musical vul-
nerabilities of the performance processes we have witnessed in this example were exactly what I had in mind. Erving Goffman calls such
repairs *face work,* by which he means a social process in which human
beings act collaboratively to sustain a flow of sociability and save or

enhance one another's faces (Goffman 1967, 5–45). To Goffman, the rules of social interaction are often revealed in the breach—that is, when a gaffe occurs.

> When a face has been threatened, face work must be done, but whether this is initiated and primarily carried on by the person whose face is threatened, or by the offender, or by a mere witness, is often of secondary importance. Lack of effort on the part of one person induces compensative effort from others; a contribution by one person relieves the others of the task. . . . Resolution of the situation to everyone's apparent satisfaction is the first requirement; correct apportionment of the blame is typically a secondary consideration. (27–28)

There is something very personal about jazz improvisation at its best, something very moving, both literally and figuratively. However much a musician may desire to prove himself or herself the best in relationship to his or her peers, most jazz performances involve a fundamental dependence on the cooperation of others in achieving this end. Goffman emphasizes that face is a social construct, rather than a solely individual attribute.

> A person may be said to *have,* or *be in,* or *maintain* face when the line he effectively takes presents an image of him that is internally consistent, that is supported by judgments and evidence conveyed by other participants, and that is confirmed by evidence conveyed through impersonal agencies in the situation. At such times the person's face clearly is something that is not lodged in or on his body, but rather something diffusely located in the flow of events in the encounter and becomes manifest only when these events are read and interpreted for the appraisals expressed in them. (6–7)

While much literature about jazz has emphasized the competitive or cutting quality of the relationships between jazz musicians, it is also important to remember that solidarity and emotional bonds with other musicians are emphasized when players talk about what they love best about performing, what they love most about being a part of a musical community.

Music and Emotion

Anthropologists Lila Abu-Lughod and Catherine Lutz have recently argued for a *discursive* concept of emotion, by which they mean exploring "the many ways emotion gets its meaning and force from its location and performance in the public realm of discourse" (Lutz and Abu-Lughod 1993, 7). Their thinking draws on Michel Foucault's idea that discourses should be viewed more as "practices that systematically form the objects of which they speak" than as "groups of signs" that "designate things" (Foucault 1972, 49; Lutz and Abu-Lughod 1993, 9). The discursive approach sees emotion less as an internal state than as a form of social action, with particular attention to how emotion is "*created in,* rather than shaped by, speech" (Lutz and Abu-Lughod 1993, 11–12). Borrowing Foucault's language, Abu-Lughod and Lutz are interested in the way in which emotion is constituted or constructed through social practices, especially those making use of language in socially interactive contexts. Music, it seems to me, is a particularly powerful constructor of emotion, and when I speak of music as discourse, I am adding to our idea of conversation the notion that music is a powerful activity that can produce a "community of sentiment" binding performers and audiences into something larger than the individual (Appadurai 1993).

Lutz and Abu-Lughod confirm the common-sense idea that working together as musicians, performing on stage, and being on the road can lead to strong interpersonal bonds that have as their axis competition, respect, love, hate, or solidarity. Often it is through performance, in fact, that such bonds are formed. The story of the Lennie's engagement is a case in point. Jaki Byard originally wanted to hire Richard Davis for this gig. Davis was not available, but he recommended George Tucker, who was then playing bass with Earl Hines (Gitler 1965). Byard did not have strong bonds with Tucker before the Lennie's engagement.

In choosing to use "Bass-ment Blues" as an example, I unwittingly walked into the tragedy that surrounded its release: approximately six months after the recording, George Tucker died of a cerebral hemorrhage while performing with guitarist Kenny Burrell.[15] In an obituary for Tucker, "Bass-ment Blues" and two other tunes recorded at Lennie's were cited as particularly memorable examples of Tucker's playing style (Hunt 1968). Shortly before this, Byard had also experienced the deaths of two other musicians with whom he had worked closely: alto saxophonist Eric Dolphy, who died on 29 June 1964; and trumpeter Booker Little, who died on 5 October 1961. In subsequent years, several other musicians Byard worked with in this period passed away as well: drummer J. C. Moses and tenor saxophonists Booker Ervin and Joe Farrell.[16]

After having watched Byard's enthusiasm as he listened to "Bassment Blues," I was surprised when he said that he didn't have any favorites among the musicians he plays with now: "I am able to play with anybody. . . . Now in order to satisfy *my* ego I have to adopt that attitude. That satisfies my ego—to say that I can play with anybody. I can play with anybody and I don't have any favorites" (Byard 1990). Every player I interviewed except Byard had responded to this question by identifying the individuals he or she felt especially close to musically. But then Byard continued:

> I don't want to fall in love with anybody in the business because—because, well, a situation like this. Fall in love with George Tucker and Joe Farrell and they're gone. See, so you can't fall in love with them, but you can enjoy playing with them and reaching [musical] excitement with them. . . . Oh, you're getting me into some *heavy, heavy* stuff. . . . That's one of the main reasons why after these guys passed away—Eric [Dolphy], Booker Ervin, Joe Farrell, George Tucker, and a drummer named J. C. Moses. . . . All these guys are *tremendous* musicians, and we had a ball playing with each other, you know. Now when I hear that, I say, "Oh, I feel so sad that he's gone." But he did document this, thank the powers for electricity. (Byard 1990)

Later, Byard explained that part of the reason he devoted the next phase of his career to solo piano playing was "because the guys were dying" (Byard 1991).

The depth of feeling that Byard had for the memory of this performance illustrates one aspect of the power of music to create emotion in those who make it. The point for our larger discussion is that the musical conversations we have been talking about do not concern communication solely in an abstract, semiotic sense; to conceive of music and emotion as created through interactive activities provides a way to think about musical conversations in time and over time as something other than simply linguistic properties. The relationships between interactive performance and intermusical associations are not merely "in the head" but also in the heart and the body. They are part of the process by which communities grow out of the social activities and emotions of real people.

Byard was also not the only musician who spoke of love, emotion, and family relationships in connection with favorite musical experiences. Joanne Brackeen, for example, spoke of her musical relationship with Cecil McBee: "We're close, we're extremely close, but we never talk about it. Between tunes we talk about something else. We might talk, but it's not about [music], . . . but musically it's very, very close" (Brackeen 1989). McBee remarked that "the drummer and the bass must literally develop a marriage, have a marriage on the stage, you know" (McBee 1990). The marriage metaphor recurs in Wilbur Campbell's memories of a band he had with Ira Sullivan, Nicky Hill, and Donald Garrett: "That is the unique, uncanny thing about that band; we all thought alike. We really hung together. I guess, to some extent, you could say we was all married" (Campbell 1980). Milton "Mezz" Mezzrow's recollections also make use of this image: "If you could catch a couple of cats that just met each other talking about certain musicians they know or humming a riff or two to each other, before you could call a preacher they'd be practically married" (Mezzrow and Wolfe 1946, 61).

When I asked Ralph Peterson Jr. about the dedication to Dannie Richmond that appears on his album *V* (Peterson 1988), I expected to hear talk of musical influences:

> Shortly before I signed with Toshiba, I had the honor of
> meeting Dannie and the experience for a week, a week
> and a half, was so *enriching* and so *memorable* that, quite
> frankly, I'd fallen in love with Dannie Richmond. . . . Be-
> cause his spirit seems to be very much in line with a lot of
> the things I was feeling about the music, about business,
> about the way drummers are looked at and perceived, re-
> spected or lack thereof. He gave me a lot of strength in my
> convictions." (Peterson 1989a)

The type of emotional connection identified here has most usually been glossed as male bonding or camaraderie, with the implicit assumption that the friendships stem from hanging out while in clubs or on the road. My interest is in the way the music itself contributes to the creation and maintenance of emotions and friendships between players—or, conversely, to animosities.

Richard Davis, for example, relayed a story about the "father–son" relationship that existed between Duke Ellington and tenor saxophonist Paul Gonsalves. Gonsalves evidently offended Ellington very badly one day, and when he arrived for rehearsal the next day he found Ellington playing a tune on the piano. "As hung over as he was, [Gonsalves] took his saxophone out of the case very slowly and played along with the piano player. . . . And the woman who told me the story . . . said never before in her life has she heard someone express through their instrument an apology. Like, 'Father, forgive me for I know not what I do'" (Davis 1989).

Jaki Byard provided another example of an unsuccessful attempt to mediate a conflict through playing music. He introduced the story by explaining why his wife didn't like coming to his performances with the Charles Mingus band: "It's funny to say, my wife came to the club *once,* while we were at the Five Spot and that was the last time. She didn't come any more to see us, because she didn't like the way that Mingus used to *harass* musicians, the public and me. . . . I just usually ignored him, you see. I *knew* what his temperament was all about, see, so in order to stay with him, I just tolerated some of his so-called nonsense to people." But by early 1965, Byard had had enough. Explaining that Mingus was very upset when he resigned from the band that year, Byard relayed one of the famous stories about Mingus and fire axes.[17]

> When I left him it was weird. [He] came backstage and
> took the axe and said, "Wait a minute!" I walked off the
> stand and said, "I've had it," cause I was contracting hives
> and everything. . . . So finally . . . I picked up the fire extin-
> guisher, said "Go ahead," and I pointed it at him. So he
> threw the axe down, said, "C'mon, man, let's play some
> blues." I was shaking like a *leaf,* you know. I said, "Sorry,
> I can't make it, I got to go home." (Byard 1990)

In this case, music was not enough to mediate the conflict. My point for purposes of our larger discussion, however, is that music can be centrally involved not only in the production of performances but in the establishment and maintenance of human and/or spiritual relationships.[18] I believe the creation of emotional bonds is tied to the historical contexts of performances as well.

In an interview with Dan Morgenstern that appeared in *Down Beat* (Morgenstern 1965), Byard talked about growing up in Worcester, Massachusetts, in the 1920 and 1930s.[19] He frequently went to hear the bands that came through town, among them those of Fats Waller, Fletcher Henderson, Count Basie, Jimmie Lunceford, Chick Webb, and Earl "Fatha" Hines. But, Byard commented, "The one band that really intrigued me was Fatha Hines" (Morgenstern 1965, 18). Several types of musical gestures in Earl Hines's piano-playing style—as well as the type of arrangements used in his big band—are transformed in Byard's accompaniment and solo styles. These gestures include (1) the use of stride piano style,[20] (2) thickly voiced harmonies that include harmonic tensions,[21] (3) right-hand tremolos as an accompaniment device for intensification,[22] (4) the accompaniment of horn solos with riffs, and (5) a virtuosic level of pianistic skill.

Byard was certainly familiar with the pianistic styles of Fats Waller and Art Tatum as well. Of course verbal interjections and the use of riffs as accompaniments pervaded big band performances of their period. Byard explained to Dan Morgenstern why he enjoyed making use of older piano styles:

> I can't sit there and just play single lines all night and go away satisfied. I can't play one way all night; I wouldn't want to, and I wouldn't want the public to hear me that way. If you stay in one groove, you can't reach the people. (Morgenstern 1965, 38)

Moments of resemblance between what Byard plays in "Bass-ment Blues" and the performances of Earl Hines or other big bands are primarily at the level of gesture rather than direct quotation, but Hines may have been particularly in Byard's mind since in March of 1965 Charles Mingus's band (in which Byard was still employed) and Earl Hines's band shared a week at New York's Village Vanguard. In fact, the preliminary idea for recording at Lennie's was conceived during that week. Hines was greatly impressed by Byard, and the two developed a considerable amount of rapport during the week. Hines even asked Byard to show him some of his musical ideas. As Gitler observed, "Because Hines plays as if he is a big band, it seemed to inspire

Byard to emphasize his own leanings in this direction when he got to Lennie's" (Gitler 1965).

In "Bass-ment Blues" (musical example 17), the riff figures that begin in chorus 9 (m. 97), the densely voiced shout-style passages in choruses 10 (m. 107) and 11 (m. 119), and the send-off chorus structure in choruses 12 (m. 131) and 13 (m. 143) are all in the style of the big band arrangements of the 1930s and 1940s, a repertoire that was and is very familiar to Byard. As producer Don Schlitten remarked,

> He was like a 16-piece band. One second he would be playing the piano part, and then he would resolve and sound like a saxophone section. Behind Joe Farrell he became a punching trumpet section. Throughout the whole thing he was a bandleader. Here was a quartet that sounded like three times that many. (Gitler 1965)

The tremolo figure in chorus 13 (mm. 143–45), used as something like a right-hand pedal point against which the other instruments intensify, is a device that Byard may have learned from Hines but is not a direct quotation of any particular passage, illustrating that intermusical moments are far from confined to quotation. Byard was well aware that he was drawing on tradition. When I played musical example 4 (see chapter 2) to him, he said, "That's *old,* that's a riff; it's an old big band riff" (Byard 1990).

Repertoire

We have seen that shared musical and cultural knowledges play an important part in interacting appropriately in a jazz ensemble. I would like for a moment to consider how such knowledges are acquired. Most pedagogical literature in jazz focuses upon how an individual learns to improvise, and most—like the formulaic literature—centers upon learning harmony and how to build longer melodies from smaller units. The acquisition of repertoire seldom rates more than a peripheral mention in the standard how-to books on improvisation, yet it is as important as any other element of the learning process.[23] Additionally, it is of importance in the transmission of the larger-scale conventions of musical intensification.

Since musicians most typically improvise within the context of a particular tune, a prerequisite to successful participation within a jazz

group is a repertoire of tunes that may be called by other musicians—
and the ability to play them in more than one key. While musicians do
use collections of lead sheets known as fake books and can be seen
reading these tunes from them, there are certain standard jazz compositions that musicians are expected to be able to play without their aid.
In fact, a significant loss of face occurs if a player has to read a tune
that everyone else in the band knows. Older musicians generally know
a lot more repertoire than younger musicians and can embarrass
younger players by calling a tune they don't expect.

Jaki Byard's career can serve as an illustration of how repertoire is
learned. Byard's first professional jobs in the forties were in big bands
that required him to be familiar with the repertoire of particular well-
known bands, among them those of Jimmie Lunceford and Artie Shaw
(Morgenstern 1965, 19).[24] In addition, from 1947 to 1949 he played
with Earl Bostic's big band. The conventions of big band arrangements
and accompaniments, as well as particular pieces, were consequently
extremely familiar to him. In addition, Byard has a long history of
composing for big bands and has taught orchestration and arranging
at several major conservatories.[25] By the mid-forties, Byard was also
learning the repertoire and improvisational styles of Charlie Parker
and Bud Powell, two leaders in the emerging bebop movement. Byard's
facility in bebop piano style, in fact, led to friction with Earl Bostic,
who preferred to hear more traditional playing styles from his musicians (Morgenstern 1965; Byard 1991).

By 1965, as noted previously, Byard was toward the end of an intensive three-year stint with Charles Mingus. Mingus's drummer Dannie
Richmond reported that in 1959, when Byard first played with Mingus,
there had been a high turnover of pianists in the band (Priestly 1982,
110). Mingus may have been particularly hard on pianists, since he
had very specific ideas about what he wanted the piano to do (77).
When Byard officially joined Mingus in 1962, he became a member of
a rhythm section that featured a very tight musical connection between
Mingus on bass and drummer Dannie Richmond; they were referred
to as the "Dynamic Duo" (75, 143). After Byard joined, this duo became the "Almighty Three." Although Byard apparently coined this
term, Dannie Richmond confirmed the band's high esteem for Byard
by referring to him as a genius, along with Mingus and Eric Dolphy
(143, 159).[26] On the liner notes to *Portrait* (Mingus 1965), Byard described playing with the Mingus rhythm section:

Every time we played one of those tunes, you had to be
alert and ready for constantly varying situations. Patterns
would change from time to time, and if perchance any of
us were caught off guard—watch out!! (Priestly 1982, 143)

Mingus's music frequently changed grooves and tempos, and he demanded that performances achieve great musical intensity.[27] Mingus also made verbal remarks to the musicians during performances (78–79).[28] Byard's comment about the "constantly varying situations" testifies to the degree of musicianship needed to negotiate Mingus's metric changes (frequently from 4/4 to 6/4 and back) and extreme tempos. In addition, Byard reported that as a bassist, Mingus would drop out with no warning when he wanted to rest (Byard 1991).

Mingus dictated parts to musicians by singing them or playing them on the piano and did not want the musicians to notate them. These parts were frequently very intricate and challenging for many musicians to remember (Priestly 1982, 77). Mingus was particularly well known for stopping the band during performances and publicly humiliating musicians who failed to meet his performance standards. Dannie Richmond, in fact, got his first chance to play with the band after Mingus stopped to castigate drummer Willie Jones for failing to maintain an extremely fast tempo on the tune "Cherokee" (74–75).[29]

Byard's drive for intensification in "Bass-ment Blues" is most certainly informed by the musical resources he developed while working with the often unpredictable Mingus. As noted earlier, he even included a direct quotation from Mingus's "Fables of Faubus" in chorus 2 (mm. 17–19). The point for our larger discussion is that when Jaki Byard sat down to play "Bass-ment Blues" on 15 April 1965, he brought with him at least twenty-five years of musical experience as a player, listener, and composer. Alan Dawson, George Tucker, and Joe Farrell likewise brought their individual playing and listening histories to bear on their performances. The particular course of events during any performance thus clearly depends upon a whole range of intermusical as well as synchronically interactive conditions.

Social Pragmatics and Musical Analysis

Putting all of the elements of this chapter together, I am suggesting that interactive musical conversation in real-time performance, combined with the intermusical and intercultural associations musicians and audiences bring to the conversation over time, have much to do with where the feeling in rhythmic feels comes from. The testimony of musicians and a close analysis of a performance confirm many common-sense intuitions we have about the emotional power of music, its interactive character in jazz improvisation, and the aesthetic centrality of linking sound to an ethos, cultural identity, and communities of participation. It is more difficult to talk about these issues in theoretical terms, but it seems to me that examining the implications of musicians' ideas about saying something in music requires thinking about what an interactive, relational theory of music and meaning might address. We are left, after all, with the perennial problem of the relationship of formal structures to contextual and cultural issues.

In the remainder of this chapter, I consider what one of the foremost theoreticians in linguistic anthropology, Michael Silverstein, might have to contribute to the debate between formalism and contextualism in musical scholarship. In approaching this well-traveled issue, I propose to take as a point of departure the idea that the formal features of musical texts are just one aspect—a subset, so to speak—of a broader sense of the musical, which also includes the contextual and the cultural. Rather than being conceived as foundational or separable from context, structure is taken to have as one of its central functions the *construction* of social context. In other words, there is a mutually defining relationship between structure and context, rather than one of autonomy. In taking this position, I am adapting Michael Silverstein's work on the metapragmatics of spoken language to the specific conditions of interactive musical improvisation. In theorizing about the contextual aspects of language use, Silverstein has developed a model that systematizes many of the issues we have been talking about more informally. At issue is the capacity of aural signs to signify in multiple directions—their ability to simultaneously constitute structure and a broader field of human relationships through a communicative discourse such as language or music.

Silverstein has argued that the categories of formal linguistics were designed to describe only the referential function of language, despite the fact that "the sign modes of most of what goes on in the majority of speech events are not referential" (Silverstein 1976, 15). To illustrate how the referential functions of language are context-dependent even in the most mundane of everyday speech events, Silverstein cites the contextual presuppositions of a verbal statement in the past tense: for example, "The cat ate the rat." To assert that something happened in the past presupposes the time of the present verbal statement as a point of comparison against which the time of the past is estimated, "so the referential meaning of . . . 'tense' . . . depends upon a comparison of the time referred to with the time of utterance in each speech event incorporating the token" (Silverstein 1976, 24).[30] Another example of a context-dependent index comes from the so-called deictics (*this/that, these/those*), whose meaning depends on the location of the speaker who is using them. Both examples fall under the linguistic category of shifter (or indexical denotational form), for which "the reference 'shifts' regularly, depending upon the factors of the speech situation" (24).[31] Indexicality, for Silverstein, is present in any sign (regardless of whether it is also involved in iconic or symbolic modes of signification) in that "each signal form indexes its own context-of-occurrence," either presupposing something about the context or entailing (creating) something (Silverstein 1993, 36).

The simultaneous presence of both referential and pragmatic (contextual, indexical) meaning in the same speech segment illustrates the multifunctionality of linguistic signs and the possibility that analysis of a speech segment can yield contrasting analyses from different functional points of view. Silverstein further argues against privileging the purely referential functions of language:[32]

> Once we realize that distinct pragmatic meanings yield distinct analyses of utterances, we can sever our dependence on reference as the controlling functional mode of speech, dictating our traditional segmentations and recognitions of categories. We can then concentrate on the manifold social pragmatics that are common to language and every other form of socially constituted communication in society. (Silverstein 1976, 20)

It is from this point of view that Silverstein argues that semantic (referential) meaning is a special case of pragmatic meaning—that is, the broader class of communicative meanings that may include both referential and nonreferential modalities.

In music, the traditional objects of analysis have been the parameters of musical sound most amenable to Western notation—pitch, rhythm, counterpoint, harmony—and their combinations, relations of inclusion, structural properties, and architectonic shapes. These features of musical structure and the categories in which they have been analyzed in the most widely known schools of music theory, I would argue, are epistemologically analogous to the referential function about which Silverstein speaks. They are those features of a musical text that lend themselves most readily to segmental formalization, analytic systematization, abstraction from context, and structural analysis. That these same musical features may simultaneously participate in more pragmatic musical functions is a point I wish to emphasize.

In chapter 4, I talked about the issue of musical quotation, in which the quoted musical material serves to index a prior performance iconically and place it in juxtaposition to the present.[33] This intermusical moment of allusion points to the indexical capacity of music—that is, its ability to establish through aural means a point of spatio-temporal reference relative to its context of occurrence. Indexical musical moments can also be entailing: they can point to something that may be about to occur or otherwise set up a feeling of expectation, often through metrical or harmonic means.[34] The musical token in the present (the quote or other stylistic reference) need bear no deictic or similar formal referential marking, however, and it communicates only to those who have the aural knowledge to recognize the index. In contrast to Nattiez (1990a) and Abbate (1991, 1989), therefore, I am arguing that music does indeed have the functional equivalent of a past tense and that this indexical, intermusical capacity is crucial to thinking about the constitution of social meaning through music.[35]

To the extent that musical styles sound within (or outside) a tradition, I would argue that the perception of stylistic (dis)continuities, as well as the more obvious example of explicit quotation, turns exactly on this indexical and hence highly pragmatic aspect of musical communication. That such musical moments may simultaneously articulate a harmony, a rhythmic closure, or a point of symmetry is in no way a contradiction to these more contextual concerns. In fact, the metapragmatic indexicals in interactive improvisation frequently do triple duty: they simultaneously generate musical shapes, interpersonal bonds in the ensemble, and intermusical associations for a community of listeners. It is important to note here that Silverstein's more formal framework is extremely compatible with Bakhtin's literary notion of internal dialogism, which I used to frame the discussion of intermusicality in chapter 4.[36]

More crucial to the issue of jazz improvisation is the interactive construction of the musical surface or the "interactional text," as Silverstein terms it. The overall coherence and shape of "Bass-ment Blues" clearly indicates that interactive musical participation creates something larger than local interactive exchanges in terms of both musical shape and human bonds. Silverstein asks how it is possible that a complex coherence, or "interactional text," can be constructed through language in real-time use. Central to the answer is his notion of metapragmatics, the idea that the indexical (that is, context-signaling) aspects of any sign are themselves framed or structured by higher-order pragmatic functions (that is, by linguistic signs functioning metapragmatically). Metapragmatics is thus concerned with the way in which local pragmatic events develop certain kinds of coherence through time.[37] There may be several interactional texts projected from any conceivable range of human behaviors, from bodily gestures to speech and music. Certainly the transcription of a musical performance is one such "metapragmatic representation of the facts of indexicality" (as Silverstein calls a discursive event), even though it leaves out important musical variables such as timbre, dynamics, and rhythmic tightness that may contribute to another sort of interactive text. A standard musical transcription, then, is not the only possible interactive text; a recording, which "freezes" an otherwise interactive and flexible musical environment, is another such text (Silverstein 1993, 36–38).

I have been arguing throughout this work that one of the most significant metapragmatic framing devices in jazz improvisation is the groove (or rhythmic feel), which is established by the interactive relationships among members of the rhythm section.[38] The groove is therefore one sort of interactional text within the ensemble that is dynamically related to an additional interactional text established between the rhythm section and the soloist.[39] To these interactional layers, which can be relatively visible in transcription, must be added intermusical relationships (aural references, in the literary sense), which may index something as specific as another composition or performance or as general as a cultural sensibility) and the (meta)pragmatic functions of the relatively non-notable aspects of music (sonic signaling of timbre, dynamics, and offbeat phrasing).[40] Finally, the establishment, consolidation, or liquidation of human relationships among participating players—not to mention audience members—affects all levels within the interactive musical process. In short, the intersection of all of these roles and musical framing devices contributes to the way in which interactionally produced musical texts develop, and I would like to emphasize that these interactionally produced events structure both musical and social space.[41] The metapragmatic framing of musical and social interaction seems to be particularly developed in the multiple interlocking layers characteristic of the musics of West Africa and the African diaspora, a subject that demands further consideration.[42]

Improvisational modes of music making highlight the pragmatic aspects of music most visibly, for what is crucial in the creative process is that improvisers in differentiated musical roles continuously monitor and react to the metapragmatic, pragmatic, and formal aspects of performance. While music theory has bequeathed to us extremely complicated means of approaching the resultant musical scores and work-internal relationships, including the measurement and mapping of all kinds of musical spaces (Lewin 1987), this essential interactive component of improvisation, with its emergent musical shapes and historical as well as socially constructive dimensions, has not been an object of theoretical inquiry. Structural relationships must, of course, be included within the discussion of how music communicates, but they do not operate independently of—and in fact are simultaneous with— the contextualizing and interactive aspects of sound. The total musical fact, from this perspective, is never reducible to structural description alone, nor to descriptions of context that ignore the role of musical signs in achieving musical (as well as social) structure.

Silverstein's terminology would not be necessary if we had a vocabulary in music that recognized the complexity and simultaneity of contextual issues in music. While some music theorists have addressed the context dependence of harmonic utterances within works (Rahn 1987), and those interested in the cognitive dimensions of music have moved away from music as a textual phenomenon to stress instead the perceptual images constructed in the brain (Lewin 1986), general musicological discussions have often presumed that dealing with "the music" means resorting to the tools of traditional musical theory or parallels to the analytic tasks of referential/propositional linguistics (Lehrdahl and Jackendoff 1983).[43] The sustained inquiry into the relationship among context, formal structure, and the constitution of social relationships in cultural terms that has been carried on in linguistic anthropology and sociolinguistics has been largely absent in musicology, music theory, and ethnomusicology—in part, I would argue, because of the overwhelming complexity of the task. We continue to have rather unproductive debates over whether the cultural contexts or "the music" should predominate in our scholarship, as if it were actually possible to make some clear separation. Contextual and cultural issues are considered by some to be rather "soft" areas of inquiry, in contrast to the "harder" methodologies of both music theory and manuscript-centered musicology. Postmodernists, however, have demonstrated an equally disappointing tendency to dismiss close readings of musical texts on the grounds that they privilege formalism or modernism.[44] In their zeal to situate genres of music within the ideological, political, and historical frameworks that give them social meaning, they often treat musical sound as if it were external to the process of constituting that meaning—as if the ability to shape musical sounds were not a profoundly interactive mode that has much to do with the constitution of that social and cultural meaning. To approach sound in this meta-pragmatic manner, however, is something very different from the formalist modernism to which postmodernists and poststructuralists object.

chapter six
ethnomusicology, interaction, and poststructuralism

In recent years, ethnomusicologists have been engaging with urban popular musics from around the world that raise many of the same interactive issues that have been a topic of discussion here: cultural heterogeneity; intracultural and intercultural borrowing; the construction of social groupings through music; the mediation of musical production by mass media; and the relationship of music, economics, politics, and identity in a postcolonial world. Christopher Waterman's work on *jùjú* (1990b), Jocelyne Guilbault's work on *zouk* (1993), Peter Manuel's investigation of North India's "cassette culture" (1993), and Thomas Turino's study of urban migration from the Peruvian altiplano (1993) all offer perspectives on music and cultural practices that do not make homogeneous presumptions about the nature of culture. Working primarily in small-scale, non-urban settings, ethnomusicologists in the 1980s developed productive interpretive fields by considering metaphorically and analogically the relationship of larger cultural meanings and values to musical processes. As noted in earlier chapters, Steven Feld's work, in particular, has demonstrated the importance of metaphors and homologies between cultural domains in establishing the relationships among music, aesthetics, and other cultural activities (Feld 1981, 1982, 1984, 1988). Waterman, Guilbault, Turino, Manuel, and many others working in urban and other highly heterogeneous environments have been developing and transforming some of these ideas against the background of an anthropology and an ethnomusicology that have increasingly recognized the transnational webs of economics, politics, media, travel, and musical exchange that have rendered the idea of an isolated culture a disciplinary anachronism.

My goal in this final chapter is to consider the multiple levels of interaction that have been presented in this work in the context of jazz's position within this larger global traffic in heterogeneous yet asymmetrical cultural exchange. In so doing, I will be proceeding from the musical to the cultural theoretical, presenting the viewpoints of several musicians on aspects of these issues and considering several competing perspectives on how the study of musics ought to be conducted in the postcolonial, poststructural world. Central concerns of the chapter are the relationship of jazz to the international African diaspora; the question of what sound itself contributes to the creation of cultural meaning; and the place of human agency, lived experience, and vernacular knowledge in the interpretive acts of academia.

Grooves and the African Diaspora

Jocelyne Guilbault's exploration of the "family resemblances" among the three principal genres contributing to zouk music—*compas-direct* from Haiti, *biguine* from Guadeloupe and Martinique, and *cadence-lypso* from Dominica—illustrates the importance of rhythmic feels in thinking about continuities and differences among these mutually influencing Antillean musics (Guilbault 1993). While there are rhythms common to all three, especially audible in the maracas and hi-hat cymbal parts, Guilbault's transcriptions of the multiple, interlocked rhythmic layers reveal the subtle musical distinctions among them, especially at the level of overall rhythmic gestalt.[1] One or two of the rhythmic layers may transfer from one groove to the next, but each composite is distinct (132–33). Each of the principle tributary genres, furthermore, incorporates musical ideas from a wide variety of outside influences, including American jazz, Trinidadian calypso, Cuban and Puerto Rican salsa, and Spanish and French dances. Guilbault has argued persuasively for thinking about zouk as a coherence emerging from contradictions—not only those stemming from musical sound itself, but those deriving from differences in social use, cultural function, and position within a global musical economy. She suggests that we think of musical meaning as generated within a field of possibilities rather than within discrete works (47).

Christopher Waterman's work on Nigerian jùjú is also deeply concerned with the problem of heterogeneity.

> I was fascinated by the melding of "deep" Yoruba praise
> singing and drumming, guitar techniques from soul music,
> Latin American dance rhythms, church hymns and
> country-and-western melodies, pedal steel guitarlicks and
> Indian film music themes, and by the fact that this modern-
> ist bricolage could so effectively evoke traditional values.
> (Waterman 1990b, 2)

Waterman finds that an "irreducible core of Yoruba dance rhythms" (produced in an interlocking, role-differentiated layer of patterns) is the framework that facilitates the incorporation and transformation of diverse influences while maintaining a "traditional" sound (161). Waterman's work underscores a point I wish to emphasize in connection with jazz improvisation: that the identity and meaning of a genre is tied not only to the existence of characteristic rhythmic feels but also to *how* they are put into use by social actors. Waterman's description of a Yoruba àríyá celebration highlights the interactive and participatory richness of these neotraditional social events. Against a multi-layered groove established by interlocking guitars, membranophones, idiophones, and bass, a talking drum introduces proverbs and social commentary into a social event that thrives on direct interaction between musicians and the audience (180–212). Since Yoruba is a tone language, talking drums (*dùndún* or *àdàmòn*) quite literally talk by producing musical phrases that are speech surrogates by virtue of their mimicry of the tonal levels and rhythms of spoken Yoruba. The playing and singing of praise lyrics (which often contain statements attacking the enemies of the person being praised), the use of guitar motifs to signal changes in musical sections (183), the importance of improvisation, and the intensive engagement of participants in hearing what is going on all have more than a little in common with the interactive processes we have seen in jazz improvisation: there is a simultaneous articulation of social and musical space, and the emergent musical shapes and social events have an intensely interpersonal quality. But Yoruba music is also notably different from jazz: the contents of the rhythms that are interlocked are different; English is not a tone language (so jazz drummers "talk" more metaphorically than literally);

jazz musicians generally do not play in performance contexts like the àríyá; and the shape of the Nigerian music industry and social infrastructure contrasts greatly with those of North American cities.

The linkages between interactive musical processes and the social networks, sentiments, aesthetics, and cultural identities in which they participate potentially provide a more precise way to talk about African diasporean musical connections that are simultaneously deeply connected and widely divergent. One of the most remarkable things about African American music in general and jazz in particular is the way in which they have re-invented the deeply participatory, interactive, heterogeneous, and socially constitutive musical processes of West Africa in a vastly different context and with very different musical content. African American musicians have taken these processes and transformed them with new rhythms, new songs, new instruments, new harmonic and melodic concepts, and new spiritual symbols. They have invented genres that articulate particularly American social contradictions and have had a very powerful effect on American culture, despite every effort to control or eradicate what is African in America.

Shuffle Rhythms and Genre Boundaries

The boundaries among African American musical genres are fluid in much the same way as those found among cadence-lypso, biguine, and compas-direct—that is, overlapping in some respects yet distinctive overall. While writers have generally treated jazz, rhythm and blues, and gospel as separate genres, it is common—if not typical—for jazz musicians to have performance experience in several different African American genres. As in zouk, rhythms from one layer of a rhythmic feel may appear in another genre but with contrasting bass lines or different comping rhythms. Bassist and guitarist Jerome Harris spoke with me about the importance of R&B and Motown as well as jazz in his development as a musician, and in so doing he took me through a discussion of various inflections of the shuffle rhythms (Harris 1992).

While the classic ride-cymbal rhythm can be used in either R&B or jazz settings, Harris cited the importance of playing a strong backbeat in emphasizing the popular (R&B) feeling (musical example 18). He also mentioned that the amount of repetition is an important point of demarcation between the emphasis of a jazz or an R&B aspect of any given shuffle rhythm or bass line. While the backbeat "has pretty much

Musical example 18. Jerome Harris singing R & B bass line with backbeat.

got to be there pretty consistently" in R&B settings, it "might be there sometimes but not all the time" in jazz. Harris added that the walking bass line in musical example 8 (see chapter 2) would sound more jazz-like if the bassist "would free it up notewise" from time to time with less obvious harmonic pitch choices (Harris 1992).

Harris stressed that "people seem to be using these influences, you know, kind of back and forth wherever they are appropriate to the song or to the intentions of the arranger or what have you" (Harris 1992). He mentioned Lee Morgan's "Sidewinder" (1963) as an example of a tune that contains aspects of jazz and rhythm and blues. This piece made the pop charts in the sixties but nevertheless is firmly entrenched in the jazz repertory by virtue of the superb improvisation delivered by an ensemble that included Lee Morgan, Joe Henderson, Barry Harris, Bob Cranshaw, and Billy Higgins. Higgins plays a ride cymbal rhythm whose second and fourth beats have nearly even eighth notes (musical example 19); the two-beat bass line leans in the direction of R&B; the melody of the piece begins with a comping riff; and Higgins's two-bar backbeat riff (snare) repeats literally throughout the ensemble portion of the arrangement.

"Sidewinder" and other *soul jazz, funky jazz,* or *hard bop* tunes (as the style has variously been labeled) have generally enjoyed less prestige with modernist-oriented jazz critics, including Gunther Schuller and Amiri Baraka. Baraka lamented hard bop's deviation from the track of "high art" undertaken by bebop and even went so far as to suggest that it was a music suited to a black middlebrow audience (Baraka 1963, 222). He found the rhythmic repetition "amazingly static and regular when compared to the music of the forties" (217). In general, grooves and rhythmic feels have been important boundary markers in the debates over what should and should not be counted as jazz. The closer a rhythmic feel comes to an even duple subdivision of the

Musical example 19. "Sidewinder." Lee Morgan.
(*Sidewinder*. Blue Note BST 84157.
Recorded: Englewood Cliffs, NJ, 21 December 1963.)

Trumpet (Lee Morgan) and Tenor Sax (Joe Henderson)

Drums (Billy Higgins)

Bass (Bob Cranshaw)

beat, the more likely that some musicians and audiences will find that the music has left the realm of jazz and entered the sphere of rock and roll or contemporary funk.[2]

Ralph Peterson Jr., for example, commented that "a lot of what people our age know as jazz is nothing more than good instrumental R&B, good instrumental pop; but not to say that it's not good music, it's just not jazz." The reception of Miles Davis's electric improvisations over more duply subdivided grooves—*Bitches Brew* (1969a), *In a Silent Way* (1969b), *Decoy* (1983)—provides another example.[3] Musicians vary in where they draw boundaries between jazz and other genres, with some challenging the need for a jazz label at all, as both Michael Carvin and Jaki Byard did in chapter 4. Ralph Peterson Jr. takes a tolerant yet critical position on musical boundaries:

> I don't agree with what a lot of people are playing or say-
> ing, but what I will do is defend their right to say it and
> play it and never try to take another's ideas as being less se-
> rious than mine unless it's evident that . . . they haven't
> thought the process out. (Peterson 1989b)

When I began my research, I wanted to include musicians who performed in a wide range of playing styles, from mainstream to avant-garde. Originally I had intended to include individual representatives from each end of the continuum, but I found that most working musicians play in a diversity of styles—indeed *must* be fluent in several styles, for economic reasons—and that trying to map one style on any particular player was problematic.

A few examples illustrate the flexibility of jazz musicians. Billy Higgins is known as a consummate master of mainstream drumming, whose work with Dexter Gordon, Lee Morgan, and Sonny Clark is a virtual textbook on how to swing (Gordon 1962; Mobley 1965; Morgan 1963). Higgins also has an extensive discography of outside playing with, among others, Ornette Coleman and Cecil Taylor (Coleman 1959a, 1959b, 1960, 1987; Taylor and Neidlinger 1961). He was, in fact, a member of Coleman's original quartet, the group that most consider to have inaugurated the debate over "free jazz" in 1960. To emphasize one side of his musical aesthetic over the other would fail to do justice to the breadth of his playing. Likewise, Jaki Byard, Cecil McBee, Richard Davis, and Roy Haynes have proven themselves in multiple musical contexts, from avant-garde to straight-ahead. Don Byron might be the most eclectic performer of all, with his highly publicized participation in klezmer music as well as jazz, popular, and classical musics. When asked if they preferred one musical context over another, most musicians answered in the negative and stressed the value they place on playing in diverse musical contexts.

> My great forte and my great pleasure is to play diverse
> styles of music. . . . I'm fed by playing with different indi-
> viduals. My spirit, my musical creative spirit, is kept alive
> because I'm constantly challenged to play . . . different
> styles on my instrument. Other than that I'd be locked
> into one kind of situation which I just can't stand. (McBee
> 1990)

Such eclecticism is lamented by some members of a younger generation of musicians, who have taken Wynton Marsalis as their role model and have held mainstream jazz of the late fifties and early sixties to be the epitome of the genre. Harris observes that this aesthetic position has been aggressively marketed by record companies and that many older players "have been decrying what they say is a lack . . . of strong individual voices in this wave of young and heavily promoted players" (Harris 1992). Furthermore, recent scholarship on early jazz has documented that eclecticism—the impulse to transform and borrow from a wide range of popular musics and incorporate them into an improvisational and compositional art—has been present in jazz from the beginning (Peretti 1992; Tucker 1989).

Poststructuralism and the Politics of Race

One of the principal differences among the Antillean, the Yoruba, and the American jazz contexts is the way in which mixture is evaluated and received. Despite a considerable amount of anxiety in Guadeloupe and Martinique over the ways in which zouk's musical mixtures threaten cultural authenticity, it seems to be widely accepted, as one of Guilbault's informants reports, that the music, "like Guadeloupeans themselves, [is] the result of a mixture of races" (Guilbault 1993, 183). Guilbault views zouk as an important player in the creation of a super-ethnic *Antilliais* identity in France. In the French exile community, where a "we–they" relationship exists between Antillean and non-Antillean society, the contrast between Martinicans and Guadeloupeans diminishes, and zouk fulfills a "we" function for both groups (201). Christopher Waterman (1990a) also speaks of the ways in which jùjú has participated in the construction of a Pan-Yoruba identity among social groups who formerly considered themselves separate. While African American musics and cultural practices have likewise constructed a unity from the disparate African ethnicities forcibly brought together under the terms of chattel slavery (and later immigration), the taboo on racial intermixture in the United States has been of such force that constituencies on either side of the black/white divide have had ample historical reason for wishing to deny or de-emphasize the heterogeneous character of both African American and European American cultural practices.

During the Jim Crow era, the "one-drop rule" held that the presence of one black relative in the family—no matter how remote—made a person legally black, irrespective of physical appearance.[4] While white male transgression of the color line through the taking of black mistresses is generally acknowledged to have been the primary generator of the gradations in complexion among African Americans, the greatest taboo from the perspective of mainstream white society was against unions of white women and black men. Protecting (or policing) the "purity" of white women, Neil McMillen has explained, was crucial in ensuring that the legal descendants of white men remained unassailably white (McMillen 1989, 15). No space in between "black" and "white" could legally be acknowledged under the imperatives of racial segregation, which were most severe in the sixty years after 1890 (exactly the period in which jazz developed and became the national popular music, par excellence). An individual had to be defined as a member of one category or another for enforcement of separatist laws. Nevertheless, there were many individuals who were "white enough" in appearance to confound segregationists. Burton Peretti describes the case of New Orleans bandleader Jack Laine, who fired a musician who was physically white after discovering that the man's father was black. The father had married a white woman and lived in the "can't-tell ward" of New Orleans, where there was a great deal of racial intermixture (Peretti 1992, 31). Jazz musicians who were light in complexion, such as Count Basie band member Earle Warren, were often able to buy food for other band members at whites-only grocery stores and restaurants (193). My point for our larger discussion is that the American historical commitment to the maintenance of a pure white race and the idea of mixture as degradation form a crucial context for untangling the debates about universality, authenticity, heterogeneity, and ethnic particularity that circulate within in jazz world as well as in the cultural studies literature.[5]

The way concepts of universality are invoked within the jazz world must be read against the goal of an integrated, colorblind society that was the principal ideology driving the mainstream Civil Rights movement. Since difference in color was a morphological marker that was socially interpreted to justify discriminatory treatment against Americans of African descent, the ideology of integration de-emphasized difference in pursuing social equality under the banner of universal brotherhood. As Kwame A. Appiah has recently argued (1992), differences in human skin color and bodily shape are more morphological than genetic, and the concept of race is unimportant—indeed suspect—in explaining the biological differences between people with contrasting skin colors, hair, and bone.[6] It is not surprising, then, that one stream of thinking in the jazz world (embraced by white musicians as well as black) has emphasized the universality of jazz and its ability to transcend ethnic difference.

Joanne Brackeen, for example, emphasized the colorblind aspects of the music:

> I don't hear music according to race because music is
> something that you hear with your ears. It isn't something

that, you know, you take a picture of. You can't really take a picture of music, and therefore I can't be limited to a white or black or yellow or anything else. It just is. So I wouldn't dare try to put my finger on it and touch it and call it this or that or the other. (Brackeen 1989)

Jaki Byard talked about how "music is music, you know," just as Michael Carvin did in chapter 3. Noting that race was "too painful to talk about, so why bother?" he pointed out that "Ray Charles was blind, it was all dark to him, do you know what I mean?" Musicians who have performed internationally (as has everyone who participated in this study) often extend such observations to include a global perspective. As Cecil McBee said of the music,

> It's the universal language . . . it's a language that permeates every order of thing in the universe. . . . I've had people around the world understand what I was saying from my heart musically. I'm . . . nine thousand miles away and I'm on the stage and I play. . . . That's a very powerful force and you must appreciate it. (McBee 1990)

McBee's comment also illustrates how easily a colorblind vision dovetails with modernist notions of autonomous universal art that have had such legitimating appeal to bebop and post-bebop musicians. The importance of the rhetoric of artistic modernity in the jazz world, I would argue, must be contextualized against this broader historical backdrop of racial discrimination—a topic I hope to pursue more fully in a future work.

While it has been the purview of modernist musicologists to critique nonclassical repertories with classical ("universal") aesthetic categories, jazz musicians have sometimes inverted this practice with a "counteruniversality," evaluating classical music with jazz aesthetic categories. Jerome Harris, for example, pointed out the importance of grooving in non-jazz music:

> I mean, a Sousa march should groove. Viennese waltzes groove. Someone playing . . . a Bach solo violin sonata should be grooving. . . . You should feel . . . from phrase to phrase and within phrases . . . a forward rhythmic flow. (Harris 1989)

When emphasis on universality is used to gloss over ethnic tensions or to deny the African American origins and leadership of the music, however, musicians are quick to emphasize the ethnic particularity of jazz. Don Byron protested the "de-ethnicization" of the music through these "universal" sentiments and the institutionalization of jazz performance programs run by European Americans. To him, the music's originality is vitally related to its African American identity:

> I think the feeling of being outside the society is the ulti-
> mate inspiration. . . . I just think the feeling of being con-
> scious of yourself as part of a people that are both totally
> necessary to a society, only no one admits that, and totally
> *reeling* from it is the ultimate inspiration for doing some-
> thing totally different. (Byron 1989).

Richard Davis, likewise, explained the development of bebop as an explicit assertion of African American identity:

> In the forties came a revolution of a type. "We don't care
> to entertain you [white audiences] anymore and play for
> your dances. Matter of fact, this music is so fast you can't
> dance to it. And we don't care if you want to come and
> hear the band, you got to sit down and *listen* to this mu-
> sic. It's concert music and you got hear it and check it
> out." (Davis 1989)

Once again, the confluence of the struggle for racial justice and modernist notions of art is in evidence. Davis continued:

> In the sixties Max Roach was a real hero because he was
> outspoken. And his wife Abbey Lincoln was saying things
> that people *wanted* to say but . . . weren't in a position to
> be heard. Max Roach was in a position to be heard. King
> was in a position to be heard. Malcolm X was in a posi-
> tion to be heard. So he voiced opinions for a lot of
> people's heartfelt things. (Davis 1989)

Universalist and ethnically assertive points of view, it must be emphasized, often coexist in the same person and are best conceived as discourses upon which musicians draw in particular interactive contexts. An individual speaking to an interlocutor who underplays the role of African American culture in the music, for example, might choose to respond with ethnically assertive comments. In a context in which something closer to racial harmony prevails, a musician might choose to invoke a more universalistic rhetoric. These are two sides of a tension between universality and cultural particularity that perhaps explains the wide range of apparently contradictory opinions that can be expressed about these issues in the jazz world. On the one hand, performers are proud to play music that inspires musicians and audiences beyond its culture and country of origin; on the other, many object to the attempts of non–African Americans to gloss over the African American cultural origins and leadership in the music through the language of equality.

Since whiteness tends to be a sign of inauthenticity within the world of jazz, the appeals of white musicians to universalistic rhetoric can be perceived as power plays rather than genuine expressions of universal brotherhood. If jazz is one of the few cultural activities in which being African American is evaluated as "better" or more "authentic" than being non–African American, a white musician's appeal to a colorblind rhetoric might cloak a move to minimize the black cultural advantage by "lowering" an assertive African American musician from his or her pedestal to a more "equal" playing field. It is this use of colorblind rhetoric that often provokes African Americans to take more extreme positions on ethnic particularity.

Postmodern academic discussions have undertaken a sustained critique of the ethnically assertive "Afrocentric" literature for its essentializing and homogeneous notions of race and culture, and it is important to examine some of the principal outlines of this debate. Molefi K. Asante's project in *The Afrocentric Idea* was to "critique the Eurocentric ideology that masquerades as a universal view" by valorizing the African heritage of African American cultural practices, especially the communicative and expressive practices of language and music (Asante 1987). Afrocentricity, in his view, inverts the hegemony of Eurocentric views by "placing African ideals at the center of any analysis that involves African culture and behavior" (7). Asante's construction of "an African concept of communication rooted in traditional African philosophies," with particular attention to Akan traditions (59), is a creative attempt to re-invent and valorize a lost hereditary and cultural relationship to Africa, which he views as the true home, the true origins of African American culture (125).

Because he described this African heritage in mythic terms, Asante, along with other Afrocentric writers, has been criticized for simply reversing the ideologies of racial hegemony rather than challenging

and reshaping the fundamental racial categories in which they participate. As noted previously, Kwame A. Appiah has called for an aban-
donment of the very concept of race, arguing that it is a biologically
meaningless term that confuses socially constructed descent systems
and prejudice with biological heredity. Kinship systems that tend to
count relatives through either the mother's or the father's side "drasti-
cally underrepresent the biological range of our ancestry" (Appiah
1992, 31). If race is a genetically meaningless concept, however, color
has been of unquestionable significance as a morphological characteristic facilitating the hierarchical classification of bodies and their unequal treatment. It is unlikely, then, that the terms *black* and *white*
will fade in their relevance to describing various African and African
diasporean cultural histories.[7]

Appiah wishes also to challenge the idea that what persons with
similar skin, hair, and bones (which is all that "race" biologically accounts for) share is a "common history" (by which he means, I would
suggest, something closer to a "common biological ancestry"). Appiah
objects that when the heterogeneity and particularity of African cultures and experiences are collapsed into a simplistically unified African
racial essence, people fail to recognize the multiple ways in which it
is—and has been—possible to be African. In his detailed analysis of
W. E. B. Du Bois's concept of race, he attempts to demonstrate that
despite Du Bois's claims to the contrary, he remained caught in a conception of race and culture that held differences in "temperament, be-
lief, and intention" to be heritable in the biological sense that Appiah
develops (45). From here he goes on to critique what he terms *nativism,*
an ideology that answers Eurocentric deprecations of African cultural
productions and claims to purity and universality with a counterclaim
to a pure African ancestry and authenticity that partakes of the same
nationalist ideological presumptions as those upon which European
racism was founded. Appiah chides African nationalists with an un-
flattering analogy:

> The Western emperor has ordered the natives to exchange
> their robes for trousers: their act of defiance is to insist on
> tailoring them from homespun material. Given their argu-
> ments, plainly, the cultural nationalists do not go far
> enough; they are blind to the fact that their nativist de-
> mands inhabit a Western architecture. (60)

At times Appiah sounds as if he does not support the investigation of African histories, or as if the concept of ancestors was not a vital component in many African societies. His principal point, however, is that those of African descent should resist a reactive self-conception in favor of building a Pan-African critical practice that recognizes three things: (1) the heterogeneity of African cultural texts and practices, including the effects of the colonial encounter; (2) the continuities that nevertheless remain among precolonial, colonial, and postcolonial cultural productions and African histories; and (3) the necessity of challenging the presumption of Western cultural superiority (60). As with the similarities and differences between Yoruba and African American interactive musical practices, there is a very real basis for thinking about an African diaspora while at the same time acknowledging vast differences between cultural groups that share the same skin tones.

In emphasizing the invisible operation of ideologies that might condition people to articulate reactive counterideologies that reproduce hegemonies in inverted form, Appiah takes a position resembling that of several critical theorists writing from a postcolonial perspective, including, most notably, Gayatri Spivak. In a series of often cited articles, Spivak has deprecated the importance of documenting vernacular points of view by arguing that the ideological overdeterminations of a world capitalist system have rendered "subalterns" voiceless and duped them into various forms of false consciousness, from which, presumably, it is the task of the postcolonial intellectual to save them (Spivak 1988a, 1990, 1992). On the one hand, both Appiah and Spivak (as intellectuals whose worlds bridge the metropolitan and the postcolonial margins) argue for a recognition of the heterogeneity of discourses in which they are fluent ("We talk like Defoe's Friday, only much better" [Spivak 1990:225]) and against the expectations of Western intellectuals that they fulfill the exoticized role of "Other" by producing "antiquarian history" or "museumized identities" that amount to "roots in aspic" (Spivak 1992, 798). On the other hand, this emphasis on ideology constructs an extremely exalted role for the postmodern intellectual, whose knowledge of some of the most rarefied philosophical, scientific, and critical texts of the West enables him or her to "see through" the ideological overdeterminations that saddle the "mere" person on the street. In this sense, I would argue that Spivak's intellectual elitism inhabits its own extremely Western architecture. My concern here is for how aspects of this poststructuralist line of thinking provide a rationale for a new sort of armchair intellectual—this time, however, dressed up in a radical activist's pose.

The deprecation of the individual voice is philosophically grounded in both Michel Foucault's and Jacques Derrida's critiques of Western humanism, which emphasize the "discursive" construction of human experience on the one hand and human subjectivity and consciousness as dispersed in systems of signification and representation on the other. The biggest "sin" in either philosophical approach is to suppose that some "originary," undivided, essential self (or objective reality) exists outside of these systems of signification or discourse.[8] The way in which Foucault employs the term *discourse* in *The Archaeology of Knowledge* (1972), however, contrasts greatly with the use of the term in the sociolinguistic and anthropological literature I have employed here, with the former operating at a far more general level than the latter. A considerable confusion regarding the idea of discourse (in either sense) has emerged in the debate about postmodernism and music in recent years. Perhaps the most useful aspect of Foucauldian notions of discourse and Derridean ideas about writing has been their implications for rethinking the concept of culture—for moving from a totalizing, coherent, homogeneous idea to one that takes heterogeneity and the crosscutting of cultural identities with the contradictions (discourses) of race, gender, and economic stratification as points of departure. Perhaps the most damaging, from the point of view of ethnomusicology, is the poststructural deprecation of the "speaking subject," vernacular knowledge, and the phenomenal world in relationship to its larger philosophical project. Michael Silverstein's work, and that of several other linguistic anthropologists, I believe, provides a way to expose several false dichotomies often present in contemporary interpretive debates, such as those between ideology and individual human experience, discursivity and the phenomenal world, the music itself and ethnomusicological interpretation, and micro and macro concepts of discourse.

When I first became aware of the concept of discourse, it was through the literatures of sociolinguistics and linguistic anthropology of the 1970s and 1980s, which concerned themselves with the microanalysis of language use in face-to-face conversational interaction (Gumperz and Hymes 1986; Gumperz 1982; Goffman 1986; Labov 1969; Levinson 1983; Ochs 1988; Schieffelin 1990; Duranti and

Goodwin 1992; Moerman 1988). Two important aspects of this work were the findings that the intelligibility of face-to-face conversation was extremely context-dependent and that transcripts of spoken language were anything but transparent windows on human consciousness. Later I encountered the more general notions of discourse and writing in the works of Foucault and Derrida that have directed attention away from the microissues of interaction and toward the macroissues of ideology, social construction shaped by hegemonic discourses, and representation.

A brief review of Foucault's and Derrida's concept of discourse and writing will help clarify the argument that follows. In selecting discourse and discursive formations as his object of historical inquiry, Foucault situated himself against a book-centered, work-centered concept of history that treated texts and their authors as transparently obvious. Foucault's mission was not to suggest that individual works were irrelevant but "to tear away from them their virtual self-evidence, and to free the problems that they pose" (Foucault 1972, 26). Foucault was more interested in the broader historical question of how particular statements or discourses were *possible* rather than in the rules that governed the internal logic of any particular work (27).

One crucial aspect of Foucault's concept of discourse is the idea that nothing is anterior to discourse; instead, social discourses "systematically form the objects of which they speak" (49). This reflexive notion of the constitution of objects, of discourses "forming" subjects, is intended to shift attention away from the transcendental individual and toward the web of social, economic, and power relationships in which a particular sort of human being is constructed. Derrida makes a similar point by drawing from a Saussurian conception of signification: "There is no presence before and outside semiological difference," he argued (Derrida 1982, 12). "Essentially and lawfully, every concept is inscribed in a chain or in a system within which it refers to the other, to other concepts, by means of a systematic play of differences" (11).[9]

While the metaphorical application of the term *discourse* to nonlinguistic phenomena such as music has been widely established, it remains true that in the process of theorizing, both Foucault and Derrida primarily had Western written texts in mind. The problem that arises when music is pressed into this metaphorical framework can be illustrated through one of the latter's formulations. In "Différance," Derrida gets much figurative mileage out of stressing that in French one cannot "hear" the difference between the title of the work spelled with an *e* and with an *a;* the conceptual difference between the terms, he emphasizes, emerges only in *writing.* In music, I would argue, the situation is usually just the reverse: difference is "heard" primarily through the physical presence of sound, not in its various written representations. It begs the question to argue that the recording of music on CDs is a mode of writing by virtue of its creation of something repeatable, for so much of the metaphor of writing in the Derridean position is dedicated to questioning the importance of the phenomenal world. Writing, for Derrida, becomes a metaphor for relationality, or mediation by systems of signification. His metaphor for that which is unmediated is speech, spoken language, sound, the voice. Spivak's critique of the idea of documenting a "native voice" is in fact grounded in Derrida's emphasis on writing over speech. The problem, she argues, is *phonocentrism,* "the conviction that speech is a direct and immediate representation of voice-consciousness and writing an indirect transcript of speech" (Spivak 1988b, 212). Speech from a living human being (or musical notes from a horn) becomes, in this framework, a metaphor for an unmediated concept of the individual, for essentialism, and for a romanticized "othering" of oppressed people.[10]

This generalization of the metaphors of writing and discourse in poststructuralist thinking, I am arguing, has limits when applied to nonlinguistic discourses (systems of signification). The overuse of these metaphors in reference to music, indeed, has tended to lead inquiry away from its discursive (relational) peculiarities. We have already encountered the famous duet between Eric Dolphy and Charles Mingus that sounds like an iconic representation of two people having a conversation. If I were to transcribe the notes and play them on the piano, they wouldn't sound very much like the conversation on the recording, for it is the relatively non-notable timbral and dynamic inflections produced by the players that are the principal means of signifying the iconicity. Various visual mappings of waveforms now available on computer are not likely to do much better in communicating the iconicity. These timbral and dynamic inflections, as Gumperz (1982) might argue, signal how the notes should be interpreted and are not restricted to iconic examples such as this one.

The phenomenology of sound, in other words, is extremely important to the *way* in which music signifies and cannot be bracketed off as irrelevant to processes of social construction. While the physical aspects of sound are nonlinguistic, they very quickly become implicated in relational discursive processes, such as intermusicality, and may in turn be commented upon by audience members with words. There is a constant interplay among sound, discursivity, language, and representations thereof that takes place when human beings make and listen to music that must be considered with its own particularities in mind. I am taking *discursive* here to mean the kind of relationalities that can be established through various linguistic and nonlinguistic modes of human communication (principally speech, music, visual images, and bodily movement). While I don't particularly like the fact that language has suggested itself as the general model of relationality, the metaphors of discourse and writing seem to be here to stay. We need to remember that they are metaphors placing language at the center of the universe and may or may not be fully applicable to nonlinguistic phenomena such as music.

The line of argument in Derrida that values writing over speech and grounds the decentering of the subject may make sense in the context of debates in Western philosophy, but I would argue that it has done considerable damage to understanding the ways in which music as a sonic phenomenon and human agency participate in the construction of social and cultural meaning. Some writers have specifically avoided engaging with musical sound or ethnographically collected opinions because of their suspicion that phenomenology of any kind will lead them into the traps of essentialism or otherwise into presuming the transparency of the human voice. Musical scholars have had an additional fear that representations of music (such as musical transcriptions) are inherently formalist, reifying, and decontextualizing—a fear that has never seemed to worry those who write about written texts (Bohlman 1993).

The poststructuralist decentering of the phenomenal world is the relevant context for how we might read Lawrence Grossberg's statement that "one cannot approach rock and roll by using anyone's experience of it, or even any collective definition of that experience" (Grossberg 1990, 113). Lived experience is trivialized here in favor of its mass representations, politics, and ideologies. This position, it seems to me, constructs a rather exalted role for the intellectual, since the scholar is absolved of worrying too much about the phenomenal world or individual agencies and is free to theorize at will. It also, sadly enough, distances scholarship from the sonic pleasures of music and the myriad ways musicians and their listeners make use of them.

As we have seen, linguistic anthropology and sociolinguistics (with its emphasis on how language mediates social experience) have long since abandoned any idea of the self-evidence of speech (transcribed or not) and the transparency of individual voices independent of their construction in social and cultural contexts. Derrida's and Spivak's quarrel is actually with a concept of speech and voice that antedates that developed by linguists whose work I have talked about.[11] By the late 1970s, John Austin's (1962) concept of the performative and its presumptions about intentionality had already been deeply critiqued by several linguists, Silverstein included (1979:210–16). Those who still carry on Derrida's objection to Austin's idea of intentionality (which was timely in 1968) are, it seems to me, beating a dead horse.

Indeed, Silverstein's work implies that the mutually constituting indexical properties of human discourses are operative from the most micro level of interpersonal interaction to the most macro level of metadiscursive textual speculation and ideology. From this perspective, there is simply no reason to imagine that engaging with what someone says (or plays) is any less significant from a social constructionist (and representational) point of view than engaging with the theoretical and ideological speculations of Foucault or Derrida. In other words, I question the opposition between social constructionism and lived experience that is frequently drawn (or presumed) in deconstructionist cultural interpretation. Thinking about the multifaceted social construction of human beings and their cultural worlds, I would argue, need not be at the expense of ideas about human agency or the phenomenology of sound.

I am suggesting that to reject the deconstructionist perspective on speech, voice, and—by extension—sound is to reject the idea the idea of a subject so overdetermined by hegemonic ideologies that she or he is unable to speak or take action on her or his behalf. This rejection, however, does not preclude a partial reconciliation between practice theory and poststructural conceptions of discourse. Like Bill Hanks (1987), I like to think of discourse genres (linguistic and nonlinguistic) as modes of action, indexically situated within a historical context, and as emergent objects that people necessarily improvise upon in social practice. If we think of actors or groups of agents consciously or unconsciously partaking of particular overlapping cultural discourses while negotiating their social statuses and positions (all conditioned, of course, by the restraints of hegemony), I think we might find a way of beginning to take what has been most useful and stimulating in recent social theory and applying it to particular cultural problems. Interdisciplinary work on music and popular culture cannot afford to pretend that sound is not an active participant in the shaping of cultural meaning and human subjectivities, however peculiar its phenomenological discursivity might be and however much music is simultaneously involved with other overlapping discourses, such as those of gender, race, and class. We need, rather, to invent ways to get at the power of sound and the ways in which it shapes and is shaped by other cultural practices.

This phenomenological discursivity of music, I think, has much to do with the creation of emotion through music. Many of the non-notatable aspects of jazz improvisation—including tone color, phrasing, dynamics, rhythmic coordination, and intensity—as well as the intermusical connections that listeners hear in a jazz performance are among the seemingly ineffable physical qualities that produce emotional reactions in listeners. These visceral reactions become immediately involved in processes of discursive and cultural interpretation that may result in the attachment of an emotional label to the "feeling." Although recordings facilitate the dislocation of a performance from its historical contexts of production, these reactions must be historicized.

I realize that I have overstated my case for the importance of sound in direct proportion to the centrality of instrumental and vocal sound in jazz as compared to other genres. In music with verbal texts, the problem is complicated by the relationship of words to the sound of the voice, as well as to nonvocal instrumental sound. There is a shifting balance between words, voice, and instruments that varies greatly across cultures. In many West African musics, for example, the boundaries between language and music are much blurrier, since speech may literally be spoken through instruments, most usually drums. In this case, the tonal aspects of speech and music must be addressed, not to mention the relationship of both types of sound to the nonlinguistic discourse of dance. In some musical traditions and genres, however, sound may be quite secondary to its function of carrying text—as, for example, in Quranic chant, which is not even considered music by culture bearers. Another example can be found in the Japanese Zen Buddhist practice of *shakuhachi* playing. While sound may seem centrally important to a Westerner listening to the shakuhachi, more important to Zen Buddhist practitioners is its function in gaining control of the breath. The shakuhachi and its sound are considered primarily spiritual tools rather than musical phenomena. My discussion of sound, then, is not intended to unilaterally elevate sound to an importance it may not possess cross-culturally. Rather, I mean to suggest that insofar as it is present in cultural practices, its role, relative importance, intersection with other communicative media, and ability to index broader cultural discourses ought to be assessed.

Methodologically, I would argue that the issues of sound and agency are interrelated, for intersubjective and historical research remain crucial to ethnomusicological scholarship, however vexed by the inherent asymmetries in power relationships between the studiers and the studied. To engage in data-driven research, I would argue, is not the equivalent of presuming that socially constructed facts are a transparent window on reality. It seems to me that watching videos, listening to records, reading popular magazines, and engaging with other mass-produced cultural representations (all of which are part of the research process) can never really replace the obligation to document actively the everyday life experiences, histories, opinions, self-representations, and practices of real people that ethnomusicologists and anthropologists have generally taken to be their methodological and ethical responsibility.

Poststructuralist and postmodern emphasis on representation and the discursive production of subjectivity seems to have had the paradoxical effect of moving academic discourse in a direction of greater ivory-tower isolation while ostensibly engaging society's most mundane cultural productions. When I see that the viewpoints of people outside academia are deprecated because they have not incorporated insights derived from the debates of Western philosophy, or when the people holding these opinions are ridiculed for believing in the validity of their lived experience, I can only marvel at the sophistication of this new rationalization for elitism in people who genuinely pride themselves on their commitment to social engagement. If all this talk of heterogeneity and diversity and empowerment is used primarily to augment the status of the academic elite and silence the "ontologically incorrect," I think we can expect to hear a growing crescendo of ethnic and class particularity from outside academia: "Get real, please!"

The equation of the voices of the disempowered (and the various forms in which they have been represented) with the transcendental subject that is the object of Western philosophy's antihumanist critique I believe to be the weakest link in deconstructionist approaches to popular music and cultural criticism.[12] While there is much to be embraced and to stimulate in poststructuralist and postmodern thinking, the positions taken on human agency and the material world are open to question. Recognizing the heterogeneity of social determination and the mutually constituting (yet asymmetrical) relationships between macro and micro does not logically entail or methodologically justify the trivialization of human experience or its documentation but instead demands a critical rethinking of interpretive frameworks and the claims made on the basis of such evidence and agency. As I said more politely in the introduction to this book, I believe that academia *must* engage with the knowledges in circulation and the human beings outside of its walls in order to humanize, invigorate, and deepen its thinking, as well as to bring new people in. Without this dialogue, antihumanism threatens to become inhumane, and pretensions to social awareness on the part of many very well meaning academics become hollow postures indeed.

Conclusions

Discussions about music, race, gender, ethnic identities, and cultural relativity no longer respect the disciplinary boundaries in which academic training takes place. Anthropologists, ethnomusicologists, literary theorists, mass communications theorists, musicologists, cinema scholars, sociologists, and cultural historians have all found popular musics of relevance to their disciplinary concerns, with African American and other musics of the African diaspora disproportionately represented. Until recently, ethnomusicology has been only peripherally engaged with the debates on popular culture and multiculturalism that have taken place within anthropology and humanities scholarship, yet I think our collective cross-cultural experiences have much to contribute to this debate. While not sufficient for thinking about the heterogeneous contexts ethnomusicologists now face, the Boasian idea of cultural relativism, which stressed "the integrity of separate cultures which were equal with respect to their values" (Rosaldo 1993, xvi), nevertheless instilled in most of us a healthy respect for the self-definition and self-representations of others, a quality frequently missing in cultural criticism that feels entitled to judge the ideologies of others on Western philosophical grounds.

By way of summary, I would like to consider what jazz improvisation has to teach cultural theorists. Consider, for example, the musical metaphors in Pierre Bourdieu's *Outline of a Theory of Practice* (1977): *habitus* as a "generative principle of regulated improvisations" (78), schemes of thought as "the *intentionless invention* of regulated improvisation" (79), social life as "collectively orchestrated without being the product of the orchestrating action of a conductor" (72), and the "harmonization of [an] agent's experiences" through repetition and discussion (80). The image of improvisation appears often in postmodern and cultural studies, functioning as a metaphor for hybridity, for the blurriness of boundaries, and for liberation from the inhibiting confines of both hegemonic ideologies and structuralism. Yet this usage is only partly apt.

While "intentionless invention" (drawing upon the accumulated social experience of a lifetime) is certainly one aspect of improvisational process, there is, as we have seen, great interplay between conscious and unconscious modes of awareness in jazz improvisation and several interactive layers whose degrees of fixity and freedom are constantly shifting.[13] I hope to have demonstrated through a close look at interactive musical examples and what musicians have had to say about them that the organization and use of musical grooves offers a model of "coherence through contradiction" that can help us unravel some of the contentious debates about musical structures, genre boundaries, continuity and change, and the heterogeneity of cultural processes that currently rage in both academia and the postcolonial world.

If we conceive of global cultural processes as simultaneous layers of practices and ideologies that may or may not be coordinated at any particular moment in time (that may, in other words, sometimes come into an interaction that produces a coherence, sometimes not); if we remember that some layers may provide a great deal of continuity while others may simultaneously provide great tension and radical departure; if we recognize that the layers that provide continuity or change can trade places from moment to moment, then perhaps we can move

away from the dichotomous understandings of us/them, heterogeneity/
homogeneity, modernism/postmodernism, structure/agency, and radi-
calism/conservatism that continue to plague our discussions. There are
a lot of partially overlapping grooves out there, none of which has a
"monopoly on the truth" (Rosaldo 1993, xviii–xix).

This concept of grooves writ large is purposely meant to underscore
the relevance of music and its organization to the "reshaping of social analysis" (Rosaldo 1993). It suggests that grooves—as well as the
people who make them—have much to contribute to streams of
thought that have had great difficulty incorporating nonlinguistic discourses in more than a peripheral fashion. The musical image, it seems,
has much to offer in reorganizing our thinking in nonlinear and multiple directions. We have seen that shifts in musical layers and ideology
can range from partial to thoroughly transformative; that people can
construct their identities and social space with respect to a variety of
discourses, including music; and that any aspect of any layer can
"change up on you" at any time. Improvisation *is* an apt metaphor for
more flexible social thinking, but we'd better keep a basic music lesson
in mind: you've got to listen to the whole band if you ever expect to
say something.

Coda

Is this really necessary, this engagement with high-toned philosophical issues in the humanities? I am reminded of what Ralph Peterson Jr. had to say about the quality of jazz instruction in the colleges he attended:

> A lot of the teachers that are teaching in college are, are players that couldn't *hack* it, you know, for one reason or another. And therefore the students are subject to *their* inadequacies or their narrow-mindedness. (Peterson 1989b)

To the musicians who agreed to talk to me for this book—Phil Bowler, Joanne Brackeen, Jaki Byard, Don Byron, Michael Carvin, Richard Davis, Sir Roland Hanna, Jerome Harris, Roy Haynes, Billy Higgins, Cecil McBee, Ralph Peterson Jr., Kenny Washington, and Michael Weiss—much of what I have presented about musical roles in the ensemble, processes of group interaction, and racial politics in the United States is elementary and self-evident. They do not need to have the importance of interaction and irony and parody in improvisation explained to them! While Peterson's comments primarily referred to teachers of performance in colleges, I know that he is right: most of us who teach music history and ethnomusicology—even if once we may have come close to "hacking it"—have compromised our musical development by spending more time reading books and preparing lectures and articles than we do practicing. Nevertheless, in books such as this, we convey a seemingly exaggerated notion of our own self-importance that is in part conferred upon us by virtue of our positions in universities and in part constructed by the public nature of publishing and the authoritative look of the word in print.

In writing *Saying Something,* I have been very aware of the conflicting needs of the three audiences I have most wanted to reach: musicians, listeners, and academics. I am quite convinced that what is of most interest to musicians and listeners is of least interest to academics, and vice versa. I only hope that what emerges is the complex way in which the daily lives of musicians and the sounds they produce are connected to issues that extend well beyond the musical community. Music has become a fashionable topic for interpreters of popular culture, in part because musical performance makes visible some of the most hotly contested aspects of American and transnational culture: race, gender, sexuality, politics, and economics. Indeed, a history of twentieth-century popular music as a cross-cultural encounter between black and white—and between black and the rest of the world—would go a long way toward summarizing the most intractable dilemmas in American culture. Yet there has often been little understanding of music to accompany the many insights on politics and economics in such literature. While it may be intuitively obvious to musicians and listeners that musical sound has a great effect on people, non-musicians, for the most part, remain quite mystified by how this happens.

The perspectives that musicians gave me in 1989 and 1990 and in the ongoing conversations I have had with some of them since inaugurated my search through histories, interpretive theories, musical theories, ethnographic work, and mass media to see how their perspectives intersected with other discussions taking place about culture, politics, and style. The continual emphasis by the musicians who participated in this project on the importance of their expertise, the inadequacies of the jazz literature that has ignored it, and the centrality of the music itself made it imperative for me to address the deeper implications of these positions for some of the most abstract debates in academia, particularly those about voice, human agency, and the ethics of academia. The fact that it has become necessary to make a case for the relevance of vernacular voices (musical and linguistic) to cultural interpretation illustrates how far thinking in the humanities has moved away from the classic emphasis on insider, or *emic,* perspectives in ethnomusicology (Burnim 1985; Feld 1981; Stone and Stone 1981). Ethnomusicologists, it seems to me, cannot afford to stand on the sidelines of this debate.

I recognize that there are many in the musical community who may find the language of this debate alienating and off-putting, in part because of the futility of using language to describe the emotional and spiritual dimensions of musical experience. Either you hear it or you don't, you feel it or you won't. Nevertheless, I feel there is value in attempting to flesh out the implications of what musicians are saying and playing for those in other walks of life.

When I re-read my talk with Joanne Brackeen, I realized that she was trying to tell me things that turned out to be very important to the themes of this book, but at the time I was deaf to her more mystical way of putting them.

> Well, everything you do relates to everything else. [a hint of exasperation at my literal-minded questions] You see, everything is just energy, it's just energy moving in different ways. So everything you do, everything you think, everything you feel goes into what you produce. So, you know, it's a funny thing. There's not so many words to describe it. But it's a very definite thing. It's not that [musical energy is] not definite. It's more definite than things that are described by words in a definite form. You know, the only reason that we think something is definite is that we put on the clothes of language to it and then, you know, people read books and all it is is language. (Brackeen 1989)

The clothes of language, it seems, do much to mute the sounds of music, and this book (after all is said and done) is mostly language. There are, therefore, only so many claims I would care to make for its definiteness or authority. If I began by exploring the implications of language metaphors for musical interpretation, I am ending upside down by suggesting the implications of musical sounds for discourse. My mode has been one of saying, which certainly isn't as much fun as playing (and certainly not as moving), but "Shaw 'Nuff" (Gillespie and Parker 1945) it won't be the last word.

N O T E S

Introduction

1. Major works written or compiled by independent scholars or those with partial academic affiliation include Baraka 1963; Bruyninckx 1980; Chilton 1989; Collier 1978, 1983, 1989; Priestly 1982, 1987; Schuller 1968, 1986, 1989; Sidran 1986; Williams 1970, 1983, 1985; and Wilmer 1977.

2. Accounts of the melodic, rhythmic, harmonic, structural, and formulaic characteristics of individual improvisers—including Charlie Parker (Owens 1974), Lester Young (Porter 1985b), John Coltrane (Porter 1985a; Kernfeld 1981), Sonny Rollins (Blanq 1977), Clifford Brown (Stewart 1973), and Bill Evans (Smith 1983; Larson 1987)—have established the musical complexity of jazz improvisation through the use of musical analysis. The best and most important musicological works on jazz in recent years include Tucker 1989 and DeVeaux 1985.

3. The principal works in this area include Treitler 1974; Tomlinson 1984, 1991, 1993a, 1993b; and McClary 1990.

4. I have struggled to find an appropriate term for Western composed, notated, nonimprovised music to contrast with jazz composition and improvisation and have found all the possibilities wanting. The term *Western classical music* may seem to imply that jazz, by comparison, is not a classical music, which to many it is. Indeed, jazz has been described as "America's classical music" (Sales 1984). The term *Western art music* raises the same problem, for within the jazz community jazz has been viewed as an art music since at least the 1940s. In view of this terminological impasse, I have decided to use the term *Western classical music* to mean composed, notated music informed by the high-art aesthetic traditions of Western Europe. What we know as jazz blends the aesthetics of African, African American, Western European, and non–African American musics, and no single term will ever capture its fullness.

5. Among the most important works on ethnotheories are Feld 1981, 1982, 1988; and Zemp 1978. Feld and Zemp, who worked in relatively egalitarian societies, also distinguished themselves from ethnomusicologists studying cultural sys-

tems with high-art traditions (such as those of India, Indonesia, and Japan) by arguing for the legitimacy of non-Western musics that lack literate bodies of musical theory.

Chapter One

1. Although Jerome Harris was at the New England Conservatory around the same time I was there, I did not know him.

2. WBGO is New York's principal jazz radio station. Its studios are in Newark, New Jersey. Pulliam produces NPR's *Jazz Set with Branford Marsalis.*

3. Sometimes I used the term *musicologist* since the prefix *ethno-* carries a potentially marginalizing and racializing meaning. Musicians do not see why the more general term (*musicology*) should be reserved for Western classical music. A similar complaint has been made by scholars of Indian music: to call the study of the music of India ethnomusicology reeks of a hierarchical conception that places the West at the center. Ethnomusicologists have been searching for a new name for the field for many years, with no obvious candidate emerging. "The anthropology of music" is one suggestion. The methodological and interpretive sense of "music as a cultural practice" does not distill into an alternative disciplinary name very easily.

4. I mean to recognize the excellence of many journalists as interviewers.

5. Jackie McLean's "Fidel," which I discuss in chapter 2, was one of the examples Washington chose.

6. Large Checker Cabs have been favorites among musicians because of their capacity for lots of instruments, including basses and drums.

7. Briggs's work is part of a much larger literature in linguistic anthropology concerned with the cultural variability of language and communicative assumptions. For an overview of some of this literature, see Duranti 1992, Hanks 1989, and Lucy 1993.

8. Of course there has been much discussion of the problem of talking about music itself, most notably in Charles Seeger's work on the "linguocentric predicament" (Seeger 1977, 23, 45–50).

9. Conversation analysts have even devised special notational conventions for the transcription of conversation. See Goodwin 1981.

10. Compare Brown 1979; Ochs 1988, 26–29; and Moerman 1988, 3–13. Ochs and Moerman take contrasting positions regarding the universality of conversational organization, with Moerman defending the universalistic view.

11. I am using "standard" here in the linguistic sense of a standard language: "A *standard language variety* is a variety that has been designated as such and for which a set of forms has been identified and codified in dictionaries and grammars" (Finnegan and Besnier 1989, 496).

12. For this reason, I chose to use standard spelling in the title of this book— *Saying Something* rather than *Sayin' Something.*

13. I transcribed all of the musical examples myself but enlisted help in revising and correcting them. I thank Michael Kocour for thorough revisions to the piano voicings in "Bass-ment Blues" (musical example 17). His extraordinary ear for complex voicings greatly improved the quality of the musical example. I also thank Becca Pulliam and Greg Burrows for proofreading and correcting the piano and

drum parts in "Bass-ment Blues." I thank Michael Weiss for proofreading and suggesting corrections to my piano voicings in musical example 5.

Chapter Two

1. For additional discussion of rhythm section roles, see Berliner 1994, 314–47.

2. The importance of time holds regardless of tempo. Many musicians told me that a slow ballad is the hardest to play with good time. Out-of-time sections, in which the sense of pulse is effaced or suspended, contrast with the pulsed version of time musicians talk about here.

3. Discussions of classical tonal works in music theory, by contrast, generally emphasize tonal plan, with a view toward demonstrating how diverse musical elements serve to reinforce and support that plan. Jan LaRue terms this relationship *concinnity* (LaRue 1970, 16). Some jazz works are centrally concerned with tonal plan, however. Lewis Porter has uncovered evidence of long-range tonal planning in John Coltrane's *A Love Supreme* (Porter 1985a). Duke Ellington's compositions also stand out in this regard. As composers of tunes and other frameworks for improvisation, jazz musicians are certainly concerned with tonal issues. Improvisation within a typical jazz song form, however, provides the improviser with a predetermined tonal organization. Although musicians can and do deviate from this plan with great originality, the central point is that within such a framework, musical interest and large-scale development frequently derive from elements other than large-scale tonal plan.

4. A medium-tempo $\frac{4}{4}$ swing feel is presumed by this description. At faster tempos, a bass player may go into cut time and play bass notes that are half notes in duration. Musicians call this *playing in two*. Even at medium tempo, the bass player may begin in two and switch to four after one or two choruses to intensify the rhythmic texture. The prevailing bass motion in medium-tempo jazz tunes is generally in four, however (Michael Weiss 1990).

5. He's talking about the B section of an AABA tune here.

6. For further musical examples of the bass, see Berliner 1994, 607–16.

7. For further discussion of riffs, see Schuller's discussion of Count Basie (Schuller 1989, 242–44) and Berliner 1994, 102, 346. An excellent recorded example of riffs can be found on Basie's *Volcano* (1939).

8. The term *"Rhythm" changes* refers to the standard harmonic progression on George and Ira Gershwin's "I Got Rhythm" (Gershwin and Gershwin 1930). In B-flat, it is as follows:

A section: ‖: B♭ maj7 G7 | c-7 F7 | B♭ maj7 G7 | c-7 F7 | f-7 B♭7 | E♭ A♭7*
$$1. \underline{\hspace{1.5cm}} \quad 2. \underline{\hspace{1.5cm}}$$
| d-7** G7 | c-7 F7 : ‖ B♭maj7 ‖

B section: | D7 | D7 | G7 | G7 | C7 | C7 | F7 | F7 |

The form of the tune is AABA.

*Eo7 in some lead sheets.

**B♭major 7 in some lead sheets.

See Berliner 1994, 76–82, for further explanation of tunes used as harmonic prototypes in jazz.

9. The choice of this G diminished triad produces the effect of a blue note because D-flat is a lowered third in the key of B-flat. The use of diminished triads in this passage, however, makes it tonally ambiguous, especially since the bassist discontinues playing in measure 1.

10. For further musical examples of piano accompaniment and comping, see Berliner 1994, 629–49.

11. I would like to emphasize that my line of questioning in the interviewing process guided each musician to talk about the role of his or her instrument. Had I asked directly whether that instrument was the only important one in the ensemble, the answer in every case would have been no.

12. For an account of the development of the drum set and its early use in jazz, see Brown 1976, 89–131.

13. Pianists often combine stable with freer parts as well—for example, comping with the left hand while playing a solo melody line with the right.

14. Washington's characterization of Higgins's cymbal beat as "wide" probably has to do with the timbre of the cymbal as well as the open feeling with which he articulates the rhythm. Higgins uses a sizzle-type cymbal for his ride, which sustains the cymbal sound. A sizzle cymbal has holes drilled around the edges through which rivets are placed. These rivets cause the cymbal to sustain the sound when it is struck, giving it its characteristic sizzle (Brown 1976, 507).

15. The Smithsonian Institution sponsored the interviews, known as the Jazz Oral History Project. They are housed at the Institute for Jazz Studies, Rutgers University, Newark, New Jersey.

16. See also Charles Keil's (1972) discussion of the relationship between bass players and drummers, in which he explains the difference between "chunky" and "stringy" bass styles. Drummers in particular are very conscious of their ability to influence the tempos and pulse of the other instrumentalists in the band. See also Keil 1995.

17. For further examples of ride rhythms, fills, and drum punctuations, see Berliner 1994, 617–22.

18. Common talk about a drummer's limb use assumes that the player is right-handed. Among left-handed players, the ride cymbal is played by the left hand while the right hand plays rhythms on the snare.

19. Washington did not cite specific recordings. Among others, Vernell Fournier and Ahmad Jamal appeared together on Jamal 1961; Wynton Kelly and Jimmy Cobb on Kelly 1959; Sonny Clark and Philly Joe Jones on McLean 1958.

20. While some drummers tune their drums to particular intervals (low, middle, and high tom-tom in fourths, for example), others avoid definite pitches, since they may clash with the harmony or the soloist. Tuning preferences are highly individual, but achieving a good sound is an important aesthetic consideration for most drummers.

21. He's talking about the cymbal sustaining while he breaks from playing time to play fills.

22. The Moms Mabley reference is also a widely known sexual joke.

23. In his role as drum teacher, Carvin frequently uses stories, anecdotes, and what he calls "parables" to explain musical processes to his students.

24. This explanation of the image of the drum as a woman contrasts with the more explicitly sexual imagery of Duke Ellington's (1956) suite of the same title. The opening stanza of the lyrics to that composition are as follows:

> A drum is a woman
> Who won't stay out of your blood.
> A drum is a woman
> Its beat is like the quickening of a heart in love.
> Each beat caresses you
> Like the soft words you only hear
> When a woman caresses you.

This image has also been commented upon from a feminist perspective. Jayne Cortez's poem "If the Drum Is a Woman" (1984) uses the image to deplore violence against women:

> If the drum is a woman
> then understand your drum
> your drum is not docile
> your drum is not invisible
> your drum is not inferior to you
>
> . . .
>
> if the drum is a woman
> don't abuse your drum don't abuse
> your drum
> don't abuse your drum.

25. A feel is synonymous with a groove in the sense that both refer to the rhythmic gestalt created by multiple rhythmic parts. The word *feel*, however, stresses the emotional state created by the gestalt, while the term *groove* refers specifically to the physical grooves in 78s and LPs. The terms *groove* and *in the groove* appear to have come into usage in the 1930s. Robert Gold (1975) dates the term *swing*, which can also be a synonym, to 1888. All of these dates derive from the appearance of these terms in published sheet music and in the European and American jazz press, which may not reflect actual use among musicians.

26. The boundaries of the noun and verb usages are not absolute. For example, the concept of being in the groove is a noun usage related to the aesthetic sense of the term: being in the flow of something that is grooving.

27. Historian Douglas Henry Daniels suggests that "to swing people . . . is to move them emotionally" (Daniels 1985, 319). *Swing* is, of course, a synonym for this sense of *groove.*

28. When I later showed Weiss this quotation, he wanted to revise the wording to make it more like written prose—a common reaction to transcripts of speech (see chapter 1). I have included his aural version in the text (as I have done for everyone) but would like to include his own edits here for comparison: "Every bass player, drummer, and piano player feels the beat his or her own way and some are more sensitive or flexible than others. . . . It's . . . not unlike when you meet somebody and you discover an immediate compatibility that's just there."

29. Weiss explains "hitting" in another rewording: "A lot of times it's just a matter of having chosen the right tempo."

30. I am thinking specifically of the drummer's highly subdivided rolls and of rhythmic figures that are played on one or more of the drums. Improvisational lines played by soloists are not as frequently subdivided into 32nds or 16th sextuplets.

31. He means whether a note is consonant or dissonant with respect to the prevailing harmony. "Wrong," however, carries a positive aesthetic evaluation here. Effective use of dissonance is implied by the notion of placing a "wrong" note properly within the musical flow.

32. I have frequently heard musicians say that the soloist's role should be to "float on top" of the rhythm section. I have also heard rhythm section players say that soloists must participate in defining the groove by phrasing in a rhythmically effective manner. One musician expressed disdain for soloists who spend too much time "floating" and do not understand the effect they can have on the flow of the rhythm section.

Chapter Three

1. See Berliner 1994, 348–86.

2. The literature on the relationship between music and language is vast. There are several useful overviews, including Powers 1980; Feld 1974; and Nattiez 1990a, 1990b.

3. Turner gives the example of "the frontspiece to Hobbes's *Leviathan,* in which the giant body of the sovereign is made up of the bodies of his subjects" (Turner 1991, 158). For more on Charles Seeger's framework, see Feld 1984.

4. Once improvisations are recorded, however, they become sonic texts, a topic discussed further in chapter 4. I am limiting my discussion here to the playing that occurs during improvised solos, although there is much improvised interaction from the rhythm section during the playing of the tune or composition as well. For a detailed discussion of the relationship between composition and improvisation, see Berliner 1994, 63–94, 170–91.

5. For a cross-cultural overview of language and music, see Powers 1980.

6. Other cultures make a *langue* and *parole* distinction as well. Feld and Schieffelin (1982) discuss this concept in relation to language in the culture of the Kaluli of Papua New Guinea.

7. Gates's summary of the sociolinguistic literature on signifying is perhaps the most concise currently available (Gates 1988, 44–88).

8. For a discussion of the concept of intertextuality in literary theories, see Hutcheon 1991, 23, 37, 87.

9. Schuller's criticisms of Count Basie's "riff-cum-blues" formats, for example, center on the problems of repetition, lack of harmonic innovation, and clichés (Schuller 1989, 222–62).

10. Most of these articles can be found in the Institute for Jazz Studies (IJS) clippings files under "Jazz Terminology."

11. In 1946, Cab Calloway published a "Hepster's Dictionary" (Calloway 1946) that some (Feather 1952) have credited for encouraging the trend of jazz word

lists, dictionaries, or lexicons that was to intensify in the 1950s and 1960s (Shaw 1950; Morris 1954; "Jive Talk" 1954; Burley 1955; Horne 1961; Lees 1962; Gold 1975).

12. The musician requested that this quote be unattributed.

13. Lincoln and Mamiya (1990) discuss this aspect of African American worship practice as well (5–6). The response of a member of a congregation may also be in song (349).

Chapter Four

1. In this groove, each beat of the slower moving 4/4 can be felt as a 3/4 bar whose quarter notes (eighth of triplet = quarter in 3/4) are moving three times as fast. The bass part moves in quarter or half notes against the cymbal pattern, which (in combination with a vocal line in 4/4) prevents the faster 3/4 feeling from predominating.

2. I thank Nahum Chandler for referring me to this essay.

3. I thank Douglas Bruster for referring me to Hutcheon's work.

4. For further discussion of the issues of irony and humor in African American studies, see Gates 1988, 103–7; Lawrence Levine 1977, 298–366.

5. *The Sound of Music* opened at the Lunt-Fontanne Theater in New York City on 16 November 1959.

6. Alain Gerber discusses the "silly" (*niais*) character of standards chosen by both Sonny Rollins and John Coltrane, as well as providing an extended interpretation of "My Favorite Things" (Gerber 1985, 65–74).

7. I did not mention "My Favorite Things"; Harris brought up the subject on his own.

8. For an account of the lunch counter sit-ins and the general escalation of the Civil Rights movement in 1960, see Branch 1988, 271–311. This was also the year in which Ornette Coleman became nationally known and the controversy over "free jazz" began to develop (Spellman 1985). In October Charles Mingus recorded his version of "Fables of Faubus" (Mingus 1960) with lyrics explicitly protesting Governor Orval Faubus's refusal to allow nine black students to enroll in Little Rock's Central High School (Branch 1988, 222–25). By 1962 there were public expressions of serious racial and political divisions within the jazz world. See, for example, Gitler 1962a, 1962b.

9. It does not matter that the musical theater song was not intended to live up to the standards of classical music.

10. The liner notes to the album (Kirk 1965) mention that there are also electronically produced sounds in the coda to "Rip, Rig, and Panic." Kirk reportedly produced them by shaking an amplifier.

11. A preference for serious expression, however, does not preclude the existence of irony and humor in Western classical music; Varèse provides one example among many. The point here is that irony and parody are more central and expected means of aesthetic expression in the African American tradition.

12. Modern jazz musicians almost universally read music; the transmission of many features of musical style, however, is accomplished aurally.

13. I have in mind here musical relationships uncovered primarily through analysis, such as Schoenberg's use of row forms.

14. Indeed, the use of the metaphor of discourse to describe the inter-related, contingent aspects of music has generated much confusion as an application of poststructural and postmodern concepts to a nonlinguistic social practice. This topic is more fully explored in chapter 6.

Chapter Five

1. My discussion here is indebted to Peretti 1992 and DeVeaux 1991.

2. I also do not mean to suggest that I am the only one who has been dissatisfied with the state of jazz historiography and has been working on alternatives. For a more exhaustive treatment of intellectual trends in jazz historiography, see De-Veaux 1991, Radano 1993, and Berliner 1994.

3. Lennie's on the Turnpike operated from 1963 to 1971 (Kernfeld 1988, 2:237). A discrepancy exists regarding the spelling of the club's name. The Prestige recording (Byard 1965) lists it as "Lennie's on the Turnpike" and the owner's name as Lennie Sogoloff; Kernfeld records it as "Lenny's on the Turnpike."

4. I credit Travis Jackson's paper "'Takin' It to Another Level': Creating Flow in 'Jazz' Performance" (1995) with reminding me of this usage.

5. The f-natural is diatonic to the G dominant seventh chord—the first chord in a blues in G.

6. Bass is notated an octave above actual pitch. This melodic idea lays comfortably on the bass (Chevan 1995).

7. I do not mean to suggest a thematic analysis on the basis of these ideas; I only want to point out that these are melodic figures that recur throughout Tucker's solo. I thank Matthew Butterfield for commentary concerning this point.

8. Byard's first recorded engagement with Mingus was on 12 October 1962 at Town Hall (Priestly 1982, 273). Priestly reports that Byard had played occasionally with Mingus as early as 1959 (110). "Fables of Faubus" appeared regularly in live recordings (Mingus 1964a, 1964d).

9. Byard called this quarter-note, broken-chord accompaniment *Boston:* "Now what I'm playing there, that's called 'Boston.' The Boston background. . . . The leader would say, 'Play Boston, man, play Boston'" (Byard 1990). In an interview with Johnny St. Cyr, William Russell credits the term *Boston rhythm* to drummer Baby Dodds, who used it to describe playing on the offbeats only (St. Cyr 1958, 37). *Boston* has been used in another sense as well: in the 1930s, "to take a Boston" meant "to take a solo" or be featured on a particular piece (Pelote 1991). John Clement's liner notes to Ellington (1953) use the term as follows: "Finally, Russell Procope takes his Boston on 'Please Be Kind' to end this LP by the greatest orchestra in jazz—Duke Ellington's."

10. See Wright 1982 for scores to several big-band compositions.

11. Examples of send-offs (or *lead-ins,* as they are sometimes called) can be found in Rayburn Wright's *Inside the Score* (1982). The score to Sammy Nestico's "Basie—Straight Ahead" features a four-measure lead-in that introduces the piano solo at rehearsal letter H (20). A two-measure send-off occurs in Thad Jones's

"Three and One" (68). Ensemble passages that introduce the soloist in what ordinarily would be the first few measures of the solo are frequently heard in big band arrangements. They usually occur just once, at the beginning of the solo.

12. These remarks were in the liner notes to volume 1; "Bass-ment Blues" was included on volume 2. However, as noted earlier, "Bass-ment Blues" was recorded on the same evening as the materials included in volume 1 (Byard 1965). The tendency for hyperbole in liner notes should be noted, as well as Giller's modernist aesthetic.

13. I've omitted the names in this case, since there is no point in embarrassing anyone.

14. The relative lack of attention to errors in Western classical music performance must certainly be seen as a product of the scholarly emphasis on scores over performance. Leonard Meyer, however, devoted an entire chapter of *Emotion and Meaning in Music* to the issue of "deviation in performance" (Meyer 1956, 197–232). He even considered the expressive potential of such deviations (200).

15. Tucker, who was born on 10 December 1927, died on 10 October 1965. He collapsed on the bandstand on the night of 9 October 1965 (Hunt 1968, 15). He was thirty-seven years old at the time.

16. Alto saxophonist, flutist, and bass clarinetist Eric Dolphy lived from 20 June 1928 to 29 June 1964; tenor saxophonist and flutist Joe Farrell lived from 16 December 1937 to 10 January 1986; trumpeter Booker Little lived from 2 April 1938 to 5 October 1961; drummer John Curtis (J. C.) Moses lived from 18 October 1936 to 1977; Booker Ervin lived from 31 October 1930 to 31 August 1970 (Kernfeld 1988).

17. An incident with a fire axe got Mingus thrown out of the Duke Ellington band in 1953. After making a racist insult, trombonist Juan Tizol had to defend himself with a machete when Mingus attacked him with a fire axe (Priestly 1982, 50–51). There are several versions of this story in circulation. Mingus's own account can be found in his autobiography, *Beneath the Underdog* (Mingus 1971, 323–25). According to this account, Tizol hurled a racial slur at Mingus and attacked him with a "bolo knife" after accusing him of not being able to read his bass part. Mingus claims he retaliated by slashing Tizol's chair in two with a fire axe. Nat Hentoff, on the other hand, describes Mingus as going after Tizol with a heavy steel pipe after he had questioned Mingus's understanding of the rhythm patterns of an Ellington piece (Tucker 1993, 366). Commenting on his penchant for axes, Mingus later said that he told young musicians: "First thing you do is check out the acoustics in the hall, and then find the fire-ax" (Mingus 1978, 53).

18. What I am calling emotion or feeling here could also be thought of as spiritual. To fully explore this theme, however, would require another book.

19. Byard was born in Worcester, Massachusetts, on 15 June 1922.

20. Examples from Hines's solo recordings include "Rosetta," "Child of a Disordered Brain," and "My Melancholy Baby," which are all included on a Bluebird reissue (Hines 1939). These selections were recorded in 1939, 1949, and 1941, respectively. Byard's use of stride style can be heard during his piano solo on "Bassment Blues" as well as in many of the recordings he made with Charles Mingus—

for example, "A.T.F.W.U.S.A. (A.T.F.W.Y.O.U.)" (Mingus 1964b, 1964c). The "A.T." and "F.W." in the title stand for Art Tatum and Fats Waller (Priestly 1982, 156).

21. For example, Hines's recording of "On the Sunny Side of the Street" (Hines 1939) includes parallel augmented triads built on the whole-tone scale.

22. Gunther Schuller has noted that Hines's right-hand octave tremolos were "legendary" (Schuller 1989, 290n). He says that the right-hand tremolo is difficult to master and that few pianists can play prolonged tremolos. Examples of Hines's tremolos used in a big band context can be heard on "Boogie Woogie on *St. Louis Blues*" (Hines 1939). In this tune the tremolo is used both as an accompaniment against the saxophone section (lasting approximately 20 seconds) and in call-and-response exchanges between the piano and the bass near the end of the arrangement. Schuller cites Art Tatum, Oscar Peterson, and Erroll Garner as pianists who also had this facility.

23. For a discussion of many of these pedagogical works, see Smith 1983, 62–90. For a comprehensive discussion of jazz learning processes, see Berliner 1994.

24. From 1941 to 1944 Byard was in the army (Morgenstern 1965, 18).

25. Some of Byard's big band compositions can be heard on *Jaki Byard and the Apollo Stompers* (Byard 1984). Byard has taught at the New England Conservatory of Music, Hartt College, the Manhattan School of Music, and the New School.

26. Composer, pianist, and theorist George Russell has also referred to Byard as a genius (Brown 1979, 15). The tenacity of the romantic idea of genius among musicians is apparent.

27. Dannie Richmond's observations about musical development and making rhythmic transformations can be found in Priestly's biography (1982, 84–85).

28. Perhaps the most famous instance of Mingus's verbal showmanship done expressly for the band is found on *Charles Mingus Presents Charles Mingus* (Mingus 1960). Mingus talks as if the recording were being made live in a nightclub setting. He asks people to refrain from clinking their glasses and ringing the cash register, and he introduces each tune as if from the stage. The recording, however, was done in a studio.

29. "Cherokee" (Noble 1938) is a jazz standard that was frequently played at very fast tempos by bebop musicians. Additional examples of Mingus's behavior toward band members are found throughout Priestly's biography (1982).

30. *Token* here means an example of a verb in past-tense form—*ate*, for example.

31. There are also nonreferential linguistic indexes that describe something about the structure of a speech event but contribute nothing to the propositional value of a statement. Linguistic tokens that, for example, reveal the gender of a person speaking or indicate a relationship of deference between speaker and addressee are examples of such nonreferential indexes (Silverstein 1976, 30–31).

32. *Reference* in linguistic usage excludes figurative and indexical aspects of more informal usages of the term, such as were employed in chapter 4.

33. By defining a quotation semiotically as an indexical icon, I mean to say that a quoted musical phrase points to a prior performance through a musical phrase that resembles (is an icon of) a passage in the prior work.

34. The linguistic literature (by Jakobson in particular) talks about the "co-text" established through metric means (Silverstein 1993, 50–51). In the jazz rhythm section, clearly, there are several overlapping and intersecting rhythmic parameters (metricalized co-texts) that are further metapragmatically constrained by harmonic and melodic considerations.

35. Abbate's and Nattiez's idea of "past tense" is actually more specific: they raise the question of whether music can *narrate* something, by which they mean whether it can literally tell the story of something like Dukas's *The Sorcerer's Apprentice*. Narration in Silverstein's framework would require of music the ability to "reportively calibrate" an event, and Silverstein cites the "so-called historical present" tense as an example (Silverstein 1993, 49–50). Musical narration in this sense would require propositional as well as indexical signification. Abbate recognizes the possibility of intermusicality but rejects the intertextual musical argument as interpretively promiscuous, a charge to which I plead guilty. She argues that under very limited circumstances music can narrate (Abbate 1991). Nattiez argues that music quite simply cannot narrate in the literary sense.

36. These are simply different conceptual frameworks from which to view the same phenomena. For those particularly interested in exploring the interface between musical analysis and context, Silverstein's notion of indexicality is particularly useful.

37. This is a point similar to that made by Goodwin in her discussion of format tying.

38. Remember that the establishment of the rhythmic feel includes the establishment of the harmonic context as well.

39. In this example I am presuming the typical piano–bass–drums–soloist configuration. In the case of a solo by one of the rhythm section members, the number of interactive layers establishing the groove would be reduced, but the fundamental idea that there may be multiple interactional layers at any given time remains.

40. All of these can potentially carry intermusical meaning as well. I am well aware of the capacity of recent computer software to generate envelope shapes, timbral spectra, and the like. My apologies to any music theorist who has successfully incorporated them into a systematic analysis. My discussion presumes musical analysis in the more traditional sense of working from standard Western notation.

41. See Hanks 1990 for an intriguing and suggestive discussion of the way in which language deictics structure social space among the Maya.

42. The cohesive performance of a Western classical musical score requires a similar sort of aural communication, anticipation, and cooperation among musicians—without, however, requiring the actual production of new musical material in performance.

43. By "traditional music theory" I mean harmonic and pitch-centered, score-based analyses of tonal and nontonal music. I thank Richard Cohn for drawing my attention to recent literature in music theory and for a critical reading of this section of the chapter.

44. See, for example, the exchange between Gary Tomlinson (1993a, 1993b) and Lawrence Kramer (1993).

Chapter Six

1. Guilbault includes transcriptions by three collaborating authors as well: Édouard Benoit, Gage Averill, and Gregory Rabess (Guilbault 1993). For Guilbault's identification of the Caribbean dance rhythms related to zouk, see page 132 of her study.

2. Even eighth notes in "Latin" grooves are a separate question.

3. See Tomlinson 1991 for a discussion of *Bitches Brew.*

4. For an overview of the issue of racial mixture in the era of Jim Crow, see McMillen 1989, 14–23. The literature on the topic of miscegenation more broadly is vast. The OCLC worldwide data base lists 670 citations under the topic. For a discussion of racial intermixture and early jazz see Peretti 1992, 193–94.

5. I am well aware that the dislike of mixture has a long history in European culture and would require a much larger discussion to be adequately contextualized within European and American ideas of modernity. See Gilman 1985 for a comparative discussion of stereotypes of race, gender, and madness.

6. Appiah cites the work of several well-known geneticists in asserting that two people within the same racial category have an 85.7 percent chance of having the same characteristic at a random chromosomal locus while two people from different "races" have an 85.2 percent chance (Appiah 1992, 36). There is then only a 14.3 to 14.8 percent chance that two individuals taken at random from the world population will have a different gene at any particular site on a chromosome. The differences between the "races," then, are primarily morphological.

7. See Gilroy 1991 for an articulation of this opinion with respect to the politics of race in Britain.

8. For this reason, these philosophies are sometimes described as "antihumanist." See Spivak 1988b, 212, for this usage.

9. This general point is also similar to Bakhtin's notion of dialogism.

10. See also Spivak 1990, 1992.

11. See, for example, Duranti and Goodwin 1992; Hanks 1987, 1989; Lucy 1993; Ochs 1992; Schieffelin 1990; Silverstein 1976, 1993.

12. There is a large body of literature on popular culture and music that incorporates poststructuralist and postmodern themes to varying degrees. See, for example, Schwichtenberg 1993, Ferguson 1990, and Bhabha 1994. I do not mean to critique this work as a whole but to question aspects of its approach to the issues of subjectivity and agency.

13. See also Berliner 1994, 221–85.

INTERVIEWS

Bowler, Phil. 1989. Interview by author. Tape recording. New York, NY, 17 April 1989.

Brackeen, Joanne. 1989. Interview by author. Tape recording. New York, NY, 9 December 1989.

Byard, Jaki. 1991. Interview by author. Tape recording. New York, NY, 20 February 1991.

———. 1990. Interview by author. Tape recording. New York, NY, 12 & 19 February 1990.

Byron, Don. 1992. Personal communication. Chicago, IL, 10 December 1992.

———. 1989. Interview by author. Tape recording. Bronx, NY, 10 April 1989.

———. 1987. Interview by author. Tape recording. New York, NY, 8 May 1987.

Carvin, Michael. 1992. Interview by author. Tape recording. Chicago, IL, 12 December 1992.

———. 1990. Interview by author. Tape recording. New York, NY, 10 October 1990.

Davis, Richard. 1989. Interview by author. Tape recording. New York, NY, 6 July 1989.

Hanna, Sir Roland. 1989. Interview by author. Tape recording. New York, NY, 25 October 1989.

Harris, Jerome. 1992. Interview by author. Tape recording. Brooklyn, NY, 24 August 1992.

———. 1989. Interview by author. Tape recording. Brooklyn, NY, 29 May 1989.

Haynes, Roy. 1990. Interview by author. Tape recording. New York, NY, 4 June 1990.

Higgins, Billy. 1990. Interview by author. Tape recording. New York, NY, 6 August 1990.

McBee, Cecil. 1990. Interview by author. Tape recording. New York, NY, 24 May 1990.

Peterson, Ralph Jr. 1989a. Interview by author. Tape recording. New York, NY, 17 April 1989.

———. 1989b. Interview by author. Tape recording. New York, NY, 28 November 1989.

Washington, Kenny. 1990. Interview by author. Tape recording. Brooklyn, NY, 25 January 1990.

Weiss, Michael. 1990. Interview by author. Tape recording. Brooklyn, NY, 13 August 1990.

RECORDINGS

Basie, Count. 1939. *Volcano.* Los Angeles: 6 November 1939. CBS 66101 (53971).

Blakey, Art. 1958. *Moanin'.* New York: 30 October 1958. Blue Note CDP 7 46516 2.

Byard, Jaki. 1965. *The Jaki Byard Quartet: Live!* West Peabody, MA: 15 April 1965. Prestige PCD-24121-2. Originally issued as vol. 1, PR-7419, and vol. 2, PR-7477.

Coleman, Ornette. 1987. *In All Languages.* New York: February–March 1987. Caravan of Dreams CDP 85008.

———. 1960. *Free Jazz.* New York: 21 December 1960. Atlantic SD 1364.

———. 1959a. *The Shape of Jazz to Come.* Los Angeles: 22 May 1959; New York: 8 October 1959. Atlantic SD 1317.

———. 1959b. *Change of the Century.* New York: 8–9 October 1959. Atlantic SD 1327.

Coltrane, John. 1960a. *Coltrane's Sound.* New York: 24, 26 October 1960. Atlantic SD 1419.

———. 1960b. *John Coltrane: Coltrane Plays the Blues.* New York: 24 October 1960. Atlantic SD 1382.

———. 1960c. *My Favorite Things.* New York: 21, 24, 26 October 1960. Atlantic SD 1361.

Davis, Miles. 1983. *Decoy.* New York: 31 June, 7 July, 5 September, 10 September 1983. Columbia CD 38991.

———. 1969a. *Bitches Brew.* New York: 19–21 August 1969. Columbia C2K 40577.

———. 1969b. *In a Silent Way.* New York: 18 February 1969. Columbia CK 40580.

———. 1964. *Miles in Berlin.* Berlin: 25 September 1964. CBS/Sony CSCS 5147.

Ellington, Duke. 1956. *A Drum is a Woman.* New York: September–December 1956. Columbia JCL 951.

———. 1953. "Please Be Kind." Duke Ellington and His Orchestra. Portland, OR: 29 April 1953. Stardust.

Franklin, Aretha. 1972. *Amazing Grace.* Los Angeles: 14 January 1972. Atlantic SD 2-906.

Gillespie, Dizzy, and Charlie Parker. "Shaw 'Nuff." *The Smithsonian Collection of Classic Jazz.* Hollywood, CA: 29 December 1945. The Smithsonian Collection R033 P7-19477.

Gordon, Dexter. 1962. *A Swingin' Affair.* Englewood Cliffs, NJ: 29 August 1962. Blue Note CDP 7 84133 2.

Griffin, Johnny. 1983. *Call It Whachawana.* Berkeley, CA: 25–26 July 1983. Galaxy GXY-5146.

Hawkins, Coleman. 1939. "Body and Soul." *The Complete Coleman Hawkins: Volume I (1929–1940).* New York: 11 October 1939. RCA Editeur FMX1 7325.

Hines, Earl. 1939. *Earl Hines: Piano Man, 1939–1942.* RCA (Bluebird reissue) BMG 6750-2-RB.

Jamal, Ahmad. 1961. *At the Blackhawk.* San Francisco: 1961. Chess 515002.

Kelly, Wynton. 1959. *Kelly Blue.* New York: 19 February, 10 March 1959. Original Jazz Classics OJC-033.

Kirk, Rahsaan Roland. 1965. *Rip, Rig, and Panic.* Englewood Cliffs, NJ: 13 January 1965. Limelight (LS) 86027.

McLean, Jackie. 1958. "Fidel." *Jackie's Bag.* Hackensack, NJ: 18 January 1958. Blue Note CDP 7 46142 2.

Mingus, Charles. 1965. *Portrait.* Minneapolis: spring 1964, 5 May 1965. Prestige P 24092.

———. 1964a. *Charles Mingus Live in Paris, Vol. 2.* Paris: 18 April 1964. ESOL-DUN FCD 110.

———. 1964b. *Charles Mingus—Town Hall Concert.* New York: 4 April 1964. Prestige P24092.

———. 1964c. *Charles Mingus Sextet Live in Europe, Vol. 1—Hope So Eric.* Bremen: 16 April 1964. Ingo (It) 10.

———. 1964d. *Charles Mingus Sextet Live in Europe, Vol. 2—Fables of Faubus.* Bremen: 16 April 1964. Ingo (It) 13.

———. 1960. *Charles Mingus Presents Charles Mingus.* New York: 20 October 1960. Candid BR-5012.

Mobley, Hank. 1965. *Dippin'.* Englewood Cliffs, NJ: 18 June 1965. Blue Note CDP 7 46511 2.

Morgan, Lee. 1963. *Sidewinder.* Englewood Cliffs, NJ: 21 December 1963. Blue Note BST 84157.

New York Jazz Quartet. 1975. "Well You Needn't." *In Concert in Japan, Volume 1.* Tokyo: 23 March 1975. CBS ZK 40934.

Peterson, Ralph Jr. 1988. *V.* New York: 19–20 April 1988. Blue Note CDP 91730 2.

Rodgers, Richard, and Oscar Hammerstein II. 1959. *Sound of Music: Selections.* New York: 1959. Columbia LP 5450.

Taylor, Cecil, and Buell Neidlinger. 1961. *New York City R&B.* New York: 9–10 January 1961. Candid CCD 79017.

Thornton, Big Mama. 1967. "Ball N' Chain." *The Roots of Jazz: The Blues Era.* 1967. MU Jazz Classics MLP3-9001.

BIBLIOGRAPHY

Abbate, Carolyn. 1991. *Unsung Voices: Opera and Musical Narrative in the Nineteenth Century.* Princeton: Princeton University Press.
————. 1989. "What the Sorcerer Said." *Nineteenth Century Music* 12: 221–30.
Abrahams, Roger D. 1970. *Deep Down in the Jungle: Negro Narrative Folklore from the Streets of Philadelphia.* 1st rev. ed. Originally published 1964. Chicago: Aldine Publishers.
Abu-Lughod, Lila. 1991. "Writing against Culture." In *Recapturing Anthropology: Working in the Present,* edited by Richard G. Fox, 137–62. Santa Fe, NM: School of American Research Press.
Aldwell, Edward, and Carl Schacter. 1989. *Harmony and Voice Leading.* 2d ed. New York: Harcourt Brace Jovanovich.
Alexander, Elizabeth. 1992. "Collage: An Approach to Reading African-American Women's Literature." Ph.D. diss., University of Pennsylvania.
Appadurai, Arjun. 1993. "Topographies of the Self: Praise and Emotion in Hindu India." In *Language and the Politics of Emotion,* edited by Catherine A. Lutz and Lila Abu-Lughod, 92–112. Cambridge and Paris: Cambridge University Press and Editions de la Maison des Sciences de l'Homme.
Appiah, Kwame Anthony. 1992. *In My Father's House: Africa in the Philosophy of Culture.* New York: Oxford University Press.
Asante, Molefi Kete. 1987. *The Afrocentric Idea.* Philadelphia: Temple University Press.
Austin, John L. 1962. *How to Do Things with Words.* Cambridge, MA: Harvard University Press.
Bakhtin, Mikhail. 1981. "Discourse in the Novel." In *The Dialogic Imagination: Four Essays,* edited by Michael Holquist, 259–422. Originally published 1935. Austin: University of Texas Press.
Baraka, Imamu Amiri (LeRoi Jones). 1963. *Blues People: Negro Music in White America.* New York: William and Morrow.

Beaudry, Nicole. 1978. "Toward Transcription and Analysis of Inuit Throat Games: Macro Structure." *Ethnomusicology* 22(2): 260–73.

Berliner, Paul F. 1994. *Thinking in Jazz: The Infinite Art of Improvisation.* Chicago: University of Chicago Press.

Bernard, Jonathan W. 1987. *The Music of Edgard Varèse.* New Haven: Yale University Press.

Bernstein, Charles M. 1983. "The Traditional Roots of Billy Higgins." *Modern Drummer* 7(2): 20–23+.

Bhabha, Homi K. 1994. *The Location of Culture.* London and New York: Routledge.

Blanq, Charles Clement III. 1977. "Melodic Improvisation in American Jazz: The Style of Theodore 'Sonny' Rollins, 1951–1962." Ph.D. diss., Tulane University.

Blom, Jan-Petter, and John J. Gumperz. 1986. "Social Meaning in Linguistic Structures: Code-Switching in Norway." In *Directions in Sociolinguistics: The Ethnography of Communication,* edited by John J. Gumperz and Dell Hymes, 407–34. Originally published 1972. Oxford: Basil Blackwell.

Bohlman, Philip V. 1993. "Musicology as a Political Act." *Journal of Musicology* 11: 411–36.

Bourdieu, Pierre. 1977. *Outline of a Theory of Practice.* New York: Cambridge University Press.

Branch, Taylor. 1988. *Parting the Waters: America in the King Years, 1954–63.* New York: Simon and Schuster.

Briggs, Charles L. 1986. *Learning How to Ask: A Sociolinguistic Appraisal of the Role of the Interview in Social Science Research.* Cambridge: Cambridge University Press.

Brown, Penelope, and Colin Fraser. 1979. "Speech as a Marker of Social Situation." In *Social Markers in Speech,* edited by Klaus R. Scherer and Howard Giles. New York: Cambridge University Press.

Brown, Richard. 1979. "Jaki Byard: Romping, Stomping and Waiting for THE Break." *Down Beat* 45(5): 15–16+.

Brown, Theodore. 1976. "A History and Analysis of Jazz Drumming to 1942." 2 vols. Ph.D. diss, University of Michigan.

Bruyninckx, Walter. 1980. *Sixty Years of Recorded Jazz: 1917–1977.* Belgium: Walter Bruyninckx, Lange Nieuwstraat 121–2800.

Burley, Dan. 1955. "Time Out for Cool Talk: The Dilemma of Little Louie Hopp." *Tan* 5(7): 10–11+.

Burnim, Mellonee. 1985. "Culture Bearer and Tradition Bearer: An Ethnomusicologist's Research on Gospel Music." *Ethnomusicology* 29: 432–44.

Calloway, Cab. 1946. "Cab Calloway's Hepster's Dictionary." *Disc* 1 (August 1946).

Cameron, William B. 1954. "Sociological Notes on the Jam Session." *Social Forces* 33: 177–82.

Campbell, Wilbur. Interview by J. B. Figi. 29 April 1980. Oral History. Chicago Jazz Archive. University of Chicago, Regenstein Library, Chicago, IL.

Chandler, Nahum. 1992. "The Problem of Purity: The Question of Social Difference and African American Identity in the Early Work of W. E. B. Du Bois,

1895–1915." Unpublished dissertation prospectus, Department of Anthropology, University of Chicago.

Chapman, John. 1935. "Mainly about Manhattan." *Chicago Tribune.* Clippings files. Institute for Jazz Studies. Rutgers University, Newark, NJ.

Charron, Claude. 1978. "Toward Transcription and Analysis of Inuit Throat Games: Micro Structure." *Ethnomusicology* 22(2): 245–60+.

Chevan, David. 1995. Personal communication. 4 November 1995.

Chilton, John. 1989. *Billie's Blues: The Billie Holiday Story, 1933–1959.* Originally published 1975. New York: Da Capo.

Clarke, Kenny. 1977. Interview by Helen Oakley Dance. 9 September 1977. Jazz Oral History Project. Institute for Jazz Studies. Rutgers University, Newark, NJ.

Clifford, James. 1988. *The Predicament of Culture: Twentieth-Century Ethnography, Literature, and Art.* Cambridge, MA: Harvard University Press.

Clifford, James, and George E. Marcus, eds. 1986. *Writing Culture: The Poetics and Politics of Ethnography.* Berkeley and Los Angeles: University of California Press.

Cole, David. 1991. Personal communication.

Collier, James Lincoln. 1989. *Benny Goodman and the Swing Era.* New York: Oxford University Press.

———. 1983. *Louis Armstrong: An American Genius.* New York: Oxford University Press.

———. 1978. *The Making of Jazz: A Comprehensive History.* Boston: Houghton Mifflin.

Comaroff, Jean, and John Comaroff. 1991. *Of Revelation and Revolution: Christianity, Colonialism, and Consciousness in South Africa.* Vol. 1. Chicago: University of Chicago Press.

Condon, Eddie. 1947. *We Called It Music: A Generation of Jazz.* New York: Holt.

Cortez, Jayne. 1984. *Coagulations: New and Selected Poems.* New York: Thunder's Mouth Press.

Daniels, Douglas Henry. 1985. "Lester Young: Master of Jive." *American Music* 3(3): 313–28.

DeMichael, Don. 1966. "The Varied Peripteries of Drummer Roy Haynes or They Call Him Snap Crackle!" *Down Beat* 33(26): 18–19+.

———. 1962. "John Coltrane and Eric Dolphy Answer the Jazz Critics." *Down Beat* 29 (12 April): 20–23.

Derrida, Jacques. 1982. "Différance." In *Margins of Philosophy,* 1–27. Translated by Alan Bass. Originally published 1968. Chicago: University of Chicago Press.

DeVeaux, Scott. 1991. "Constructing the Jazz Tradition: Jazz Historiography." *Black American Literature Forum* 25(3): 525–60.

———. 1985. "Jazz in Transition: Coleman Hawkins and Howard McGhee, 1935–1945." Ph.D. diss., University of California, Berkeley.

Dillard, J. L. 1972. *Black English: Its History and Usage in the United States.* New York: Vintage Books.

Du Bois, W. E. B. 1985. "Beyond the Veil in a Virginia Town." In *W. E. B. Du Bois: Against Racism: Unpublished Essays, Papers, Addresses, 1887–1961,* edited by

Herbert Aptheker, 49–50. Originally published 1897. Amherst: University of Massachusetts Press.

————. 1969. *The Souls of Black Folks.* Originally published 1903. New York: New American Library.

————. 1910. "The Souls of White Folks." *Independent* 69 (August 18): 339–42.

Duranti, Alessandro, and Charles Goodwin, eds. 1992. *Rethinking Context: Language as an Interactive Phenomenon.* Cambridge: Cambridge University Press.

Feather, Leonard. 1952. "Feather's Nest." *Down Beat* (October 8): 16.

Feld, Steven. 1988. "Aesthetics as Iconicity of Style or 'Lift-Up-Over Sounding': Getting into the Kaluli Groove." *Yearbook for Traditional Music* 20: 74–113.

————. 1984. "Communication, Music and Speech About Music." *Yearbook for Traditional Music* 16: 1–18.

————. 1982. *Sound and Sentiment.* Philadelphia: University of Pennsylvania Press.

————. 1981. "'Flow Like a Waterfall': The Metaphors of Kaluli Music Theory." *Yearbook for Traditional Music* 13: 22–47.

————. 1974. "Linguistic Models in Ethnomusicology." *Ethnomusicology* 18: 197–217.

Feld, Steven, and Bambi B. Schieffelin. 1982. "Hard Words: A Functional Bias for Kaluli Discourse." In *Analyzing Discourse: Text and Talk,* edited by Deborah Tannen, 350–70. Washington, D.C.: Georgetown University Press.

Ferguson, Russell. 1990. *Out There: Marginalization and Contemporary Culture.* Cambridge, MA: MIT Press.

Fernandez, James. 1986. *Persuasions and Performances: The Play of Tropes in Culture.* Bloomington: Indiana University Press.

Finnegan, Edward, and Niko Besnier. 1989. *Language: Its Structure and Use.* San Diego: Harcourt Brace and Jovanovich.

Floyd, Samuel Jr. 1991. "Ring Shout! Literary Studies, Historical Studies, and Black Music Inquiry." *Black Music Research Journal* 11(2): 265–87.

Foucault, Michel. 1972. *The Archaeology of Knowledge and the Discourse on Language.* Translated by A. M. Sheridan Smith. New York: Pantheon Books.

Gates, Henry Louis Jr. 1988. *The Signifying Monkey: A Theory of African-American Literary Criticism.* New York: Oxford University Press.

————. 1987. "Dis and Dat: Dialect and Descent." In *Figures in Black: Words, Signs and the "Racial" Self,* edited by Henry Louis Gates Jr., 167–95. New York: Oxford University Press.

————. 1984. "The Blackness of Blackness: A Critique of the Sign and the Signifying Monkey." In *Black Literature & Literary Theory,* edited by Henry Louis Gates Jr., 285–321. New York: Methuen.

Gerard, Charley. 1989. *Salsa: The Rhythm of Latin Music.* Crown Point, IN: White Cliffs Media.

Gerber, Alain. 1985. *Le cas Coltrane.* Paris: Editions Parenthèses.

Gershwin, George, and Ira Gershwin. 1930. *I Got Rhythm.* New York: New World Music.

Gershwin, George, and Du Bose Heyward. 1935. *Summertime.* New York: Gershwin Publishing Corp.

————. 1930. *But Not for Me.* New York: New World Music Corp.

Giddens, Anthony. 1984. *The Constitution of Society: Outline of the Theory of Structuration.* Cambridge: Polity.

Gillespie, Dizzy, and Al Fraser. 1979. *To Be or Not to Bop: Memoirs of Dizzy Gillespie with Al Fraser.* New York: Da Capo Press, Inc.

Gilman, Sander L. 1985. *Difference and Pathology: Stereotypes of Sexuality, Race, and Madness.* Ithaca: Cornell University Press.

Gilroy, Paul. 1993. *The Black Atlantic: Modernity and Double Consciousness.* Cambridge, MA: Harvard University Press.

————. 1991. *"There Ain't No Black in the Union Jack": The Cultural Politics of Race and Nation.* Chicago: University of Chicago Press.

Gitler, Ira. 1967. "Liner Notes." *The Jaki Byard Quartet Live!, Vol. 2.* Recorded West Peabody, MA: 15 April 1965. Prestige 7477; PCD-24121–2.

————. 1965. "Liner Notes." *The Jaki Byard Quartet Live!, Vol. 1.* Recorded West Peabody, MA: 15 April 1965. Prestige 7419; PCD-24121–2.

Gitler, Ira, Max Roach, Abbey Lincoln, et al. 1962a. "Racial Prejudice in Jazz, Part 1." *Down Beat* (15 March 1962): 20–26.

————. 1962b. "Racial Prejudice in Jazz, Part 2." *Down Beat* (29 March): 22–25.

Goffman, Erving. 1986. *Frame Analysis: An Essay on the Organization of Experience.* Originally published 1974. Boston: Northeastern University Press.

————. 1967. *Interaction Ritual: Essays on Face-to-Face Behavior.* New York: Pantheon Books.

Gold, Robert. 1975. *Jazz Talk.* Indianapolis, IN: The Bobbs-Merrill Company, Inc.

Goodwin, Charles. 1981. *Conversational Organization: Interaction between Speakers and Hearers.* New York: Academic Press.

Goodwin, Marjorie H. 1990. *He-Said-She-Said: Talk as Social Organization among Black Children.* Bloomington: Indiana University Press.

Green, Freddie. 1977. Interview by Helen and Stanley Dance. 9 August 1977. Jazz Oral History Project. Institute for Jazz Studies. Rutgers University, Newark, NJ.

Green, John, and Edward Heyman. 1930. *Body and Soul.* New York: Harms, Inc.

Grossberg, Lawrence. 1990. "Is There Rock after Punk?" In *On Rock: Rock, Pop, and the Written Word,* edited by Simon Frith and Andrew Goodwin, 111–23. New York: Pantheon Books.

Guilbault, Jocelyne. 1993. *Zouk: World Music in the West Indies.* Chicago: University of Chicago Press.

Gumperz, John J. 1982. *Discourse Strategies.* New York: Cambridge University Press.

Gumperz, John J., and Dell Hymes, eds. 1986. *Directions in Sociolinguistics: The Ethnography of Communication.* Originally published 1972. Oxford: Basil Blackwell.

Hacker, Andrew. 1992. *Two Nations: Black and White, Separate, Hostile, Unequal.* New York: Charles Scribner's Sons.

Hanks, William F. 1990. *Referential Practice: Language and Lived Space among the Maya.* Chicago: University of Chicago Press.

————. 1989. "Text and Textuality." *Annual Review of Anthropology* 18: 99–101.

———. 1987. "Discourse Genres in a Theory of Practice." *American Ethnologist* 14: 668–92.

Hartman, Charles O. 1991. *Jazz Text: Voice and Improvisation in Poetry, Jazz, and Song.* Princeton: Princeton University Press.

Harvey, Holman. 1936. "It's Swing." *Delineator* (February): 10–11+.

Hood, Mantle. 1960. "The Challenge of 'Bi-Musicality.'" *Ethnomusicology* 4(2): 55–59.

hooks, bell. 1989. *Talking Back: Thinking Feminist, Thinking Black.* Boston: South End Press.

Horne, Elliot. 1961. "The Words for the Music." *New York Times* (25 June 1961): section VI, 39.

Hunt, David C. 1968. "Unforgettable." *Jazz Monthly* 162: 14–15.

Hutcheon, Linda. 1991. *A Theory of Parody.* Originally published 1985. New York: Routledge.

Jackson, Travis A. 1995. "'Takin' It to Another Level': Creating Flow in 'Jazz' Performance." Paper presented at the annual meeting of the Society for Ethnomusicology, 18–22 October 1995, Los Angeles, CA.

Jairazbhoy, Nazir A. 1977. "The 'Objective' and 'Subjective' View of Music Transcription." *Ethnomusicology* 21: 263–73.

"Jive Talk." 1954. *Rhythm and Blues* (December 1954 and February 1955): 15.

Keil, Charles. 1995. "The Theory of Participatory Discrepancies: A Progress Report." *Ethnomusicology* 39(1): 1–19.

———. 1972. "Motion and Feeling through Music." In *Rappin' and Stylin' Out: Communication in Black Urban America,* edited by Thomas Kochman, 83–100. Originally published 1966. Urbana: University of Illinois Press.

Kenney, William H. 1993. *Chicago Jazz: A Cultural History, 1904–1930.* New York: Oxford University Press.

Kerman, Joseph. 1985. *Contemplating Music: Challenges to Musicology.* Cambridge, MA: Harvard University Press.

Kernfeld, Barry, ed. 1988. *The New Grove Dictionary of Jazz.* 2 vols. London: Macmillan Press Limited.

———. 1981. "Adderly, Coltrane, Davis at the Twilight of Bebop: The Search for Melodic Coherence." Ph.D. diss., Cornell University.

Kochman, Thomas. 1986. "Strategic Ambiguity in Black Speech Genres: Cross-Cultural Inference in Participant–Observation Research." *Text* 6(2): 153–70.

———. 1983. "The Boundary between Play and Nonplay in Black Verbal Dueling." *Language in Society* 12(3): 329–37.

———. 1981. *Black and White Styles in Conflict.* Chicago: University of Chicago Press.

Kramer, Lawrence. 1993. "Music Criticism and the Postmodernist Turn: In Contrary Motion with Gary Tomlinson." *Current Musicology* 53: 25–40.

Labov, William. 1972. "Rules of Ritual Insults." In *Rappin' and Stylin' Out: Communication in Black Urban America,* edited by Thomas Kochman, 265–314. Urbana: University of Illinois Press.

———. 1969. *The Logic of Nonstandard English.* Monograph Series on Languages and Linguistics. Washington: Georgetown University.

LaRue, Jan. 1970. *Guidelines for Style Analysis: A Comprehensive Outline of Basic Principles for the Analysis of Musical Style.* New York: W. W. Norton and Company.

Larson, Steven Leroy. 1987. *Schenkerian Analysis of Modern Jazz.* Ph.D. diss., University of Michigan.

Lees, Gene. 1962. "A Show Business Lexicon." *Show Business Illustrated: 57.*

Lehrdahl, Fred, and Ray Jackendoff. 1983. *A Generative Theory of Tonal Grammar.* Cambridge, MA: MIT Press.

Leonard, Neil. 1987. *Jazz: Myth and Religion.* New York: Oxford University Press.

Levine, Lawrence W. 1977. *Black Culture and Black Consciousness: Afro-American Folk Thought from Slavery to Freedom.* New York: Oxford University Press.

Levinson, Stephan C. 1983. *Pragmatics.* Cambridge: Cambridge University Press.

Lewin, David. 1987. *Generalized Musical Intervals and Transformations.* New Haven: Yale University Press.

———. 1986. "Music Theory, Phenomenology, and Modes of Perception." *Music Perception* 3(4): 327–92.

Lincoln, C. Eric, and Lawrence H. Mamiya. 1990. *The Black Church in the African American Experience.* Durham: Duke University Press.

List, George. 1974. "The Reliability of Transcription." *Ethnomusicology* 18(3): 353–78.

Locke, David. 1987. *Drum Gahu: A Systematic Method for an African Percussion Piece.* Crown Point, IN: White Cliffs Media.

Lucy, John A. 1993. "Reflexive Language and the Human Disciplines." In *Reflexive Language: Reported Speech and Metapragmatics,* edited by John A. Lucy, 9–32. Cambridge: Cambridge University Press.

Lutz, Catherine A. 1988. *Unnatural Emotions: Everyday Sentiments on a Micronesian Atoll and Their Challenge to Western Theory.* Chicago: University of Chicago Press.

Lutz, Catherine A., and Lila Abu-Lughod, eds. 1993. *Language and the Politics of Emotion.* Cambridge and Paris: Cambridge University Press and Editions de la Maison des Sciences de l'Homme.

Mann, Alfred. 1986. *The Study of the Fugue.* Originally published 1958. New York: Dover Publications.

Manuel, Peter. 1993. *Cassette Culture: Popular Music and Technology in North India.* Chicago: University of Chicago Press.

McClary, Susan. 1990. *Feminine Endings: Music, Gender, and Sexuality.* Minneapolis: University of Minnesota Press.

McMillen, Neil R. 1989. *Dark Journey: Black Mississippians in the Age of Jim Crow.* Urbana: University of Illinois Press.

Mercer, Kobena. 1990. "Black Hair/Style Politics." In *Out There: Marginalization and Contemporary Cultures,* edited by Russell Ferguson, Martha Gever, Trinh T. Minh-ha, and Cornel West, 247–64. Cambridge, MA: The MIT Press.

Merriam, Alan, and Raymond Mack. 1960. "The Jazz Community." *Social Forces* 38(3): 211–22.

Meyer, Leonard B. 1956. *Emotion and Meaning in Music.* Chicago: University of Chicago Press.

Mezzrow, Milton "Mezz," and Bernard Wolfe. 1946. *Really the Blues.* New York: Random House.

Milkowski, Bill. 1988. "Ron Carter: The Elder Statesman of the Bass Keeps Swinging without a Safety Net." *Musician* 112: 60–63+.

Mingus, Charles. 1978. Interview by Sy Johnson. 19–22 February 1978. Jazz Oral History Project. Institute for Jazz Studies. Rutgers University, Newark, NJ.

———. 1971. *Beneath the Underdog: His World as Composed by Charles Mingus.* New York: Alfred A. Knopf.

Mitchell, Henry. 1970. *Black Preaching.* Philadelphia: J. Lippincott Company.

Mitchell-Kernan, Claudia. 1986. "Signifying and Marking: Two Afro-American Speech Acts." In *Directions in Sociolinguistics: The Ethnography of Communication,* edited by John J. Gumperz and Dell Hymes, 161–79. Originally published 1972. Oxford: Basil Blackwell.

Moerman, Michael. 1988. *Talking Culture: Ethnography and Conversation Analysis.* Philadelphia: University of Pennsylvania Press.

Monson, Ingrid. 1991. "Musical Interaction in Modern Jazz: An Ethnomusicological Perspective." Ph.D. diss., New York University.

Morgan, Marcyliena H. 1991. "African American Women's Discourse." Unpublished paper.

Morgenstern, Dan. 1965. "Ready, Willing, and Able: Jaki Byard." *Down Beat* 33(October 21): 18–19+.

Morris, William. 1954. *The Real Gone Lexicon.* New York: Self-published.

Morrison, Toni. 1992. *Playing in the Dark: Whiteness and the Literary Imagination.* Cambridge, MA: Harvard University Press.

Murphy, John P. 1990. "Jazz Improvisation: The Joy of Influence." *The Black Perspective in Music* 18(1): 17–19.

Nattiez, Jean-Jacques. 1990a. "Can One Speak of Narrativity in Music?" *Journal of the Royal Musical Association* 115: 240–57.

———. 1990b. *Music and Discourse: Toward a Semiology of Music.* Translated by Carolyn Abbate. Princeton: Princeton University Press.

Noble, Ray. 1938. *Cherokee (Indian Love Song).* London: Peter Maurice.

Obenhaus, Mark. 1986. *Miles Ahead: The Music of Miles Davis.* Film.

Ochs, Elinor. 1992. "Indexing Gender." In *Rethinking Context: Language as an Interactive Phenomenon,* edited by Alessandro Duranti and Charles Goodwin, 335–58. Cambridge: Cambridge University Press.

———. 1988. *Culture and Language Development: Language Acquisition and Language Socialization in a Samoan Village.* New York: Cambridge University Press.

Owens, Thomas. 1974. "Charlie Parker: Techniques of Improvisation." 2 vols. Ph.D. diss., University of California, Los Angeles.

Panassie, Hugues. 1942. *The Real Jazz.* Translated by Anne Sorelle Williams. New York: Smith & Durrell.

Pelote, Vincent. 1991. Personal communication.

Peretti, Burton. 1992. *The Creation of Jazz: Music, Race, and Culture in Urban America.* Urbana: University of Illinois Press.

Poling, James W. 1936. "Music after Midnight." *Esquire* (June): 92, 131–32.

Porter, Cole. 1944. "Everytime We Say Goodbye." New York: Chappell & Co.

Porter, Lewis. 1985a. "John Coltrane's *A Love Supreme:* Jazz Improvisation as Composition." *Journal of the American Musicological Society* 38: 593–621.

———. 1985b. *Lester Young.* Boston: Twayne Publishers.

Potter, Jeff. 1986. "Roy Haynes." *Modern Drummer* 10(2): 16–21+.

Powers, Harold S. 1980. "Language Models and Musical Analysis." *Ethnomusicology* 24: 1–60.

Preston, Dennis R. 1985. "The L'il Abner Syndrome: Written Representations of Speech." *American Speech* 60(4): 328–36.

Priestly, Brian. 1987. *John Coltrane.* London: Apollo Press Limited.

———. 1982. *Mingus: A Critical Biography.* New York: Da Capo Press.

Radano, Ronald M. 1993. *New Musical Figurations: Anthony Braxton's Cultural Critique.* Chicago: University of Chicago Press.

Rahn, John. 1987. *Basic Atonal Theory.* New York: Schirmer Books.

Ratner, Leonard. 1956. "Eighteenth-Century Theories of Musical Period Structure." *Musical Quarterly* 42(4): 439–54.

Read, Gardner. 1979. *Music Notation: A Manual of Modern Practice.* 2d ed. New York: Taplinger Publishing.

Rodgers, Richard, and Oscar Hammerstein II. 1959. *My Favorite Things.* New York: Williamson Music Co.

Rosaldo, Renato. 1993. *Culture and Truth: The Remaking of Social Analysis.* Originally published 1989. Boston: Beacon Press.

Sales, Grover. 1984. *Jazz: America's Classical Music.* Englewood Cliffs, NJ: Prentice-Hall.

Saussure, Ferdinand de. 1986. *Course in General Linguistics.* Translated by Roy Harris. Originally published 1922. LaSalle, IL: Open Court.

Schegloff, Emanuel A. 1986. "The Routine as Achievement." *Human Studies* 9: 111–51.

Schenker, Heinrich. 1973. *Harmony.* Originally published 1906. Cambridge, MA: MIT Press.

Schieffelin, Bambi B. 1990. *The Give and Take of Everyday Life: Language Socialization of Kaluli Children.* Cambridge: Cambridge University Press.

Schoenberg, Arnold. 1978. *Theory of Harmony.* Translated by Roy E. Carter. Originally published 1911. Berkeley and Los Angeles: University of California Press.

Schuller, Gunther. 1989. *The Swing Era: The Development of Jazz, 1930–1945.* New York: Oxford University Press.

———. 1986. "Sonny Rollins and the Challenge of Thematic Improvisation." In *Musings: The Musical World of Gunther Schuller. A Collection of His Writings,* 86–97. New York: Oxford University Press.

———. 1968. *Early Jazz: Its Roots and Musical Development.* New York: Oxford University Press.

Schwichtenberg, Cathy, ed. 1993. *The Madonna Collection: Representational Politics, Subcultural Identities, and Cultural Theory.* Boulder: Westview Press.

Seeger, Charles. 1977. *Studies in Musicology 1935–1975.* Berkeley and Los Angeles: University of California Press.

Shaw, Arnold. 1950. *Lingo of Tin-Pan Alley.* New York, NY: Broadcast Music, Inc. (BMI).

Sher, Chuck, and Bob Bauer, eds. 1988. *The New Real Book.* Petaluma, CA: Sher Music Co.

Sidran, Ben. 1986. *Black Talk.* Originally published 1971. New York: Da Capo.

Silverstein, Michael. 1993. "Metapragmatic Discourse and Metapragmatic Function." In *Reflexive Language: Reported Speech and Metapragmatics,* edited by John A. Lucy, 33–58. Cambridge: Cambridge University Press.

———. 1984. "On the Pragmatic 'Poetry' of Prose: Parallelism, Repetition, and Cohesive Structure in the Time Course of Dyadic Conversation." In *Meaning, Form, and Use in Context: Linguistic Applications,* edited by Deborah Schiffrin, 181–99. Georgetown: Georgetown University Press.

———. 1979. "Language Structure and Linguistic Ideology." In *The Elements: A Parasession on Linguistic Units and Levels,* edited by Paul R. Clyne, William F. Hanks, and Carol L. Hofbauer, 193–247. Chicago: Chicago Linguistic Society.

———. 1976. "Shifters, Linguistic Categories, and Cultural Description." In *Meaning in Anthropology,* edited by K. Basso and H. Shelby, 11–55. Albuquerque: University of New Mexico Press.

Smith, Gregory E. 1983. "Homer, Gregory, and Bill Evans? The Theory of Formulaic Composition in the Context of Jazz Piano Improvisation." Ph.D. diss., Harvard University.

Smitherman, Geneva. 1977. *Talkin' and Testifyin': The Language of Black America.* Boston: Houghton Mifflin.

"Speaking of Pictures . . . Swing Music Produces These." 1938. *Life* (21 February): 4–5+.

Spellman, A. B. 1985. *Four Lives in the Bebop Business.* Originally published 1966. New York: Limelight Editions.

Spivak, Gayatri Chakravorty. 1992. "Acting Bits/Identity Talk." *Critical Inquiry* 18 (summer): 770–803.

———. 1990. "Poststructuralism, Marginality, Postcoloniality and Value." In *Literary Theory Today,* edited by Peter Collier and Helga Geyer-Ryan, 219–44. Ithaca: Cornell University Press.

———. 1988a. "Can the Subaltern Speak?" In *Marxist Interpretations of Literature and Culture: Limits, Frontiers, Boundaries,* edited by Larry Grossberg and Cary Nelson, 271–313. Urbana: University of Illinois Press.

———. 1988b. *In Other Words: Essays in Cultural Politics.* New York and London: Routledge.

St. Cyr, Johnny. 1958. Interview by William Russell. 27 August 1958. Digest. William Ransom Hogan Jazz Archive. Tulane University, New Orleans, Louisiana.

Stewart, Milton. 1973. "Structural Development in the Jazz Improvisational Technique of Clifford Brown." Ph.D. diss., University of Michigan.

Stix, John. 1978. "Roland Hanna: Versatile Mainstream Pianist." *Contemporary Keyboard* 4(5): 10+.

Stone, Ruth, and Vernon Stone. 1981. "Event, Feedback and Analysis: Research Media in the Study of Music Events." *Ethnomusicology* 25(2): 215–26.

Stowe, David W. 1994. *Swing Changes: Big Band Jazz in New Deal America.* Cambridge, MA: Harvard University Press.

"They're Killing Swing: More Editorial Blah on the Subject of Swing." 1938. *Metronome* (November).

Thomas, J. C. 1975. *Chasin' the Trane: The Music and Mystique of John Coltrane.* Garden City, New York: Doubleday.

Tirro, Frank. 1974. "Constructive Elements in Jazz Improvisation." *Journal of the American Musicological Society* 27: 285–305.

Tomlinson, Gary. 1993a. *Music in Renaissance Magic: Towards a Historiography of Others.* Chicago: University of Chicago Press.

———. 1993b. "Musical Pasts and Postmodern Musicologies: A Response to Lawrence Kramer." *Current Musicology* 53: 18–24.

———. 1991. "Cultural Dialogics and Jazz: A White Historian Signifies." *Black Music Research Journal* 11(2): 229–64.

———. 1984. "The Web of Culture: A Context for Musicology." *Nineteenth Century Music* 7: 350–62.

Treitler, Lèo. 1974. "Homer and Gregory: The Transmission of Epic Poetry and Plainchant." *Musical Quarterly* 60(3): 333–72.

Tucker, Mark, ed. 1993. *The Duke Ellington Reader.* New York: Oxford University Press.

———. 1989. *Ellington: The Early Years.* Urbana: University of Illinois Press.

Turino, Thomas. 1993. *Moving Away from Silence: Music of the Peruvian Altiplano and the Experience of Migration.* Chicago: University of Chicago Press.

Turner, Terence. 1991. "'We Are Parrots.' 'Twins Are Birds': Play of Tropes as Operational Structure." In *Beyond Metaphor: The Theory of Tropes in Anthropology,* edited by James W. Fernandez, 121–58. Stanford: Stanford University Press.

Varèse, Edgard. 1958a. *Ionisation, for Percussion Ensemble of Thirteen Players.* New York: G. Ricordi.

———. 1958b. *Poème électronique.* Recorded Brussels. CBS mp 38773.

Waterman, Christopher A. 1990a. "'Our Tradition Is a Very Modern Tradition': Popular Music and the Construction of Pan-Yoruban Identity." *Ethnomusicology* 34(3): 367–79.

———. 1990b. *Jùjú: A Social History and Ethnography of an African Popular Form.* Chicago: University of Chicago Press.

West, Cornel. 1993. *Race Matters.* Boston: Beacon Press.

Williams, Martin. 1985. *Jazz Heritage.* New York: Oxford University Press.

———. 1983. *The Jazz Tradition: New and Revised Edition.* Oxford: Oxford University Press.

———. 1970. *Jazz Masters in Transition, 1957–1969.* New York: Da Capo Press.

Wilmer, Valerie. 1977. *As Serious as Your Life: The Story of the New Jazz.* New York and London: Serpent's Tail.

Wilson, Olly. 1992. "The Heterogeneous Sound Ideal in African-American Music." In *New Perspectives on Music: Essays in Honor of Eileen Southern,* edited by Josephine Wright, 327–38. Warren, MI: Harmonie Park Press.

———. 1990. "Musical Analysis of African American Music." Paper presented at the Pre-Conference Symposium of the Society for Ethnomusicology, 7 November 1990.

Wright, Rayburn. 1982. *Inside the Score: A Detailed Analysis of Eight Classic Jazz Ensemble Charts.* Delavan, NY: Kendor Music.

Zemp, Hugo. 1978. "Aspects of 'Are 'Are Musical Theory." *Ethnomusicology* 23(1): 37–67.

INDEX

Abbate, Carolyn, 188, 229n.35
Absolute music, 4, 134
Abu-Lughod, Lila, 178
Africa, 203–5; music, 82, 126, 190, 194, 211; —, talking drums, 194, 211; —, Yoruba, 92–93, 194–95, 199
African American: aesthetics, 88, 90, 104, 111–12, 115–23, 129–31; African heritage, 203–4; Christian denominations, 95; double-consciousness, 121 (see also Du Bois, W. E. B.); leadership in jazz, 75, 90, 137, 201, 203; relationship to European American music, 104; spirituality, 96, 195, 218
African American English: representation of, 22–23; signifying, 86–88; speech genres, 86; verbal dueling, 86–88, 94
African diaspora, 9, 193–95, 205, 213
Afrocentricity, 203
Agency, 9, 14, 193, 209, 210, 213
Alexander, Elizabeth, 100
Allen, Geri, 77, 80, 89, 128
Anthropology, 5, 24, 192, 213; concept of culture, 131; linguistic, 20, 190, 206, 210; of emotions, 178

Anticipation. *See* Interaction (musical)
Appiah, Kwame Anthony, 200, 204–5, 230n.6
Armstrong, Louis, 134–35
Asante, Molefi K., 203
Austin, John, 210
Authenticity, 200, 203, 204

Backbeat. *See* Rhythm
Bakhtin, Mikhail, 8, 81, 87, 98–100, 125
"Ball N' Chain," 98
Baraka, Amiri, 196
Basie, Count, 28, 56, 61, 69, 200
Bass: harmonic role, 30–32; importance of, 50; in relation to piano, 49; ostinato, 33, 113; pedal point, 29, 32–37; register shift, 34, 40–42; role of, 29–43; timbral contrast, 38–40, walking bass, 29–30, 32, 33, 44, 54, 56, 68, 196
"Bass-ment Blues," 8, 19, 178–79, 183, 185, 189; analysis of, 137–77, 183; correcting chorus structure, 156–70
Bebop, 52, 56, 57, 126, 201
Bechet, Sidney, 102, 124
Berliner, Paul, 4–5, 73